Duel Between the First Ironclads

Duel Between the First Ironclads

William C. Davis

STACKPOLE
BOOKS

Published by
STACKPOLE BOOKS
5067 Ritter Road
Mechanicsburg, PA 17055

Printed in the United States of America

Second hardcover edition

Originally published by Doubleday & Company, Inc., in 1975.

10 9 8 7 6 5 4 3 2 1

Library of Congress Cataloging-in-Publication Data

Davis, William C., 1946–
    Duel between the first ironclads / William C. Davis. — 2nd
hardcover ed.
        p.   cm.
    Includes bibliographical references and index.
    ISBN 0-8117-0536-6
    1. Hampton Roads (Va.), Battle of, 1862.   2. Monitor (Ironclad)
3. Merrimack (Frigate)   I. Title.
E473.2.D36   1994
973.7'52 — dc20   93-26867
                                                                          CIP

Contents

List of Illustrations

Preface

The explosion of significant new research and discoveries that has hit almost all facets of the Civil War story in the past two decades has also struck naval studies of the war. No aspect of that oft-neglected story has seen more new information come to light than the dramatic events at Hampton Roads, Virginia, in March 1862, when the CSS *Virginia* — for which scholars and buffs alike still cling tenaciously to its earlier name *Merrimack* — nearly destroyed a Yankee fleet one day, and then battled for hours with another iron antagonist, the USS *Monitor,* on the next.

Not long before this book first appeared in 1975, the wreck of the *Monitor* was finally discovered lying on the bottom several miles off Cape Hatteras. Since *Duel Between the First Ironclads* first appeared, repeated expeditions to the wreck have yielded a rich trove of information, supplemented by continuing archival investigations.

In 1978 I had an opportunity to participate in one of the submarine dives on the site. It was an eerie feeling, going more than 200 feet to the ocean bottom, where the light is so dim that visibility extends no more than a few feet. Suddenly out of the gloom appeared the rim of the deck, lying upside down. Slowly the submersible glided along the wreck only two or three feet away from it, until the turret came into view, beneath the deck. I could see the dents in the turret plates where the *Virginia's* shots struck, only to bounce away harmlessly. I could see the gun ports from which the *Monitor's* 11-inch Dahlgren guns belched forth their own fire. It was an experience never to be forgotten. The sense of majesty was overawing.

Making the experience even more unforgettable was the fact that I was in a submarine that held two men in the control compartment, and two in a diving "lock-out" in the rear. I was in back, with a diver who quickly went over with me the emergency procedures in case the pilot and observer in the front should lose control or, worse, be swamped in their compartment. The instructions were only a little less clear to me than nuclear fission would be to a Great Dane. It hardly helped when the diver told me that a few months earlier a man had suffocated in that same compartment when the submersible tangled for hours in underwater cables.

And on top of that, I was bleeding. The sea is high off Hatteras. That day it was moderate—waves about six feet high, in other words. In jumping from a pilot boat onto the larger launching vessel, I misjudged a wave, and came down hard on a bulwark, splitting my knee open. I merrily bled through the ensuing dive, then transferred over to the other research vessel where Jacques Cousteau's former ship's physician sewed up my leg without benefit of anesthetic. I did not even get a bullet to bite into. Thanks to that experience I think I have rather a special understanding of what some Civil War soldiers felt like when being treated by their surgeons. So far as I am aware, not even the most fanatically correct of today's re-enactors and living history folk submit themselves to a doctor's needlepoint without a little something first. At least my surgeon did manage to share a little pain killer afterward when we got back to the hotel bar.

Alas, there is no wreck of the *Virginia* to find. But scholars are continuing to find more and more about it from long-neglected archives. Repeatedly talk arises of building a full-scale replica of the ironclad—or of both of them—both for study purposes and as learning and tourist sites. A fictionalized film based on the epic duel of the two monsters went out over the airways recently, and more investigation and celebration are planned.

This book was one of the steps in the growing awareness of the real story of these two ships, the men who designed and built them, and the daring fellows who faced battle in them. Their place in history is secure without any books. With them, that significance can be better understood. It is comforting, after nearly twenty years since its first appearance, to see *Duel Between the First Ironclads* arise once more for a new generation of readers, and encouraging as well to know that if it stimulates their interest, there is today so much more available for them to continue feeding that interest than there was in 1975.

Maybe, in time, Americans will even learn to stop calling the *Virginia* the *Merrimack*.

But I doubt it.

William C. Davis
Mechanicsburg, Pa.
May 1993

ACKNOWLEDGMENTS

Special thanks are always due to those who assist the historian at his task, and this work hardly provides an exception. Many friends and colleagues lent their aid in the research and presentation of this book. It would be difficult to name them all; I hope that all of them, named or not, realize how very much I value their contribution. For most, this is neither the first time nor the last that their assistance has been asked. One must marvel at their patience.

Some require special mention, and none more so than those connected with the manuscript collections that provided most of the basic stuff of which this book is made. Winifred Popp, Henry E. Huntington Library, San Marino, California; Joseph E. Suppiger, Lincoln Memorial University, Harrogate, Tennessee; J. Isaac Copeland, Director of the Southern Historical Collection, University of North Carolina, Chapel Hill; Colonel James Agnew and Dr. Richard J. Sommers, U. S. Army Military History Research Collection, Carlisle Barracks, Pennsylvania; and Howson Cole, Virginia Historical Society, Richmond, were particularly helpful in providing access to the rich holdings in their collections. I am much indebted.

Additionally, many people and presses graciously allowed me to use quotations from published works still under copyright, a boon greatly appreciated. Lilla M. Hawes, Director of the *Georgia Historical Quarterly;* Pearl Ann Reeder, Editor of *Hobbies* magazine; Agnes Moran of Macmillan, Inc.; Mary Ryan of W. W. Norton & Company, Inc.; Clayton R. Barrow, editor of the *United States Naval Institute Proceedings;* and William M. E. Rachal, editor of the *Virginia Magazine of History and Biography,* all kindly granted their permission for quotations drawn from books or articles. A particular word of thanks is due Thomas F. Epley, Editorial Director of the Naval Institute Press, for permission to use quotations from the invaluable book of wartime letters by Paymaster William F. Keeler, *Aboard the U.S.S. Monitor.*

Descendants of some of the chief actors in the drama of the ironclads lent their aid as well. Dr. George R. Brooke, of Lexington, Virginia, not only allowed me to quote briefly from his excellent doctoral dissertation done at the University of North Carolina, but also provided a hitherto unpublished photograph of his distinguished ancestor John M. Brooke. Mr. Alvan Macauley, of Grosse Pointe Farms, Michigan, kindly allowed me to publish photos of his ancestor Hardin B. Littlepage and of the pennant of the *Virginia;* and Jon Nielson, Orono, Maine, very graciously allowed me the full use of Littlepage's postwar reminiscences and other papers.

It is customary for historians to bring their acknowledgments to a close with an obligatory compliment to their spouses, in most cases so unimaginatively worded that the lines could be interchanged with those in a hundred books with no one noticing much difference. How unfortunate! To be sure, our helpmates may read, type, even correct or edit, our manuscripts, but their real trials on our behalf go unsung. While we cloister ourselves for months in research and writing, it is they who run the house, keep the children quiet and out of the way, tend the pets, and all the while urge us to continue. Their reward is untold hours of aloneness, boredom, solitude. They deserve better, certainly much better than a fleeting dedication or a tiresome acknowledgment between the table of contents and the text. Certainly one wife and friend, Pamela Davis, is entitled to more. Yet when all was done she paid me the compliment of reading this finished book, not to edit or criticize but simply to read. It was a gesture difficult to equal; it would be futile even to try to do so here.

DUEL BETWEEN THE FIRST
IRONCLADS

CHAPTER 1

"To Bury Us Forever"

Chance dearly loves to toy with history: A missed moment, unexpected delay, a storm, inefficiency, and of course that most frightening specter of all, bureaucracy, can and do combine to foil even seemingly inevitable appointments with destiny. And yet at the same time, through some inscrutable perversity, all the machinations of Chance often serve only to heighten the drama, to punctuate the inescapability of an event that would not be denied its place in time.

Chance seldom toiled harder at the task than on March 7, 1862. America was at war with itself. For nearly a year, the conflict between Union and Confederacy had raged indecisively. For a much longer time, far older antagonists sparred with each other. Tradition and Technology had met on a thousand battlegrounds since the Dark Ages. In this first of the "modern" wars, however, they faced each other almost daily, their fateful encounters becoming commonplace. On this day, though, something far out of the ordinary seemed imminent. An epic rendezvous was in the making, if only Chance would leave things alone.

The meeting place was settled and secure: Hampton Roads, Virginia. Here, where the James, Nansemond, and Elizabeth rivers join to flow into the Chesapeake, the flower of the Union's North Atlantic Blockading Squadron sat at anchor. These great, tall ships, rocking gently in the tidal swell, would be essential in the anticipated moment to come. They would be here, ready. Yet they were largely supporting players in what was to be essentially a cast of two. And Chance was doing her best this March 7 to keep both of them from making the curtain.

At her berth at the old Gosport Navy Yard the CSS *Virginia* was still a ship unfinished. Day and night, the workmen swarmed over her iron and fittings, her engines and machinery. Even as they worked, the vessel's stores were being carried aboard. Stumbling over the mechanics and laborers, her crewmen vainly tried to train at their tasks. Yet with all this turmoil, the ship stood essentially ready, though untried. Only one essential element was lacking to send her to that meeting in Hampton Roads. She could not get enough powder for her guns.[1]

For weeks the *Virginia*'s officers sought to find the powder they needed. The Navy could not supply it to them. Private suppliers were contracted to the limits of their capabilities and had none not already committed elsewhere. Finally, in desperation, the seamen turned to the Army. Could it not find a few hundred pounds somewhere?

At last the Army agreed and slowly began sending through the meager allotments. By the dawn of March 7 the ship's magazine was not as empty as before, but still more was needed. If it did not come, she could still meet her appointment well enough, but her guns would be mute. In the greatest naval drama of the century, in the test for which she was destined from birth, without that powder she would be silent.[2]

If the *Virginia* was having her problems, however, the other principal in the predestined appointment at Hampton Roads faced possible destruction this March 7. The USS *Monitor* stood in imminent danger of sinking.

"Our decks are constantly covered with a sea of foam pouring from one side to the other as the deck is inclined," her paymaster laboriously wrote in a letter that he might never live to post, "while at short intervals a dense green sea rolls across with terrible force, breaking into foam at every obstruction offered to its passage."

This ungainly, unlikely warship, whose deck stood barely inches above the water in calm seas, was tossing and bobbing at the mercy of an intemperate gale. Six-foot waves crashed across her deck, even breaking over her smokestacks to send gallons of salt water hissing and popping onto her boiler fires. She was riding it out better than expected, but no one knew how long she could last against the storm. "Now we scoop up a huge volume of water on one side," the paymaster bravely wrote on, "&, as it rolls to the other with the motion of the vessel, is met by a sea coming from the opposite direction, the accumulative weight seeming sufficient to bury us forever."

Then came a threat infinitely more terrible than the sea around her. Up from the engine room were brought men apparently dead. Following close behind them came odorless "carbonic-acid gas"— carbon dioxide. Imperiled by the sea around them, the men of the *Monitor* must now face invisible death within the very heart of their ship.[3]

Hampton Roads, the *Virginia,* and a rendezvous with destiny could not have seemed more remote. Chance was doing her best to foil this much anticipated appointment. But would her luck hold?

CHAPTER 2

"Iron Against Wood"

There was nothing at all revolutionary about the idea of an ironclad warship in 1861. In one form or another, the protection of a ship's decks or sides by metal armor went back centuries. In the third century B.C. the King of Syracuse supposedly built a merchant ship sheathed with lead. The first *iron*clads were the long ships of the Norsemen of the eighth through eleventh centuries. When rowing, they lined the sides of their ships with their ironbound and studded shields, indirectly providing themselves with an enhanced defense against enemy missiles.

More lead-sheathed ships followed. Then, in 1592, the Korean admiral Yi-sun repelled a Japanese naval attack with an iron-covered "tortoise ship," its hull shaped like a turtle. Its success was astonishing. With increasing frequency, variant forms of iron-clad ships were proposed, and sometimes built. The Spanish built floating gun batteries in the 1780s, the guns protected by slanting bulwarks covered with iron. The Napoleonic Wars and the War of 1812 spawned even more plans. In the 1840s, British and American iron-hulled ships were built, some intended for war service, though none were supposed to repel enemy fire. This was deemed by some to be impossible, though experiments toward finding the right mode of making impenetrable ships' armor began in Europe and the United States, continuing into the 1850s.

It was a radical development in naval ordnance that forced the ironclad to fruition. In 1824 a French artillerist, General Henri J. Paixhans, introduced the shell gun. Instead of firing a solid-iron ball at an antagonist, it sent a hollow shell filled with powder, which could explode on or after impact. The result upon wooden warships was dramatic. No longer would cannon balls simply bounce off their sides or bury themselves harmlessly in the timbers. Now they could explode and dash the wood to splinters, though it took almost thirty years before the world had a dramatic display of their power. Barely weeks after the beginning of the Crimean War, on November 30, 1853, a squadron of Turkish warships and transports en route to the front met a Russian fleet at Sinope. The Russians, armed with Paixhans's shells, completely destroyed the Turks' wooden vessels. The day of the timber ship was done. Clearly, all that could protect a ship from iron thenceforth was iron.

The lesson learned was applied somewhat even during that war, as a few thinly clad floating batteries were put into service and performed well. It remained for postwar France to undertake serious efforts to produce an ironclad warship, however. In 1859 Stanislas Dupuy de Lôme constructed the *Gloire,* a 253-foot wooden steamer of conventional design, whose sides he protected with plates of iron armor four and one half inches thick. Napoleon III and his ministers so approved of the design that by 1861 another twenty such vessels were completed or under construction.[1]

Hardly content to follow the French, the British Admiralty made plans of its own. In 1859 they began work on the *Warrior,* a 9210-ton "iron-cased" ship. An identical sister ship, the *Black Prince,* followed shortly. By some, these warships were regarded as "the admiration of the naval world." Unlike the *Gloire,* their frames and hulls were of iron, a radical departure from the French design. Still, Edward, Duke of Somerset, First Lord of the Admiralty, was not satisfied. Another, smaller class of warships were modeled after the *Defense,* and then yet another, the *Resistance* class. By 1861 the British had ten ironclads built or under construction, some sheathed in six and one half inches of iron plating.[2]

With all of this going on, the United States had been surprisingly unenterprising. The closest thing to an ironclad was the unwieldy "Stevens Battery," a 420-foot, 6000-ton monster that carried seven guns. Begun in 1854, it was still incomplete in 1861, with no prospect for the future. Its sides were partially protected by armor on iron ribbing, but not sufficiently to withstand heavy guns. Its builders were offering to finish the ship at their own expense if the government would purchase it from them when completed, but a board of naval examiners declined.

To be sure, there was interest in the construction of American ironclads. Donald McKay, the nation's foremost shipbuilder, father of her finest clipper ships, issued a call for a fleet of armored ships after seeing the European progress. "It would be easy for us to build in one year, a fleet of 500 to 600 men-of-war ships, from a gunboat to the largest class of iron-cased frigates," he declared. He suggested that as an interim emergency measure, the Navy's existing battle frigates could be cut down a deck or two and cased in iron to protect the gun decks.[3]

As is often the case, events forced action. In early 1861, with war between North and South seemingly inevitable, President Abraham Lincoln's administration faced a touchy situation with those states, such as Virginia, which had not yet taken steps to secede from the Union. The Old Dominion held valuable Federal property, particularly the Gosport Navy Yard at Portsmouth on the Elizabeth River, and the naval shops at nearby Norfolk. In berth at Norfolk sat several warships, chief among them the *Cumberland* and the pride of the Navy, the powerful new *Merrimack*. Through March and early April 1861 Lincoln and his high command feared to send troops to Norfolk to protect Federal property lest such an act provoke Virginia into secession. Yet some measures were needed to avoid losing those ships and shops should the state join the Confederacy.

Secretary of the Navy Gideon Welles desperately hoped to get the *Merrimack* in particular to safety. She was largely dismantled, her machinery out of order. When Welles asked the navy yard's commander, Commodore C. S. McCauley, how long it would take to get her ready to leave, he said a month at least. This was on April 11, with the outbreak of hostilities at Fort Sumter, South Carolina, expected almost hourly. Thinking McCauley "feeble and incompetent for the crisis," Welles sent his chief engineer, Benjamin Isherwood, to Norfolk to get the *Merrimack* ready.

Isherwood had estimated that he would have the situation in hand within a week. It actually took him only four days to get the *Merrimack*'s machinery in working order. But McCauley began to interfere at every turn. Isherwood reported that the commodore was drinking heavily; he was suspicious, meddlesome, creating delays. Partly to circumvent this, Welles had sent with Isherwood Commander James Alden to take command of the ship and bring her to Philadelphia if evacuation of Norfolk was necessary. Not entirely decided on a course of action, Welles wanted the navy yard held if possible. Whatever happened, though, the *Merrimack* must be ready.

Firing broke out at Fort Sumter on April 12. Five days later Virginia seceded. A contest for Norfolk was inevitable within a matter of days. On April 16 Alden had reported to Welles that the *Merrimack*'s machinery was working and that she could steam out the next evening, but McCauley, perhaps in his cups, refused to let her go. Desperate to protect the navy yard, or at least buy time to get the ships to safety, Welles persuaded army commander Lieutenant General Winfield Scott to send a regiment of infantry to Norfolk. From other navy yards he gathered recruits. Looking ahead to the worst, he made arrangements for Commander John A. Dahlgren to take a ship loaded with explosives to Norfolk to destroy everything that could not be gotten away. Unfortunately, Welles failed to notify timorous old McCauley that relief was on the way. Panicking in the face of the surge of events, the commodore ordered the few loyal seamen at his command to scuttle the ships in the navy yard. On Saturday morning, April 20, they sent them to the bottom. Just three hours later, one of Welles's relief ships arrived.

The commander of the relief, Captain Hiram Paulding, now decided that the navy yard must be destroyed, despite the fact that he had enough men to defend it creditably. Parties went to the task of burning the buildings and shops. The job was badly done, and some facilities, such as the graving dock for the cleaning and care of ships' hulls, were left untouched. As for the ships, some of them still sinking, Paulding ordered them fired. The wooden warships burned spectacularly, the flames in their spars flickering like candles over a scene of grotesque conflagration. Ordnance shells and tons of explosives boomed for hours around a column of hissing, rising steam as the burning ships settled ever deeper into the river. Within hours the Federals were gone, escaping with only three of the twelve vessels that had been berthed there. Only a few hours more brought Major General William B. Taliaferro's command of Virginians into Norfolk, Portsmouth, and the Gosport Navy Yard. One of the finest naval facilities in the country was theirs without a fight.[4]

The Confederates soon found that the work of destruction had been shoddily done. Over one thousand cannon were left behind unharmed. Valuable stores, ships' parts, equipment, and machinery were virtually intact. Many of the shops and their tools showed only slight damage from the fires. The graving dock was intact, and with it much of the rest of the ships' berths. Foundries and forges were unharmed. The Confederate authorities were elated by their good fortune. Few were slow to realize the importance of the capture. Two days after Taliaferro marched in, the Richmond press exulted that in the capture of Gosport "we have material enough to build a Navy of iron-plated ships." And resting on her bottom in the river, her machinery and hull saved from the fire by her sinking, they had the *Merrimack*.[5]

It was fortunate for the infant Confederacy that in Secretary of the Navy Stephen R. Mallory the South had a man well aware of the value of ironclad warships. As senator from Florida in the 1850s, he had taken a keen interest in the early stages of the Stevens Battery, being one of very few public men to evidence much concern with this new mode of warship. He followed closely the progress of the French and British with their iron-sheathed frigates and, upon taking office in Jefferson Davis' administration, one of his first concerns was to send an agent abroad to purchase armored ships based on the European designs.

Only days after the fall of Norfolk, Mallory declared,

I regard the possession of an iron-armored ship as a matter of the first necessity. Such a vessel at this time could traverse the entire coast of the United States, prevent all blockades, and encounter, with a fair prospect of success, their entire Navy.

If to cope with them upon the sea we follow their example and build wooden ships, we shall have to construct several at one time; for one or two ships would fall an easy prey to her comparatively numerous steam frigates. But inequality of numbers may be compensated by invulnerability; and thus not only does economy but naval success dictate the wisdom and expediency of fighting with iron against wood, without regard to first cost.

Mallory was emphatic. If the Confederacy was to construct such a ship, "not a moment should be lost."[6]

Since February 1861 at the latest, Mallory had been urged to look into the building of ironclads by various Confederates, but he was dismayed by his investigations into the capabilities of southern industry to do so. It appeared that none of the rolling mills in the infant nation could produce armor plating thick enough to protect a vessel. It was on the basis of this, and advice from such Confederate naval experts as Lieutenant John M. Brooke, that the Secretary at first pinned his hopes upon foreign acquisition of ironclads.[7]

In May and June 1861 the Confederate capital was transferred from Montgomery, Alabama, to Richmond, Virginia. Mallory himself arrived to set up his department on June 3. That very same night, after a most tiring day, Mallory met with Lieutenant Brooke. They discussed ironclads. Hopeful, Mallory pressed the point of whether or not the Confederacy could, after all, build its own armored ships. Brooke believed it possible, and now Mallory asked him to put together some figures, estimates, and rough plans "in regard to floating batteries." On June 7, Brooke went to work.[8]

The thirty-five-year-old Brooke was already a man of wide experience and reputation. An 1847 graduate of Annapolis, he had invented sounding apparatus for topographical mapping of the ocean bottoms, charted the little explored North Pacific, and traveled to Japan with Matthew C. Perry. Like Mallory a Floridian, Brooke was blessed with an inventive mind tempered with a mature sense of practicality. His designs were always simple, yet sound.

Within a few days he completed his preliminary studies. What they produced were body, sheer, and deck plans of an ironclad which, with no basic alterations, would eventually serve as the prototype for virtually every ironclad the Confederacy would build.

What Brooke proposed was a shallow-draft vessel, sharply pointed at the bow and rounded astern, whose deck would sit only slightly above the water line. Midway between bow and stern he placed a casemate, or iron-enclosed structure, rounded front and rear with its sides sloping upward roughly at a 45° angle. On port and starboard the sides were to slope down to the very outside edges of the deck. Ports in the casemate would allow the running out and firing of guns from within, while pivot guns in the forward and after sections would swivel to fire from ports on either side and in their front. In action, all of the machinery and vital parts of the ship would be below the water line, safe from enemy shells. The only portions of the ship exposed to enemy fire would be the deck—itself probably slightly awash in all but the calmest water—and the casemate, whose iron-covered, sloping sides would deflect almost anything thrown against it. Brooke himself described the casemate as "a shield of timber, two feet thick, plated with three or more inches of iron, inclined to the horizontal plane at the least angle that would permit working the guns." For protection, the sides, or "eaves," of the shield were to be submerged two feet. Those submerged portions of the hull extending beyond the casemate fore and aft were to give the ship stability, greater speed, and more buoyancy. The decks, like the shield, were to be protected by several inches of iron.[9]

There was nothing revolutionary in this armored, slope-sided casemate. The idea went back at least eighty years, to Europe. Nevertheless, Brooke's design presaged a future fleet of Confederate armored warships.

When shown the plans, Mallory approved heartily. Lieutenant Brooke then suggested that John L. Porter, constructor at the Norfolk yard, and Confederate Chief Engineer William P. Williamson, be brought to Richmond to help in putting the plans into execution. Mallory, however, decided to send for a "practical mechanic" from Norfolk, instead. The man was able to help in providing some details on the kinds of timbers to use, but proved wholly useless in the matter of preparing more detailed drawings and specifications for the ship. Brooke also found him "lacking in confidence and energy, and . . . averse to performing unusual duty." Mallory sent him back to Norfolk quickly, and then did as Brooke originally suggested and sent for Porter and Williamson, on June 22.[10]

Porter did not know the purpose of the proposed meeting when he received the order but, just in case, he took something along with him. Porter, a fifty-eight-year-old native of Portsmouth, had been a naval constructor for many years in the United States Navy. As far back as 1846, while working on the USS *Alleghany*, his mind had turned to ironclads. Then—he claims—he conceived of a seagoing vessel of nineteen feet draft, covered with three-inch armor on an inclined casemate much similar to Brooke's 1861 design. The idea went to the Navy Department in Washington, where nothing was done with it—and where no record of it exists—and Porter shelved his plans until 1861.

He was working at Gosport as a constructor when the Federals evacuated the place, and promptly offered his services to the Confederacy.

The outbreak of war brought Porter's mind back to his supposed 1846 ironclad plans. He went to work on them, adapting the design to fit the limitations of Confederate industry and what he saw as a primary need for harbor-defense vessels. His new plans called for a flat-bottomed vessel 150 feet long and forty feet wide. The casemate—as in a discarded Brooke design—covered the entire length of the vessel, with no projecting bow or stern, and its eaves were to extend below the water line by two feet. With the facilities at the navy yard, Porter had constructed a small-scale model of his ironclad. When Mallory's unexplained call came on June 22, Porter decided to take his model to Richmond with him.[11]

Mallory, Brooke, Porter, and North Carolinian Williamson gathered in Brooke's office on June 23. Here they first discussed the model submitted by Porter. All were impressed by the casemate design, which called for a 40° incline instead of the 45° proposed by Brooke. This would be more effective against the powerful shells now being used. "It was considered a good shield," Brooke declared, "and, for ordinary purposes, a good boat for harbor defense." Brooke and Porter were in almost perfect agreement on the salient features of the casemate, the thickness of the wood backing, the amount of iron plating, and the angle of incline. Consequently, this meeting adopted a plan for a casemate "nearly identical" to Porter's model, and including the idea independently arrived at by both him and Brooke of having the eaves extend two feet below the water line.

Mallory now turned the meeting to Brooke's design. It differed from Porter's chiefly in the extension of the bow and stern decks beyond the shield, submerged so that only the casemate would be visible to the enemy. Curiously enough, Brooke thought this would increase such a vessel's speed. "By unanimous consent," wrote Brooke, the idea of extending and submerging the deck was adopted. Mallory directed Porter to prepare new structural drawings of the design agreed upon, and ordered Brooke and Williamson back to Norfolk to investigate the availability of the necessary engines and other machinery. The Confederacy had a plan, and a good one. But now she must find a way to take it from the drafting board to the launching ways.[12]

Brooke and Williamson first went to Richmond's Tredegar Iron Works, the foremost such facility in the South. Nowhere in the

Confederacy would they find suitable engines for such an ironclad, they were told. They discussed their findings with Porter on June 25, when Williamson remarked, "It will take at least twelve months to build her engines unless we can utilize some of the machinery in the Merrimac." Here was an idea with possibilities. The *Merrimack* had been raised from the river bottom on May 30 by the Baker Wrecking Company, and Porter himself had taken charge of moving her into dry dock. He was quite familiar with her present condition, and informed his colleagues of it. Then—there is some question as to whether Porter or Williamson first made the suggestion—the thought came up that their ironclad design, with only slight modifications, might be applied to the existing hull and works of the *Merrimack*. "I can adapt this model to the Merrimac," Porter declared, "and utilize her machinery in her." He and Brooke did feel that her draft was perhaps too much, but all agreed that this offered the best means of producing an ironclad in the least time.

This same day, June 25, 1861, they submitted a report to Mallory. Use the *Merrimack*, they said. She could be adapted to an ironclad mounting ten guns, four on each side, and two pivot guns, fore and aft. The hull, boilers, and most of the engine were little damaged, and the whole work of converting and finishing her could be done for around $110,000.[13]

Mallory approved almost immediately. Porter now began preparing new drawings for the *Merrimack*'s conversion. He returned to Gosport and, with the assistance of a laborer who held the end of his tape line, he measured the raised vessel. Then began the calculations for the weight of all the ship's components to determine how much she could carry. Porter found that she could take everything and still have fifty tons' displacement to spare. This would require the addition of extra weight to keep her eaves the proper two feet below the water line. Then a problem over the size of the propeller forced him to change her draft at the stern, a modification that would require another two hundred tons of additional ballast. By July 10, the complete plans were finished, and the next day Porter himself delivered them to Mallory. There was another conference between them, with Brooke and Williamson, and Mallory ended by accepting the plans and issuing an order to Captain French

Forrest, commandant of the Gosport Navy Yard, to proceed immediately with the ship's conversion.[14]

Lying in the graving dock at Gosport, the object of all this effort, sat the remnant of the once proud *Merrimack*. She and five other ships like her had been authorized by the Thirty-third Congress and President Franklin Pierce in 1854. The *Merrimack* was the first of the six to be completed. She was launched on June 14, 1855, at the Boston Navy Yard amid "the enthusiastic huzzas" of an estimated one hundred thousand spectators. It was "altogether the most beautiful and perfectly artistic" launch the people of Boston had ever witnessed.

The frigate was not officially completed until February 25, 1856, displacing 3200 tons and powered by a mighty steam screw, or propeller. Her first service was in the West Indies but, after only a year's service, she was decommissioned in 1857 for repairs. On September 11, 1857, she went back into service as flagship of the Pacific Station and remained there until sent back to Norfolk, where, on February 16, 1860, she was decommissioned again for more extensive overhauling. And there she sat in April 1861. Her only travel since had been to the bottom of the Elizabeth River and back up again.

Hers was a curious destiny. Once the pride of the United States Navy, now she faced a possible future as the object of the best naval hopes of the Confederacy. Her fate lay in the hands of Porter, Williamson, Brooke, and Mallory for the present, but there were others to come. With them and with yet another, unborn iron monster would come the verdict on her place in history.[15]

CHAPTER 3

"There's Something in It"

Gideon Welles, Lincoln's Secretary of the Navy, was a farsighted, capable cabinet minister. Yet, perhaps because he was not nearly so experienced in naval matters and technology, he failed to grasp the necessity for an ironclad fleet as early as Mallory. In May 1861, just when Mallory was applying to the Confederate Congress for authorization to proceed with an ironclad, Welles's Navy Department had no armored vessels in the works and very few plans under consideration.

Even so, information and rumors about enemy plans came into Washington with regularity, and Welles felt compelled to bring himself up to date on the subject. His top naval advisers were skeptical about immediate ironclad prospects—even though the Army was building ironclads on the Mississippi—but still he felt enough concern to personally author a bill asking Congress for $1.5 million for experimentation and development of three prototype ironclads. He would constitute a three-member ironclad board to consider designs submitted and decide on those to be pursued. After a good deal of lobbying, the bill passed both houses of Congress on August 3 and was signed by Lincoln. A curious footnote is that one of those who voted for its passage, Kentucky Senator John C. Breckinridge, would three and one half years thence sit in Richmond as Confederate Secretary of War.[1]

Immediately, Welles appointed Commodore Joseph Smith, Commodore Hiram Paulding, and Captain Charles H. Davis to man the examining board. This was on August 8. The day before, he had issued an advertisement soliciting designs for ironclad vessels to be submitted to the board within twenty-five days. Smith was an old friend of Welles and was possessed of a sound mechanical mind receptive to new ideas, though he and the others all admitted that they knew little of ironclads. What they did not know, they soon would learn.

The proposals came in quickly, seventeen of them. The board, in its examination, winnowed them to two that showed definite possibilities. One, proposed by C. S. Bushnell and Company of New Haven, Connecticut, called for a vessel 180 feet long, of conventional design, and armored on the "rail and plate" principle, meaning simply that the iron armor was to be affixed to its sides much like the clapboard siding on a house. The board had fears, however, that her great weight would not allow her to float high enough to be stable at sea, a problem that remained for a short time unresolved. She was to cost $235,000 and eventually would be named *Galena.*

The other likely prospect was equally unrevolutionary. Presented by the Philadelphia firm of Merrick and Sons, it was a steam frigate of wood and iron. There was little new to this one either, though the board felt it "the most practicable one for heavy armor." Measuring 220 feet with a 60-foot beam, it would displace 3296 tons and make nine and one half knots. The as yet unnamed ship—she would come to be called *New Ironsides*—was projected to cost $780,000.[2]

It was the board's reservations on the seaworthiness of Bushnell's design that led to something really new. In Washington, lobbying for his ironclad, Bushnell chanced to meet Cornelius H. Delamater of New York, a leading iron founder. When informed of the doubts held about the *Galena's* stability, Delamater told Bushnell that it would do him well to visit John Ericsson in New York. The internationally known inventor and engineer might be able to help him.

Bushnell took his problem to Ericsson, gave him all the pertinent data on the ironclad and, after some calculations were made, was rewarded with the reply, "She will easily carry the load you propose, and stand a six-inch shot—if fired from a respectable distance." Then, this matter settled, the inventor asked Bushnell a question. As he later recalled it, "Captain Ericsson asked if I had time just then to examine the plan of a floating battery absolutely impregnable to the heaviest shot or shell." Since that very problem had occupied Bushnell's waking moments for the past three months, the result being the *Galena,* he agreed to take a look.[3]

John Ericsson was an archetype genius, as uncompanionable and self-centered an egotist as his profession ever produced. He was truly comfortable and at home only with his designs and his machines. Fifty-eight now, he was born in Värmland, Sweden, and there received an early education in engineering before going to London in 1826. In twelve years in England he produced an endless succession of novel inventions, including a fire engine and the prototype for a screw propeller. In 1839 he crossed the Atlantic and adopted the United States. The productivity continued unabated, as did his reputation for being personally intolerable. He designed the USS Princeton, the first American steam, screw-propelled man-of-war, several improved steam engines, and a variety of other military and domestic wonders. He was not always spectacularly successful. In 1853, amid great public interest, he proclaimed the "Age of Caloric" with his new vessel named, modestly, the Ericsson. She was powered by—and her opponents claimed was promoted by—hot air instead of steam. The principle was applicable to small, stationary engines, but the great vessel herself proved a hopeless failure and a great embarrassment to Ericsson.[4]

But the inventor was not at all displeased with the design he now presented to Bushnell. Out from its musty storage came the blueprint of a naval revolution.

In September 1854, during the Crimean War, Ericsson had sent to France's Napoleon III the plans for what he called an "iron-clad steam-battery," whose chief feature was a hemispherical revolving turret in its center, mounting one gun. France did nothing with the design, but since then Ericsson had devoted no little time to refining it until he arrived at the model now displayed to Bushnell.

It was in every way a peculiar vessel. The hull was in two parts: an upper, iron-plated portion 172 feet long and 41 feet wide, tapered to a point fore and aft; and a lower section of wood, 122 feet long and 34 feet wide. The effect, when placing the one over the other, was an armored overhang of three and one half feet on either side and roughly twenty-five feet fore and aft. Thus designed, this hull could be rammed from any direction, producing no damage to the lower, vital hull until the ram had penetrated at least three feet of armored upper hull.

The forward section—like all of the vessel—boasted a host of novel features. At its very front sat the anchor well, a covered cylindrical hole in the bow from and into which the anchor could be lowered and raised without its ever being exposed to enemy fire. The machinery for operating it lay entirely inside the armored, upper hull. This improvement alone eliminated the danger so prevalent in naval battle of losing a ship's anchor and associated gear, thereby losing its ability to remain perfectly stationary when necessary.

Immediately behind the anchor well sat the pilothouse. It stood three feet ten inches high and was rectangular in form. Its sides were composed of blocks, or "logs," of solid wrought iron a foot wide and nine inches high, bolted at the corners. One block down from the top, iron spacers five eighths of an inch thick were to be inserted between the logs, producing a narrow aperture all around for the visibility of the captain and the helmsman. The top of the pilothouse was an iron plate two inches thick resting unfastened in inlet grooves in the top rectangle of logs. In an emergency, this plate could be pushed up and aside, allowing the crew to escape the vessel.

Behind the pilothouse and below the main deck lay the berths of men and officers—a cabin and stateroom for the captain, a wardroom, eight officers' staterooms, the main berth for the crew, and a number of store lockers. With a good sense of economy, Ericsson allowed quarters for only half the crew, since at all times half would be on and half off duty. Since these quarters were almost entirely below the water line—the main armored deck over them resting only a little over a foot above the water line—ventilation posed a problem. Ericsson solved it by allowing for blowers operated by separate steam engines and capable of bringing seven thousand cubic feet of air per minute in from pipes on deck. Ingeniously, it was forced into the lower part of the hull so that it would force out the heated, fouled air above it, thereby keeping the interior as cool and fresh as possible.

Some distance to the rear of these quarters, Ericsson placed the engines, single-cylindered steam power plants with two pistons, one at either side of a partition in the middle of the cylinder. An intricate system of cranks and connecting rods allowed both to act smoothly, while the over-all construction using only one cylinder instead of the conventional two saved much needed space within the not-oversize hull. From the engines, a propeller shaft extended through the rear of the lower hull to a four-bladed propeller. This vital part of the ship was protected by a cavity in the overhanging rear upper deck, allowing the propeller to turn freely while still unexposed and protected from above by the iron deck. Just behind it he placed the ship's rudder, equally protected so that under even the heaviest fire or ramming, the ironclad's locomotion would not be endangered.

Bushnell stood impressed by all he saw thus far, but nothing so captivated his attention as what Ericsson had placed in the middle of this already innovative vessel. Resting squarely amidships sat a cylindrical iron "cupola," or turret, a great, round, flat-topped tower of metal with two ports in one side. Through them would fire two powerful naval guns. This turret alone would have made Ericsson immortal; it was the most successful innovation in nautical warfare of the century.

The idea of a turret, or armed, revolving gun tower, was, like the ironclad itself, not at all a new one. Its antecedents went back at least to the days of the French Directory. In 1798, a "floating circular citadel" was proposed to them, forming in effect a small circular castle mounting guns on all sides and surrounded by a floating parade ground boasting windmill-driven paddle wheels for locomotion, and drawbridges for passage to dry land.

In 1805, a Mr. Gillespie of Scotland devised a movable turret for land use, boasting impregnability and the ability to "take a sure aim at any object." It was also intended for use on the water, its machinery being "adapted to turn the most ponderous Mortars with the greatest ease, according to the position of the enemy." Two years later, Abraham Bloodgood devised a floating revolving turret with guns ranged all around the inside so that, as the turret turned, each cannon could be discharged successively, keeping up a steady fire. In 1843, this same feature was boasted of a revolving turret developed by an American, Theodore Timby. In Syracuse, New York, he made a model and detailed plans at a cost to himself of over five thousand dollars. President John Tyler himself examined the model, but two years later an army-navy commission recommended against its further development by the government.

The closest thing to a practical, working turreted warship was that introduced by Captain Cowper P. Coles, Royal Navy. In 1855, during the Crimean War, he built a model of an "iron-clad raft, with revolving cupola" while stationed aboard his ship *Stromboli* in the Black Sea. This was at almost the same instant that Ericsson claims he presented his first ironclad proposal to Napoleon III. Though the Royal Navy did nothing with his invention, it was much publicized in England and America during the next five years. Indeed, there were some who would accuse Ericsson of pirating Coles's design. The Swede was certainly aware of it—despite his statements to the contrary—but there is no sound reason to suppose him guilty of stealing Coles's invention. Many inventors were looking into turreted vessels. Ericsson's was only one of six to be submitted to Commodore Smith's board.

Ericsson's design was a masterpiece. His turret consisted, he said, "simply of a short cylinder resting on the deck, covered with a grated iron roof provided with sliding hatches. This cylinder is composed of eight thicknesses of wrought-iron plates, each one inch thick, firmly riveted together." The whole turret rested on a polished brass ring set in the deck, its weight upon the ring forming a watertight seal. When in battle, the turret would be raised slightly to turn freely.

A small steam engine below the deck powered the revolving turret, its controls being inside the gun tower so that, presumably, only one man would be needed to manage them. This would also allow for good communication and co-ordination between him and the gunners. The turret mounted two large-bore naval guns, to be run out and fired through ports on one side. When the guns were in and being loaded, heavy iron shutters, or stoppers, were to swing into place, closing the ports until raised again.[5]

Ericsson could be most eloquent when describing this invention of his, and he kept the enrapt Bushnell for some time in explaining it. The ship could be built cheaply, and it could be altered to meet the pressing necessities of the situation. It could be constructed quickly; it could operate in shallow coastal waters like Hampton Roads; it could operate in narrow channels, since only the turret—and not the ship—need be turned in battle.

Bushnell, despite the fact that an ironclad of his own stood before Welles's board, immediately asked Ericsson if he might advocate this novel design before the Secretary of the Navy, Ericsson himself not enjoying the best of relations with a department that, he felt, had ignored his genius. The inventor agreed. He had already written to Lincoln on August 29 and submitted plans to the board on September 3. At once Bushnell traveled to Hartford, Connecticut, where Welles had gone to see to the moving of his family to Washington. Upon seeing the Secretary, he presented Ericsson's design with the immodest claim that he had found "a battery which would make us master of the situation." Welles, too, found the plan impressive. "I was favorably impressed," he would write in his diary. The ironclad was "extraordinary and valuable."

Without delay, Welles asked Bushnell to take the model and plans to the naval board in Washington. Bushnell, however, having had experience of his own in the difficulty of getting anything new seriously considered, decided to make a stop in Troy, New York, on the way. Here he met with John A. Griswold and John F. Winslow, influential iron founders who were working with him in armoring his *Galena*. All three were men with a quick eye for profits, and all saw an opportunity in government adoption of the Ericsson plan. Since both of the manufacturers enjoyed friendly relations with the powerful Secretary of State, William Seward, they were able to get from him a letter of introduction to President Lincoln.

On September 12, 1861, Bushnell saw the President. Lincoln, who had himself dabbled in nautical invention some years before, found the proposed ironclad interesting—Bushnell claimed he was "greatly pleased" by it—and agreed to go with Bushnell to present it to the naval board the next day.

At 11 A.M. Lincoln and Bushnell met with Assistant Secretary of the Navy Gustavus Fox and Commodores Smith and Paulding. Davis was absent, though a number of unofficial navy men came to look on. Bushnell exhibited the model and the plans, and found that "all were surprised at the novelty" of it. Some of those present thought the idea possessed merit and advised its adoption. Others ridiculed it as another of Ericsson's follies. The discussion ended, with nothing settled, when Lincoln finally looked at the model and remarked, "All I have to say is what the girl said when she stuck her foot into the stocking. It strikes me there's something in it."

Welles, worried over Bushnell's mission, was back in Washington now, hoping to help. The day following the meeting with Lincoln, Commodore Smith convened the entire board, with Davis present, and Bushnell once again made his presentation. Carefully he weighed the remarks of each of the board members and went back to his hotel "quite sanguine of success." The next day, however, he learned that Ericsson's chances were slim. And there was little that Welles could do to help him. As Bushnell put it, "the air had been so thick with croakings that the Department was about to father another Ericsson failure."

Bushnell was a man of amazing tenacity. "Never was I more active than now," he wrote, "in the effort to prove that Ericsson had *never* made a failure." After considerable difficulty, he managed to obtain Smith's and Paulding's endorsement of a recommendation to build a trial Ericsson ironclad. They signed only on the condition that Davis also might be persuaded to endorse the proposal. Davis proved immovable in his opposition. "Take the little thing home and worship it," he told Bushnell, "as it would not be idolatry, because it was in the image of nothing in the heaven above or on the earth beneath or in the waters under the earth." Davis could masterfully make a simple "no" into a biting refusal.

But this man Bushnell refused to quit. Knowing that Ericsson himself, when speaking on his own inventions, could be as charming and persuasive as he was otherwise abrasive and insufferable, Bushnell determined to get Ericsson to present the plan to the board once again in person. Here was no easy task, for the engineer bore little love for the Navy Department or those of its minions who scorned his ideas. Here, at least, Welles could help. Bushnell spoke to him, and the Secretary agreed to arrange a meeting in his office between Ericsson and the board. Beyond this, Welles personally spoke to Smith and asked him to treat the sensitive Swede tenderly, to give him a full hearing. Smith happily agreed.

Now it remained to bring the mountain to Mahomet. Bushnell was no fool. He knew Ericsson would refuse to come to Washington if he knew the initial reception given his design, particularly by Davis. Consequently, Bushnell set out to deceive him. Traveling immediately back to New York, he appeared on Ericsson's doorstep at 9 A.M.

"Well! How is it?" asked the engineer.

"Glorious," lied Bushnell.

His interest, and his vanity, stimulated, Ericsson demanded impatiently, "Go on, go on. What did they say?"

"Commodore Smith says it is worthy of the genius of an Ericsson." Bushnell saw the inventor's eyes gleam with pride.

"But Paulding—what did he say of it?"

"He said, 'It's just the thing to clear the Rebs out of Charleston with.' "

Here Bushnell hesitated, and Ericsson demanded, "How about Davis?"

"Oh, Davis." Bushnell could not stop now. "He wanted two or three explanations in detail which I couldn't give him, and so Secretary Welles proposed that I should come and get you to come to Washington and explain these few points to the entire board in his room to-morrow."

Ericsson had reportedly sworn he would never set foot in the capital again after his earlier treatment by the Navy, but Bushnell had masterfully judged the engineer's ego and ambition. "Well, I'll go," said Ericsson. "I'll go to-night."

"From that moment," Bushnell recalled years later, "I knew that the success of the affair was assured."

They rode the train all night, arriving the next day, September 15, to an immediate audience with the board. Bushnell's whole ruse almost crumbled when the officers appeared to find his appearance not only unexpected but, to Davis and Paulding, unwelcome as well. As a matter of form, they stiffly asked a few questions, which he as stiffly answered, and then he prepared to leave when finally told that his plan had already been discussed and rejected. Ericsson asked why. Here Smith gave him his opportunity. It was feared, said the old commodore, that the ironclad was not possessed of sufficient stability.

At once Ericsson launched into an eloquent defense and explanation not only of the craft's stability but of all its merits. As Bushnell later told Welles, "He thrilled every person present in your room with his vivid description of what the little boat would be and what she could do." He claimed he could build the ship in three months, less time than had already been spent by the Confederates on their still unfinished ironclad at Gosport. Seeing that he was winning the board to his plan, Ericsson concluded with the characteristically immodest exclamation: "Gentlemen, after what I have said, I consider it to be your duty to the country to give me an order to build the vessel before I leave this room."

The members of the board stepped to a corner of the room for hushed consultation. They asked Ericsson to call again that afternoon at one o'clock. He did so and at Welles's behest repeated the salient features of the morning's presentation. The Secretary asked him how much his vessel would cost. The engineer showed no hesitation in replying that it would take $275,000, and this time displayed a hastily prepared diagram, showing the vessel's stability, which he had made between interviews. Welles then polled the board members individually. Davis and Smith were convinced. Paulding wanted still more explanation in the matter of stability. Ericsson went to his private office and presented yet again his arguments. Finally Paulding was convinced. "Sir," he said, "I have learnt more about the stability of a vessel from what you have now said than all I knew before." Ericsson was to call back yet again at 3 P.M.

When the tired inventor appeared at the Navy Department on the appointed hour, he was ushered immediately into Welles's private office. The board approved his plan. He would get a contract. He was to start work on this novel ironclad immediately, and the contract would be sent on to him in New York. The Navy was going to take a chance.

Ericsson returned to New York at once. In order to make the most progress in the least time, he decided not to trust the building of the entire vessel to one firm alone. Instead he gave detailed plans of it to several companies. The hull would be built by the Greenpoint, Long Island, shipyard of Thomas F. Rowland's Continental Iron Works. The turret and its accompanying works he gave to the Novelty Iron Works. Cornelius Delamater, who had originally sent Bushnell to Ericsson, would build the engines. The all-important armor plating would be rolled by the largest iron mills in the North. To each of the contractors he made it clear that only the most skilled workmen and the very best of tools would be used. Whenever possible, they were to work through the night as well as the day.[6]

Since Ericsson began the work even before his contract arrived from Washington, he needed money to advance to his contractors. Winslow and Griswold, along with Bushnell, here found their opportunity to buy a share in the anticipated profits from the design. They advanced ten thousand dollars each, Winslow in particular expecting that, if the vessel proved successful, the Navy Department would award him an exclusive contract for the building of all subsequent such ironclads. On September 27 a contract was drawn up and signed by all parties, agreeing that each would share in the profits and that, on all future government contracts for the Ericsson ironclad, they would follow this same procedure.

With these partners, the contracting became more complicated, thanks in large part to their holdings in various firms. Now some of the armor plate was to be subcontracted to Holdane and Company in New York. The port stoppers would be made by the Buffalo firm of Charles D. De Lancy and Company. The Rensselaer Iron Works of Troy, New York, in which Griswold was a partner, would make some of the rivets and bar iron for the pilothouse. The Albany Iron Works, co-owned by Winslow, would also furnish some of the armor plating as well as the angle iron for the ship's frame.

The backers' shrewdness extended beyond providing themselves the business for this ironclad and its hoped-for successors. Some of them actually felt that Theodore Timby was entitled to the credit for the revolving-turret idea. After all, in 1843 he had applied for a patent on it. Despite Ericsson's protestations, they later decided to pay Timby a five thousand dollar royalty on this and all future turreted ironclads that they might build. They hoped that this would keep him from contesting their rights in the construction of Ericsson's vessel. The engineer himself never admitted any debt whatsoever to Timby, but did finally see the business sense behind his partners' move.[7]

Meanwhile there was the matter of Ericsson's government contract. It proved slow in coming, for Welles was beginning to find that taking risks was not popular in Washington. Senior naval officers loudly proclaimed that the Ericsson boat would prove a failure and thereby disgrace the naval board for its part in the fiasco. "Amidst obloquy and ridicule," Welles later wrote, he went ahead. To protect himself, however, he made the contract a stiff one. The ironclad must be absolutely complete when delivered, it said, all in working order and capable of making eight knots. Furthermore, she must be ready within ninety days of signing. The contract also called for Ericsson to furnish masts and spars so that she might make six knots under sail, oblivious of the fact that the design made no allowance for any but steam power. The builders would be paid

$275,000, in installments roughly every two weeks depending upon the progress of the work and certification of its completion by a supervising agent from the Navy Department. Twenty-five per cent of each payment would be held back, however, to be paid within ninety days of the vessel's receipt by the government and contingent upon its trials and performance. Finally, in its most stringent clause, the contract required that the ship prove a complete success. Should she fail, the government was to be refunded all money advanced. The restrictions were tough, but neither Ericsson nor Bushnell resented them at all. They felt confident in the new ship. Winslow and Griswold, loath to part with their dollars on a failure, felt imposed upon, but they had no choice. On October 4, 1861, the contract was signed, just eighteen days after the naval board formally recommended the adoption of the designs for the *Galena, New Ironsides,* and what everyone for the time being would call the "Ericsson."

That same day, Commodore Louis Goldsborough sent Welles a dispatch from Hampton Roads. His information indicated that, without doubt, the Confederates were even then planning an early attack upon his fleet with the reconstructed *Merrimack,* now reported to be a formidable ironclad.

Welles and Commodore Smith had for some days tried to think of the most suitable test for the Ericsson ironclad. Goldsborough's letter gave it to them. This novel vessel would have to steam down to Hampton Roads, pass the Confederate batteries lining the Elizabeth River, pass up it to Norfolk, and there destroy the *Merrimack.*[8]

CHAPTER 4

"Prompt and Successful Action"

"We have the *Merrimack* up and just pulling her in the dry dock." Captain French Forrest, Confederate commandant at Gosport, wired the good news to Robert E. Lee on May 30. The decision to raise the burned frigate had been made just three weeks before. On May 11, a naval advisory board had proposed to Virginia Governor John Letcher that the ship be brought up. The firm of B. & I. Baker of Norfolk put in a bid of five thousand dollars to do the job and deliver the ship to the graving dock. Their bid was accepted and the work begun. For extra manpower, the Baker brothers called upon some of the local Confederate troops, among them men of Company G, 4th Georgia Infantry, the first troops to reach the navy yard after its evacuation. They had been eating breakfast at Portsmouth's Ocean Hotel when the ruins of Gosport were still smoking.[1]

Forrest thought the whole *Merrimack* affair a waste of time, but he had his orders and by the end of May the job was done. The raised ship looked terrible. Charred timbers arched grotesquely up from the water line. Her brass and iron railings and fittings were twisted hideously. The smokestack was ruined, most of the decking was destroyed. And as soon as she hit the air, the *Merrimack*'s iron parts from boiler to rivets began to rust. One who would be intimately associated with this ship in the ensuing months, Acting Chief Engineer H. Ashton Ramsay, declared that "when she was raised by the Confederates she was nothing but a burned and blackened hulk."[2]

Hulk or not, Mallory saw her worth. On June 10 her value in dry dock was estimated at $250,000. A month later he told the Confederate Congress that refitting her as a frigate would cost $450,000 or more, and even then she would not be able to escape the Federal blockading fleet in Hampton Roads. But as an ironclad the situation would be changed entirely, and the ship would cost only $172,523 to complete. Congress readily agreed.[3]

Even before the appropriation was approved, work on the *Merrimack* was well under way, and so was the acrimony. Porter was to oversee the construction. Brooke would manage the armor and weaponry for the vessel. Williamson was in charge of refitting her engine and other machinery. Such an arrangement, particularly where boundaries of authority overlapped frequently, as they did between construction and armoring, immediately proved unwise. Brooke and Porter in particular did not like each other. It did not help that Brooke was also to act as Mallory's inspecting officer for the whole project. There was no secret of the fact that the Floridian had the Secretary's ear and stood a favorite with him. Resentment between Brooke and Porter heightened as each claimed the authorship of the new ironclad's design, a situation complicated by at least three other claimants: Ex-Governor Henry Wise of Virginia believed that he first proposed the idea, based upon earlier models by Commodore James Barron. Engineer Williamson would later claim title to the idea and plans. And one E. C. Murray, a contractor who had submitted an ironclad plan to Mallory in April 1861 at Montgomery, declared that the *Merrimack* design was his but that Brooke got credit for it through an unexplained maneuver that Murray called "jeremy diddling."[4]

Porter's was the greater animosity, probably because he was an unhappy man. His had not been a distinguished career. In 1847 he failed the examination for a constructor's appointment with the United States Navy. Ten years later he passed it, only to be tried for neglect of duty in 1860 over faulty construction in the USS *Seminole*. He was acquitted but, embittered, he was the only naval constructor to transfer allegiance to the Confederacy in 1861. For the time being, he was all Mallory had.[5]

Work on cutting down the burned hull began even before the Congressional appropriation was approved. All of the charred upper timbers were cleared away, and her entire upper works were eliminated down to the berth deck, just over three feet above her unladen water line. Assisted by James Meads, master ship carpenter, Porter had her cut on a straight line from bow to stern and then began laying the main, or gun, deck. Over the portion that would be covered by the casemate, the deck consisted of planks laid over beams, but for the outer decks fore and aft he used solid timbers.[6]

By the end of July the deck was laid and Porter was starting work on the casemate backing. The work went at a feverish pace. The energies of almost the entire navy yard went into this one ship. Mallory had as many as fifteen hundred men working on her, oftentimes keeping them at it on Sundays and through night shifts. "The Secretary required almost impossibilities," Porter complained. Rush orders came almost daily from Richmond, along with directions for guarding the vessel against sabotage and urgent requests for progress reports. The as yet unnamed ironclad commanded more and more attention in Richmond with each passing day. "The government is constructing a monster at Norfolk," declared a War Department clerk.[7]

Meanwhile, Williamson did his job as well as could be expected. To assist him in the work, Mallory sent Acting Chief Engineer Ramsay. In the old Navy, Ramsay had been the *Merrimack*'s second assistant engineer. "I knew her every timber by heart," he claimed, and his knowledge of the ship's cantankerous engines was invaluable. "During a cruise of two years whilst I was attached to this ship in the United States service," he wrote, "they were continually breaking down, at times when least expected, and the ship had to be sailed under canvas during the greater part of the cruise." Finally, when all attempts to improve their performance had failed, the engines were condemned. The defects were so great that repair was impossible, and the ship was indeed awaiting new engines when Norfolk fell. Ramsay faced a dim prospect in trying to set things aright, but at least he did have the Navy Department's assurance that the ship, when completed, would not be sent any place where a delay caused by engine failure would endanger her safety. In all the chain of elements to compose this mighty ironclad, here lay the weakest link. To Ramsay would fall the chief burden of keeping it together.[8]

None of the three originally charged with the *Merrimack*'s conversion performed so well as Brooke. His duties encompassed overseeing the preparation of the armor plating, managing its delivery to

Norfolk, testing its strength, and determining the proper ordnance for the vessel. "He is an indefatigable fellow," wrote Lieutenant Robert Minor, "and works with head and heart for our glorious cause."[9]

On July 23, 1861, Mallory contracted with Richmond's Tredegar Iron Works to supply the iron plating for the vessel at a rate of six and one half cents per pound. They were to make one-inch-thick plates, eight inches wide and in varying lengths. This facility, formerly geared to the production of railroad engines and materials, had to convert almost overnight to the making of war machines. Many of its workmen were unskilled at their new tasks, and even some of the vital tools had to be made before rolling could begin. Some machinery had to be rebuilt to accommodate the eight-inch width specified.

This was not the only improvisation required. The necessary iron itself had to be found. Some three hundred tons of scrap iron from burned portions of the Gosport yard went to Tredegar for the job. Meanwhile, railroads in northern Virginia and captured portions of the Baltimore & Ohio were scavenged for spare rails. Other railroad iron was purchased and lifted from threatened lines too close to the enemy. These rails were taken, cut to the lengths specified, and then laid together side by side. Bars of puddled pig and scrap iron were then placed around them. The whole mass was heated to the proper temperature and then forced through the powerful rollers to the approximate dimensions. Then they were finished off ready for delivery. Brooke personally supervised and inspected the work.[10]

Tredegar soon had a quantity of one-inch plate ready. But then Brooke entertained second thoughts about his plans for the ship's armor. It had been his intention all along to clad the casemate in three layers of one-inch plate. Now, however, he began to fear that three inches of armor might not be enough. To Tredegar he sent orders in September to start making plate two inches thick. He would use two layers of this instead. For Tredegar this hardly came as welcome news. One-inch plate was easy for them to handle. It could be rolled economically, and the holes for the bolts that would mount the iron on its wooden backing were punched out without difficulty. The two-inch plate could not be punched. It must be drilled, and compounding the problem were the frequent design changes made by Porter and Brooke. Whenever they realigned the design for the overlapping layers of iron, new holes had to be drilled in order that the top layer's holes would line up with those on the bottom. Some plates had their bolt holes redrilled four times, and other changes were still anticipated. The result was a rise in Tredegar's overhead costs and a resultant rise in the price of the iron by one cent a pound.[11]

So important was this matter of the iron plating that Mallory ordered Brooke to conduct tests on it with the heavy guns of Confederate batteries at Jamestown Island. Brooke went early in October, and there met the commander of the batteries, Lieutenant Catesby ap Roger Jones. This forty-year-old Virginian was a veteran of the U. S. Navy and nephew of Thomas ap Catesby Jones, who commanded the little fleet opposing the British at New Orleans in 1814 and later anticipated the Mexican War by four years when he seized Monterey, California, in 1842. The curious "ap" in the name was actually a Welsh idiom meaning "son of," in this case "son of Roger." A capable, energetic officer, Jones immediately gave Brooke his full co-operation.

They constructed a wooden target twelve feet square, conforming to the planned construction of the *Merrimack* casemate. The wood was two feet thick, and on top of this they placed first three layers of one-inch plate. To approximate the casemate, they inclined the target at an angle of 36° and set it 327 yards from the test gun. They would use an 8-inch columbiad, a heavy iron cannon firing an 8-inch solid iron ball with a ten-pound charge of black powder. In firing seven or eight shots, they found that the ball shattered the iron plating and entered several inches into the wood. Clearly, this would be unsatisfactory for the *Merrimack*, particularly if the enemy were to use explosive shells. The shot, after penetrating the iron, would go off in the wood, shattering the casemate and probably setting it ablaze.

Now Brooke and Jones placed two layers of two-inch plating on a target. Again they fired the 8-inch gun at it, and a 9-inch columbiad as well. This time the outer plate was shattered, but the inner iron was only cracked. The balls could not reach the wood backing. This more than justified Brooke's change of mind on the plating to be used. Just to be sure, however, yet another target was built. This time they covered it with railroad T rails in two layers. Six shots were fired at it with the 8-inch gun. They found that the rails in both layers could be broken and the wood penetrated. Three shots with the 9-inch gun showed even greater damage, and with both guns the greasing of a portion of the target showed no enhanced ability of the shield to deflect the balls.

On October 12 Jones submitted an official report of the tests, in which he took a great interest. Results clearly indicated that flat iron plating was more effective than rails, and that four inches was definitely necessary for the *Merrimack*. They also showed that the angle of inclination to be given the side of the casemate assisted materially in reducing the damage done by the impact of the shot. Jones was recognized as a first-rate ordnance expert from his days in the old Navy, and his words carried weight. His consuming interest in the success of the ironclad only enhanced his reliability. "I consider the *Merrimac* the most important naval affair the country has to deal with," he wrote to Robert Minor just before the tests, "and consequently am deeply interested in her success."[12]

The Confederates knew well by now that others felt a deep interest in the success of their ironclad. The enemy was well aware of what they were doing. In an attempt to lull Federal suspicions, the Navy Department leaked to the press a report that "the iron sheeting for the Merrimac has proved, under trials made recently at Jamestown Island with Columbiads, to be almost worthless." The report appeared in many of the South's newspapers, and the department was particularly interested in getting it into the Norfolk *Day Book,* whose words would be given the most credence by the Federal blockaders in Hampton Roads.[13]

Regardless of what the papers said, the two-inch plate began to roll out of Tredegar. From September 1861 until February 1862, this iron works found itself occupied almost entirely with the *Merrimack*'s armor. "We are now pressed almost beyond endurance," complained one of Tredegar's owners on October 11, and the pace would not let up. But then arose a new problem. The available rail facilities for transporting the iron to Norfolk let them down. There was a shortage of flatcars, and some of the plate had to sit on the banks of the James River four weeks and more awaiting shipment. Nearly one hundred tons was ready by mid-October, but there it sat. Mallory hounded Tredegar to get the plate to Norfolk more quickly, and Tredegar in return sought government assistance in getting priority for shipment. Finally Forrest dispatched an officer from Gosport to oversee the movement of the iron. Whereas the iron works had expected to have most of the plate ready by the end of November, it was actually February 12, 1862, before the last shipment was delivered to Norfolk, and then only after a route was arranged that actually took the iron from Richmond to Norfolk by way of Weldon, North Carolina. In all, Tredegar furnished 723 tons of iron. Porter had estimated that one thousand tons would be necessary. Instead of seven and one half cents per pound, the final bill came to slightly over a cent higher, $123,015.[14]

Overseeing the armor was only one of Brooke's tasks. To him Mallory also entrusted the choosing of the guns for the ironclad. From the outset it was assumed that the heaviest guns practicable should be used. Jones suggested to Brooke in September that 10-inch Dahlgren smoothbores be used, but the latter settled on 9-inch guns instead. There would be six of these mounted at the broadside ports. However, Mallory specifically asked Brooke to design special guns for the other four ports fore and aft. He wanted rifles, guns that could fire heavy wrought-iron "bolts"—elongated projectiles—as well as shells.

Brooke started work on the new guns even before the armor plate was begun. By mid-September he was done. The proposed gun was a standard 7-inch tube with several heavy wrought-iron rings heated to expand and then placed tightly around its breech. When the iron cooled, it would contract, forming an extremely tight reinforcing band around the powder-chamber area. This would allow much heavier powder charges to be used, providing the force needed to fire bolts and other rifled projectiles with great power and accuracy. It was not entirely a new design. R. P. Parrott designed a much similar gun for the Union, the chief difference being that his iron band was welded into one piece. The British Blakeley and Armstrong guns also bore much similarity to Brooke's design.

With the guns designed, Mallory placed an order for two of them with Tredegar on September 21, and other orders followed in the coming months. Once again the iron works had to adapt its machinery and make new tools, to produce the desired product. Still, by late November the first guns were ready, two 7-inch and two 6.4-inch Brooke rifles. To oversee their testing, as well as to speed the snail's-pace construction of the ironclad, procure a crew, and get the whole ready for service, the Navy Department relieved

Jones at Jamestown Island. His new assignment was as executive officer of the *Merrimack*. "No more thoroughly competent officer could have been selected," declared one of her junior lieutenants.

Jones knew this ship. Like Ramsay, he had served aboard her before the war. His knowledge of ordnance was even better. He had assisted John A. Dahlgren in the original tests leading to the development of the Dahlgren smoothbore, and now he put the Brooke guns through rigorous trials, determining that they would perform accurately and safely with a fourteen-pound charge of powder. Tredegar also made the projectiles for the guns, casting only shells for them at a cost of twenty dollars each. The rifles' design allowed for the use of solid shot to penetrate iron armor, but since Brooke and Jones anticipated meeting only wooden ships in Hampton Roads or elsewhere, shells were by far the more practical.[15]

Jones's task of finding a crew for the *Merrimack* proved far more difficult than perfecting her armament. Because of its strong attachments to the land, the South really had no maritime population before the war. Whereas a great number of the officers in the old Navy were Southerners, almost all of the men came from the North. As a result, officers were not at all hard to find. People like Jones, Minor, Ramsay, and others were eager to serve aboard the experimental warship. But finding the two hundred or more common sailors who would be needed to man the vessel and its guns was another matter.

Recruiting-officers did little good, since most of the men who did have sea experience had already gone into the Army. As a result, Jones had to look to the Army for help. In January 1862 Lieutenant John Taylor Wood received orders to report to Norfolk for duty aboard the *Merrimack,* and to him Jones entrusted much of the work of finding men. There were a few seamen in Norfolk who would join. Better prospects seemed to lie in the command of Major General John B. Magruder at Yorktown. He had there two battalions of men from New Orleans that should have several seamen. Wood found Magruder most co-operative, as the general sent one of his staff to accompany the lieutenant to each of his camps to call for volunteers with sea legs. At each stop, Wood spoke to the men on parade. Out of two hundred volunteers, he found eighty who would do. Later he would visit Richmond and Petersburg on the same errand, slowly building the *Merrimack*'s muster. Eventually the necessary three hundred would step forward, but as late as February 10 the Navy Department's Office of Orders and Detail would complain that "the *Merrimack* has not yet received her crew, notwithstanding all . . . efforts to procure them from the Army."[16]

Even with the crew coming in, the unfinished state of the ironclad allowed for little or no drilling of the recruits. Every sort of delay had been encountered. Whereas the vessel was to have been completed in November, the year 1862 dawned with the entire stern portion of her still unclad. Tredegar's problems accounted for much of this. Ramsay complained that in the time it took that firm to roll her plate, "we could have rolled them at Norfolk and built four *Merrimacs*."

Changes and alterations also caused more than their share of delay. Brooke frequently visited the dry dock, and just as often suggested modifications to Mallory, who imposed them on a resentful Porter. He changed the position of the steering ropes connecting the wheel to the rudder, added more gun ports, increased the thickness of the wood backing on the casemate, and, of course, increased the plate from three to four inches. "Lieut. Brooke was constantly proposing alterations in her," Porter would complain, "and as constantly and firmly [they were] opposed by myself."

By January 1862, with the work still far from complete, the blacksmiths and finishers connected with the project signed an agreement "to do any work *that will expedite the completion of the Merrimac,* free of charge." They would work until 8 P.M. every night without extra pay. Still, as Jones lamented, "there were many vexatious delays attending the fitting and equipment of the ship." As January came to a close, he was far more blunt in describing the situation to Brooke: "Somebody ought to be hung."[17]

Just who Jones had in mind he never said, but there is no doubt he was disappointed in Porter. The constructor, however, was having his own problems. "I received but little encouragement from anyone," he lamented. "Hundreds—I may say thousands—asserted she would never float." She would turn upside down, they said; she would suffocate her crew; the firing of her guns would deafen the men; she would not steer. Porter was suffering insomnia with the multitude of constructional difficulties facing him. "You have no idea what I have suffered in mind since I commenced her," he wrote in March 1862. "Public opinion generally about here said she would never come out of the dock." Porter was not exaggerating. While Ramsay was at his work on the vessel, his friend Captain Charles MacIntosh frequently came by to watch the operation. When he finally received orders to another station, MacIntosh stopped by one last time. "Good-by Ramsay," he said from the granite curbing at the graving dock. "I shall never see you again. She will prove your coffin."[18]

Meanwhile, the officers and men filled the time as best they could as the work slowly progressed. Gun crews trained at the cannon aboard the old U.S. frigate *United States* for about two weeks, the only practice they would get. The ship's officers became popular figures in Norfolk and with the many visitors who came to see their ship. Often they were guests of ex-Governor Wise, whose son found them "mingling with us simply and unostentatiously, as if unconscious that the issues of one of the greatest struggles the world ever witnessed were committed to their keeping." They entertained Wise with accounts of the ship's progress, while they fascinated his son. There was Brooke, "taciturn and dreamy"; Jones, "a quiet man of forty"; and Robert Minor, "young, quick, and fidgety as a wren." Wise, in turn, told them all that was wrong with the way the *Merrimack* was being converted. The officers bore his remarks patiently.[19]

By late January 1862 the armoring of the vessel was complete, and on February 17 she was commissioned and launched. To the very last, the skeptics plagued Porter. Of the officers stationed at the yard or assigned to the vessel, Porter felt that only Captain Archibald Fairfax, inspector of ordnance at Gosport, really had confidence in her. Even Jones, he felt, showed "a want of faith in her ability to float." The day before the launch, Porter went to Captain Sidney Smith Lee—brother of General Robert E. Lee—and informed him that the water would be let into the dry dock the next day. Lee, executive officer at the yard, asked the constructor, "Mr. Porter, do you really think she will float?"[20]

The launch was pure anticlimax. No governors or other dignitaries were on hand; there was no band, no crowd of onlookers. The few officers present preferred the safety of the dockside to standing aboard the ship, and only one or two of the officers who would serve on her witnessed the event. When the water flowed in and the ship began to slide out into the river, only five men stood aboard her: four marine privates and a corporal. Standing on her bow, Private William R. Cline marveled at the lack of ceremony. The only event of note was her christening. The old USS *Merrimack* was commissioned CSS *Virginia,* though most navy men, including even many who served aboard her, would always call her by her former name.[21]

The *Virginia* still swarmed with workmen, far from finished with the task of her conversion, but already she seemed a formidable antagonist. From bow to stern, she measured 262 feet and nine inches. In her center sat the casemate, 178 feet three inches long at the base, and sloping upward at roughly a 36° angle. The backing of the casemate consisted of two feet of solid pine and oak extending from the water line to a point seven feet above the gun deck, itself nearly 168 feet in length. Outside of this ran the first layer of two-inch iron plate, fastened in horizontal lengths. Over this lay the second course of iron, placed vertically. Bolts ran from the outside through the iron and wood and were fastened inside by heavy nuts. The sides ran nearly twenty-four feet from water line to top, where an iron grate of two-inch square bars formed the top deck. Porter located three hatchways on this fourteen-foot-wide deck, and at the front placed a conical pilothouse made of twelve-inch-thick iron with four sight holes cut out. On each side of the casemate Porter cut four holes, or ports, to accommodate the two 6.4-inch rifles and the six smoothbores. At the ends were three ports for the 7-inch pivot rifles. Heavy iron shutters were supposed to be fitted to close the ports but were not yet in place.

The main deck extended twenty-nine and one half feet in front of the shield and fifty-five feet behind it. All of the outside decking was covered with iron, and the entire ship was ringed with one-inch plate extending from the decks' edge down to a depth of three feet. The rudder and propeller Porter considered items of special vulnerability, and these he protected with a heavy fantail. On the ship's bow, just below the water line, he installed a fifteen-hundred-pound cast-iron ram, or beak.[22]

All in all, this was a fearsome war machine, but like most innovations, it suffered from many defects, indeed more than its share. Despite the extensive calking done at all her seams, the *Virginia* leaked profusely. "There has not been a dry spot aboard of her, leaks everywhere," complained Jones on February 20. The crew found quarters aboard her damp and unhealthy, "as uncomfortable as possible," said Jones. The ventilation was bad, and nearly one third of the crew went on the sick list from one malady or another connected with their quarters.[23]

The ram was not well mounted. Porter did not entirely approve of it in the first place, but gave in to the Navy Department's insistence in the matter. From the very first, Mallory had intended for his ironclad to act as a ram as well, able to stave in the side of wooden vessels with an iron prow. Porter did a halfhearted job of installing it, however. Even as one of the *Virginia's* midshipmen looked on, the workers fastening it to the bow drove in the iron bolts that would secure it, using heavy sledge hammers. A missed blow cracked one of the flanges mounting it completely across, but nothing was done about it. Even the meddlesome Henry Wise saw that it was improperly fastened, but no one listened to him.[24]

Worst of all, however, was Porter's grave miscalculation of the ship's weight. In figuring her displacement, he forgot to subtract some weight that would be removed from the ship before she was floated. As a consequence, when the *Virginia* slid out into the Elizabeth, her fore and after decks were not under water as planned, and the casemate eaves, instead of extending two feet below the water line, barely reached below the surface. As a result, in even the slightest swell the waves would frequently expose the hull below the eaves, where the armor was only an inch thick. A well-placed shot here would penetrate with ease, flooding the ship.

Jones was furious: "The ship will be too light, or I should say, she is not sufficiently protected below the water. . . . The eaves of the roof will not be more than six inches immersed, which in smooth water would not be enough; a slight ripple would leave it bare except the one-inch iron that extends some feet below. We are least protected where we most need it. The constructor should have put on six inches where we now have one."

Porter himself brought the mistake to Brooke's attention, but never would he admit that he had made an error. He was extremely proud of his work on her. "Of the great and skillful calculations of the displacement and weights of timber and iron involved in the planning and construction of this great piece of naval architecture, . . . no other man than myself has, or ever had any knowledge," he would claim in March. But instead of admitting that he had forgotten to subtract in his calculations the weight of the masts, spars, rigging, sails, and upper decks, which were removed from the ship, he would claim instead that Brooke's changes in the armor or the placement of the propeller were responsible.

All that could be done was to add ballast to bring the *Virginia* down in the water. Hundreds of tons of pig iron were stowed bow and stern and in unused storerooms. This, plus the anticipated powder and shells and about 150 tons of coal, were expected to bring her eaves down a foot or more. Yet, by March 5, with everything but powder aboard, the fore and after decks rode barely awash and the casemate extended only about six inches below the surface. At this point, no more ballast could be added either, for fear of overstraining her bottom. If an enemy gunner aimed true, this one defect alone could prove fatal to the *Virginia*.[25]

Still, defects and all, the *Virginia* was a novelty, and Porter, Brooke, Williamson, and Mallory could all take some pride in their ersatz ironclad. Mallory was always effusive in his praise of Brooke, but here he even lauded highly the sometimes difficult Porter. He did his job with "ability, energy, and ingenuity," said the Secretary. "He is a skillful constructor and in all respects a valuable officer." To Porter, who would suffer the torture of for many years to come hearing his contributions to the *Virginia* credited to others, these were indeed welcome compliments.[26]

Even as the ship was still unfinished at her floating, so was her crew. Most of the men had been recruited, but the officers were still coming aboard. In addition to Jones, Wood, Minor, and Ramsay, orders brought aboard Lieutenants John R. Eggleston and Hunter Davidson. Surgeon Dinwiddie B. Phillips came to her. Such midshipmen as H. H. Marmaduke and Hardin Littlepage joined the officers' mess. A detachment of marines led by Captain Reuben T. Thom filled out the ship's complement.

But still the *Virginia* had no captain. With good cause, Jones entertained hopes from the first of being assigned to command her. Alas, the time-honored seniority system doomed his hopes. "Jones is not old enough," wrote Wood; "this is our system." In fact, however, it appears that Mallory did not intend to appoint anyone to actual command of the ship. Forrest and others senior to Jones had applied for the command, but Mallory held them unsuited to the task. They were also senior to the man he wanted for the job, and the only way to avoid an uproar by appointing someone junior to the command was to appoint no one. Instead, Mallory gave his man command of all the James River naval defenses, thereby placing the *Virginia* under his jurisdiction and naming it his flagship. The solution neatly circumvented the problem, accomplishing the Secretary's goal without upsetting the system. Only Jones felt greatly disappointed. Having been so intimately connected with her conversion, Jones confessed that "I was actually oppressed with the undue expectations" of being given command of her. He would never entirely reconcile himself to not receiving it, "though I endeavored to console myself by making every possible exertion and with the reflection that it is as necessary sometimes to suffer from one's friends as to fight one's enemies."[27]

The man Mallory chose to command the James River defenses, and therefore the *Virginia,* had not wanted to serve in the Confederate States Navy. Captain Franklin Buchanan was a lifelong Marylander, born September 17, 1800, the grandson of a signer of the Declaration of Independence. As a youth he resided for a time in Pennsylvania, and from this state he was appointed a midshipman in the United States Navy in January 1815. Thereafter he saw wide service aboard the *Constitution* and the *Constellation.* In 1845 he submitted a plan for a naval academy, which was approved, and the department made him the first superintendent of the United States Naval Academy at Annapolis. When the war with Mexico came, he commanded the sloop *Germantown,* fighting aboard her at Veracruz. Following the war, he served with Matthew C. Perry's Japan squadron, commanding the flagship, the *Susquehanna.* In 1855 he won appointment as a captain, and four years later took command of the Washington Navy Yard.

When the Lincoln administration took power, and war seemed inevitable, men of southern connections, such as Buchanan, immediately came under suspicion. "I was, by reliable friends, put on my guard as respected . . . Buchanan," Welles wrote, as he was "being courted and caressed by the Secessionists." Buchanan remained true to his oath, however, until the riots in Baltimore in April, when he believed that his Maryland would secede immediately. Unwilling to bear arms against his home state, he resigned his commission on April 22, 1861, and said a tearful farewell after forty-six years in the Navy. True to his duty to the last, he turned the navy yard over to John A. Dahlgren with the injunction to defend it well. But Maryland did not secede. "I never was an advocate for secession," Buchanan told a friend in June; "I am a strong Union man. . . . I have had a horror of fighting against the 'stars & stripes.' " Consequently, he asked Welles to reinstate him. "I am ready for service," he said, hoping only that he might be assigned abroad so that he would not have to fight the South. Welles, understandably distrustful, declined. "Your name has been stricken from the rolls of the Navy," he replied.

All this time, hints had come Buchanan's way that he could attain high command in the infant Confederate Navy. He did not want it. Saddened by the abrupt termination of a fine career and anxious not to fight against the old flag, he retired to his Maryland estate, hoping to live out his days farming. By September, however, he could sit no longer. Despite wide criticism of his attempt to retrieve his resigned commission in the U. S. Navy, Buchanan was immediately made a captain by Mallory and assigned to command the department's Office of Orders and Detail. It was a position that made him one of the Secretary's most trusted advisers, and Buchanan's activity and wholehearted immersion in the cause once he adopted it made Mallory sure that this was the man to direct the new *Virginia* in battle.[28]

On February 24, 1862, Mallory ordered Buchanan to take command, using the *Virginia* as his flagship. Along with the order he included his own hopes for the ironclad's future. "The *Virginia* is a novelty in naval construction, is untried, and her powers unknown. . . . Her powers as a ram are regarded as very formidable, and it is hoped that you may be able to test them." Ramming was "like the bayonet charge of infantry," he said, and it also conserved on ammunition. Indeed, "even without guns the ship would be formidable as a ram."

Mallory hoped for bigger things. The year 1862 had not proved a good one for the Confederacy thus far. The loss of Forts Henry and Donelson, in Tennessee, had opened the heartland of the South to invading Federal armies, and on February 8 Henry Wise—now a brigadier general—had had twenty-five hundred of his men captured, and lost much face, at Roanoke Island, North Carolina. The Confederacy needed something to revive its spirits. "Could you pass Old Point and make a dashing cruise on the Potomac as far as

Washington," Mallory told Buchanan, "its effect upon the public mind would be important to the cause." This was the Navy's first opportunity to strike an important blow. "Action," he concluded, "prompt and successful action—now would be of serious importance to our cause."[29]

Buchanan had visited the *Virginia* at dry dock once prior to his assignment, and even before had made recommendations of officers for her, including Jones. As soon as possible, now, he moved to Norfolk to take his new command. Everyone on the *Virginia* seemed pleased with him. Eggleston found him "a typical product of the old-time quarter deck, as indomitably courageous as Nelson, and as arbitrary. I don't think the junior officer or sailor ever lived with nerve sufficient to disobey an order given by the old man in person." It was said that during his service with Perry, Buchanan so sternly scolded a Chinese pilot that the hapless Oriental jumped overboard. Ramsay, an old hand himself, thought Buchanan "one of the grandest men who ever drew a breath of salt air." Even at sixty-one the captain was, said Ramsay, "the beau ideal of a naval officer of the old school, with his tall form, harsh features, and clear, piercing eyes." Civilians in Norfolk found him "quiet, kindly, and as unpretentious as a country farmer, but with an eye which age had not dimmed, and which even then was filled with the light of battle." Catesby Jones, however, was less effusive. The captain was, he said, "excitable."[30]

Perhaps so, but events were coming to a head. Time was getting short, and the *Virginia* had an appointment to keep. Always in the back of Buchanan's mind echoed Mallory's urgent appeal: "Action —prompt and successful action."

CHAPTER 5

"Ericsson's Folly"

John Ericsson had a contract, albeit a curious one. Aside from its highly unusual provisions for payment, it boasted certain other peculiarities. The document called for the construction of "an iron-clad, shot-proof steam battery of iron and wood" capable of making eight knots under steam. Strangely, though, it also stipulated that the vessel was to make six knots *under sail!* Just how the Navy Department ever expected this ship to mount masts and spars is a mystery. Even assuming that the turret's own guns did not accidentally blast the masts away from the deck, the pitch and sway caused by the wind's blowing into sails would have run the ship's low deck under water, swamping her. Surely this should have been obvious to those drawing up the contract, for it also called for only eighteen inches of freeboard—the height of the deck above the water line—when fully loaded. Of course the whole question was strictly academic, for the imperious Ericsson never had any intention of honoring this part of the agreement. His ironclad would never be encumbered with sail.

The contract also stipulated that no one serving in the Federal government was to share in the construction, a hopeful attempt to avert profiteering. Yet Winslow and Griswold had very good government connections, and hopes of lavish profits in the building of future ironclads. This made all the more ironic the rumors that would soon spread to the effect that they were financing the experimental vessel entirely out of their own pockets, with no promise of remuneration from the Navy.[1]

Ericsson himself personally supervised almost every facet of the construction, and he made few friends in the process. He was "an intense—a high-pressure steam engine himself," said George Robinson, an acquaintance. Bushnell called him "a full electric battery in himself." The fifty-eight-year-old Swede was short—five feet seven and one half inches tall—but, at 178 pounds, powerfully built. Rumor said that he had once lifted and carried an iron casting weighing 592 pounds and then broken it in two with a sledge hammer. It was an act characteristic of this supreme egoist. He was, as well, cruelly sarcastic, disdainfully logical. Before the war, when Delamater cordially invited him to visit Niagara Falls, Ericsson's only reply was, "Is anything the matter with them?"[2]

How interesting it is that, as the Navy Department's representative in overseeing the vessel's construction, the man Welles sent was just as officious, just as abrasive, as Ericsson. Chief Engineer Alban C. Stimers was little loved in the Navy. Just thirty-four now, his expert knowledge of steam principles and engines helped him rise rapidly, until he became a chief engineer in 1858. Having risen quickly, and displaying all the conceit and overconfidence that often accompanies such a rise, he appeared to his associates "smart but coarse—and like all of his kind, overbearing and disagreeable." Considering this, how surprising it is that Stimers and Ericsson became fast friends almost immediately, and that, in the former, the latter would find one of his chief and most vocal champions.[3]

The ship's keel was laid at the Continental Iron Works, Greenpoint, Long Island, New York, on October 25, 1861, the very same day that Ericsson signed with his subcontractors. In co-operation with Thomas F. Rowland, Continental's owner, Ericsson oversaw the entire construction of the ship's hull. Such concert of action between the two was difficult at first, for Rowland himself had designed an ironclad ship featuring a gun turret revolving on a bed resembling a railroad turntable. Ericsson could be persuasive and even diplomatic when it served his purposes, however, and he soon had Rowland convinced that Ericsson's was the earlier design.

The work proceeded around the clock, so that, within a few weeks, the basic wooden hull was completed and ready to take on the rest of the ship's works. From the Rensselaer Works came the bar iron and rivets to begin the construction of the main deck. From the Albany Iron Works came the armor plate, their supplies supplemented by additional plating from the rollers of New York's Holdane & Company and H. Abbot & Company of Baltimore. The iron pendulums for the turret's port stoppers were being fashioned at Buffalo by Charles De Lancy, and meanwhile the stoppers themselves were produced at Nashua, New Hampshire, by the Hollis Street Foundry. The crucial curved plating for the turret was entrusted to Abbot & Company. Ericsson was managing a miracle in time-saving, simultaneous construction of all the ship's vital parts. Even more astounding, every part was being manufactured from his own plans, which proved so precise that when parts that had to function together were assembled, little or no custom work or alteration was required, even though they had been produced hundreds of miles apart.[4]

One of the most vital components was the vessel's power plant, to be built by Delamater. The plans called for two Martin boilers, which were to power two "vibrating lever" engines of Ericsson's own design. Both engines were geared to turn the same drive shaft, at the end of which would be a four-bladed screw propeller of nine-foot diameter. When finished, the boilers were mounted in the hull, side by side, just below and behind the turret chamber, the area immediately below the revolving turret. Watertight bulkheads separated the chamber from the boiler room, not to protect from water leakage so much as to make an airtight seal. The boilers would depend upon forced drafts of air brought in through two large deck openings by blowers, and any air that leaked out was just that much less that would get to the boiler fires.

This system also lent itself to a serious danger, however. Should water come in through these air intakes—hardly an impossibility, with the vessel's low freeboard—it would be taken directly to the blowers. This could stop their functioning by making their drive belts slip or come off. When that happened, the smoke from the boiler fires would not have the requisite upward draft through the deck-level smokestacks. As a result, the smoke would all back up into the boiler room and, eventually, permeate through the interior of the ship, making it not only uninhabitable but deadly.

Just behind the boilers, Ericsson placed the two engines. Their horsepower combined came to 320 under full steam, on the drawing board more than sufficient to produce nine knots, instead of the required eight. The pistons were three feet in diameter. Along either side of the boiler and engine rooms ran coal bunkers capable of holding one hundred tons of fuel, enough for about eight days' steady steaming.[5]

Next in importance to the ironclad's machinery, naturally, was the turret, which would house her guns. This, too, Ericsson supervised. Indeed, the designer was constantly in motion between one subcontractor and another during November and December 1861. Abbot & Company saw a lot of him as they produced the iron for the revolving cupola. When assembled, by the Novelty Iron Works in New York, the turret stood nine feet high, its sides plated with eight inches of iron consisting of successive layers of one-inch plate bolted together. It would have produced armor of greater strength if the plates had been thicker, but one inch was the best that Abbot's rollers could provide. Long bolts ran through all eight layers—nine around the gun ports—and were fastened by heavy bolts inside.

The interior diameter of the turret was only twenty feet, unfortunately ensuring that it would be rather crowded, with two big cannon and their gun crews, when in action. When it was completed, Novelty installed the port stoppers and their cumbersome pendulums, only to discover that, due to a design error, only one could be raised at a time, cutting the ship's broadside in half. A simple modification cured this, but the stoppers remained so heavy that only block and tackle, and a lot of sweat, could raise them.

The turret would turn on giant ball bearings, ten inches in diameter, that rested on the giant brass ring. All of this was inset into the deck to protect it from damage in battle. The central, vertical drive shaft on which the turret sat, and which was responsible for turning it, was to be turned by four giant horizontal gears connected to a small steam engine. The whole mechanism was designed to be controlled by one man.

When completed, the turret was far too heavy to ship intact to Greenpoint. Consequently, Novelty disassembled it and shipped it in pieces. Once at the Continental Iron Works, the sections were reassembled on the ironclad's deck. By now it was January 1862 and the novel warship was taking shape. Already the skeptics both at Greenpoint and in Washington called it "Ericsson's folly."[6]

But many showed more faith, Welles and Commodore Smith in particular. As the date of the ship's launching approached, they began looking for a suitable commander for her. Smith soon found his man. Lieutenant John Lorimer Worden, a native New Yorker, had served in the Navy ever since his appointment as a midshipman in 1834. Serving at the United States Naval Observatory until the outbreak of war, he had been captured in April 1861 after delivering secret orders to a threatened Union force at Fort Pickens, in Pensacola Bay, Florida. Having delivered his orders, he rather foolishly tried to return north by train across the heart of the Confederacy and was taken prisoner immediately after the firing on Fort Sumter brought declared war. For seven months he remained in prison, until released in November. Curiously enough, the route by which the Confederates sent him home took him through Norfolk, where the *Virginia* was then under construction.

Smith thought he saw in Worden the sort of man he wanted. On January 11, 1862, he wrote to Worden about the new ironclad. "This vessel is an experiment," he said; "I believe you are the right sort of officer to put in command of her." That very same day, an excited Worden went to Greenpoint to see the vessel. "After a hasty examination of her," he told Smith, he was "induced to believe that she may prove a success. At all events, I am quite willing to be an agent in testing her capabilities." He asked to be ordered to her officially as soon as possible. On January 16, 1862, he reported for duty to command the as yet unnamed machine of war.[7]

With the time for launching coming fast, Assistant Navy Secretary Gustavus Fox asked Ericsson if he would care to suggest a name for the ironclad. On January 20, 1862, Ericsson replied.

Sir:

In accordance with your request, I now submit for your approbation a name for the floating battery at Green Point. The impregnable and aggressive character of this structure will admonish the leaders of the Southern Rebellion that the batteries on the banks of their rivers will no longer present barriers to the entrance of the Union forces.

The iron-clad intruder will thus prove a severe monitor to those leaders. But there are other leaders who will also be startled and admonished by the booming of the guns from the impregnable iron turret. "Downing Street" will hardly view with indifference this last "Yankee notion," this monitor. To the Lords of the Admiralty the new craft will be a monitor suggesting doubts as to the propriety of completing those four steel-clad ships [the British ironclad frigates] at three-and-a-half millions apiece. On these and many similar grounds I propose to name the new battery *Monitor*.

Your obedient servant,

J. Ericsson

Some of the best engineers in the Navy, as well as experienced constructors, believed that the *Monitor* would not float when launched. Rowland, worried himself, decided to insure her floating by installing large, wooden, airtight tanks under her stern. These would keep her up in case the buoyancy calculations were in any way incorrect. Rowland made all the arrangements for the launching, and oversaw the event. On January 30, 1862, the *Monitor* slid down the ways at Greenpoint and gently floated exactly as planned. Once again Ericsson had been right. Weighing 776 tons, she drew eleven feet four inches fully loaded. A much pleased Fox wrote to Ericsson: "I congratulate you and trust she will be a success. Hurry her for sea, as the Merrimack is nearly ready at Norfolk and we wish to send her there." Others, too, were interested in the possibility of the *Monitor* going to Hampton Roads to face the *Virginia*. Watching her launch, this January 30, was one quiet man who immediately hurried to his hotel room to make sketches of the new ironclad. Within a few days, both man and sketches would be in Norfolk advising the Confederates on what they might someday have to face.[8]

According to the terms of the contract, the *Monitor* should have been completed and delivered to the Navy by January 12. Obviously, Ericsson had missed the mark, though he had still accomplished a marvel of shipbuilding. As a result of the *Monitor* being delayed beyond January 12, however, Welles had to abandon the planned test he had devised, to send the ship to Hampton Roads, steam her up the Elizabeth River to the Gosport Navy Yard, and there have her stand off the dry dock and destroy it, the *Virginia*, and everything else within range of her guns. Welles firmly believed that the *Monitor* could easily have done it. All he could do now, however, was try to hurry the completion and fitting out of the ironclad and hold up payment of the final installment to Ericsson until the ship had proved herself in combat, wherever it might come.[9]

On January 31 Worden got the *Monitor*'s boilers under steam for the first time, even as the work of finishing her progressed at a feverish pace. Meanwhile, consulting with Stimers, Worden had been looking to shipping a crew. Calculations had to be made very carefully on how many men could fit into the turret and how many were needed to serve the various ship's components. He decided that the maximum in the turret should be nineteen. To get his gunners and other seamen, Worden asked for volunteers from the Navy receiving ships *North Carolina* and *Sabine*. He got more than he wanted, for many of the men had heard of the new ironclad and were anxious to ship aboard her. Some, however, such as Samuel Lewis, adhered to an old custom of signing on under a fictitious name. It was done, Lewis explained, "on account of danger of running afoul of bad captains or bad ships, when we might have to decamp at the first port." Consequently, aboard the *Monitor* Lewis was officially known to everyone as Peter Truscott.

The ship's roll filled quickly, numbering fifty-seven in all, a small complement for a warship expected to meet whatever the Confederacy might throw at her. Worden's executive officer was Lieutenant Samuel Dana Greene, a Marylander now just twenty-one years old. A fellow officer found Greene "a young man [with] black hair & eyes that look through a person & will carry out his orders I have no doubt." Two acting masters were signed, one of them Louis N. Stodder, who had been with the *Monitor* at Rowland's works during her building. "You had better take a good look at her now," skeptics warned him, "as you won't see her after she strikes the water. She's bound to go to the bottom of the East River, and stick there, sure." Fortunately, Stodder had seen them proved wrong so far.

In addition to the ship's ten officers, Stimers sat at the wardroom mess. Never assigned to duty on the *Monitor,* he would nevertheless stay with her for some time as an observer. One member of the officers' circle was a rank landlubber. Acting Assistant Paymaster William F. Keeler had no Navy experience at all, and only received his appointment through influence with Congressman Owen Lovejoy of Illinois. He had actually thought that he would be allowed to go to sea without wearing a uniform. Commodore Paulding set him straight on that. "Not at all, not at all, get a uniform before you go to sea." Keeler got his suit of blue, but it took a lot of getting used to.

Besides the officers, there were nine ordinary seamen, seven coal heavers—one of them, David R. Ellis, would shortly become Keeler's assistant—eight first-class firemen, and a number of petty officers, cooks, landsmen, and mates. Truscott was made a quartermaster.[10]

The men had varying reactions to their new, iron home. Stodder thought that "she was rather a hasty job, was the *Monitor*." "She was a little bit the strangest craft I had ever seen," Truscott would add. David Ellis was worried about her, and thought that some of the crew had second thoughts about their wisdom in volunteering, once they saw her. "She had not been pronounced seaworthy, and no one could safely judge of her fighting qualities," he complained. Keeler, on the other hand, was immensely pleased. Worden he found to be rather effeminate in appearance. Indeed, the lieutenant commanding was quite slim, with an alabaster complexion brought about by his months of imprisonment. "Never," said Keeler, "was a lady the possessor of a smaller or more delicate hand" than Worden's. Only a long, dark beard interfered with the impression of weakness. Keeler saw behind the appearance, though, and found that "if I am not very much mistaken he will not hesitate to submit our iron sides to as severe a test as the most warlike could desire."

As for the ship itself, Keeler felt confident, almost smug. He saw it for the first time on February 13, 1862. "I shall not attempt a description of it now," he wrote to his wife, "but you may rest assured your *better half* will be in no more danger from rebel compliments than if he was seated with you at home. There isn't even danger enough to give us any glory."[11]

Even while men and officers were bringing their effects aboard and taking up residence, the work on the *Monitor* continued. A particular concern was her susceptibility to heavy seas. Due to her low freeboard, it would take only two feet of water coming into her bottom to sink her, and that so quickly that few would likely survive. With all the vents, deck-level smokestacks, pilothouse slits, and other openings where water could seep past supposedly watertight seals, even a light sea would pose a continuing problem of water entering the hull. To combat this, a channel was built into the keel, sloping back to the stern. This would force all water aft to two bilge pumps, which could eject it.[12]

Ericsson himself saw to the appointment of the officers' rooms, and spared no expense on them. Worden's cabin sat at the very front port side of the berth deck. It was roughly ten feet square and, adjoining it on the starboard side, was his stateroom, of equal size. Immediately behind them were eight staterooms for the other officers, four on either side of the wardroom, where all gathered to take their meals. These staterooms were smaller than Worden's but still quite comfortable.

Keeler's room could serve as a model for all. About six by eight feet in dimensions, its floor was covered with oil cloth over which lay a tapestry rug and, on that, a soft goat's-hair mat. His bunk rested against one wall, and was just long enough that, when he stretched out to sleep, his head touched the wall at one end while his feet touched at the other. Above the bed, and set into the wall, were storage closets for clothing, while more storage drawers were located under the berth. On the wall by the head of the bunk sat a desk with a lid that dropped down to provide a writing surface. Beneath it was an iron chest for Keeler's pay records. On the opposite wall, between the berth and the doorway, lay a shelf into which a washbasin had been set. Beneath it was another shelf. Here holes allowed space for setting his night jar, drinking tumbler, water pitcher, soap dish, and other utensils. All were set into holes cut to fit them so that they could not roll or slide off in heavy seas. All were made of beautiful white stoneware, with "Monitor" painted on each in gilt lettering. Over the washbasin was another shelf for comb and brush, and above this hung a gilt-framed mirror reaching to the ceiling. All the woodwork in the cabin was of polished black walnut, accented with brass railings and fixtures. The bed curtains were lace and damask. A register in the floor furnished fresh air brought in from the deck above by blowers, while a waterproof glass skylight set in the deck overhead allowed light to filter into the room. This could be opened to provide additional fresh air in calm seas, or closed off from above with iron stoppers during bad weather or battle.

Keeler's only complaint was that the door was so thin that he could hear everything going on in the wardroom, which distracted him from his letter writing. Then too, with storage space at a premium, he usually had to keep his books on his bed in the day and then transfer them to the floor at night to sleep. Still, he felt fortunate. He looked on board a number of other vessels, yet had "seen no room as handsomely fitted up as ours."[13]

Of course, not everyone aboard lived so well. All but the nine principal officers slept in hammocks in an open space just aft of the officers' cabins. Ventilation was primitive for a room crowded with sleeping men, and the heat from the boilers only added to the discomfort. Aside from storage lockers, there were few facilities for the crew, and no privacy. Their only real recreation was to be found on deck. The great iron ship magnified temperatures around it, making it hotter inside than outside during the day, and nearly as cold as the ocean at night.[14]

Of course, what made things all the more uncomfortable for officers and crew was the continual noise and bustle of the finishing still being done. The pilothouse was one of the last items completed, and it brought with it some inherent weaknesses. It was lower than necessary for good visibility over a wide area, yet sufficiently high that the guns in the turret could not fire directly ahead without hitting it. Unfortunately, its only communications link with the turret was a speaking tube that was serviceable only when the turret's guns were pointed forward. This was fine for ordinary days, but in battle, when the turret would be turning, the only way to communicate back and forth would be by sending a man back and forth along the berth deck.

The guns inside that turret, of course, were a prime concern of everyone. Their selection was up to Worden, though Ericsson had strongly urged that 12-inch Dahlgren smoothbore cannon be used. Worden could not get them, however, or anything else at first. The ordnance officers at the Brooklyn Navy Yard had nothing to give, but 11-inch Dahlgrens were expected. These would have to do. In fact, they were removed from another ship, the *Dacotah,* in order to fill Worden's need. Stated very simply, the Dahlgren gun was shaped much like a bottle—hence its nickname, the "soda pop" gun —being thicker at the breech in order to allow heavy loads. Those for the *Monitor* had been cast in 1859 and were thus comparatively new. They were fired by yanking a lanyard which set off a friction primer placed in a vent in the breech. This vent led to the main powder charge, usually fifteen pounds of coarse black cannon powder, which in turn propelled a 166-pound solid-iron ball. The basic idea of using such large-bore guns was simple. An 11-inch ball weighed almost as much as those of the combined broadside guns of the standard old wooden frigates, yet concentrated it all at one point for maximum effect on the smallest spot. This was the only way Worden might hope to penetrate another ironclad. When he finally got his guns, it took four or five days to get them properly sighted in, but then the *Monitor* was almost ready.[15]

By February 15 almost everything was done. Four days later she was officially turned over to the Navy. At 2 P.M., February 19, she got up steam and moved away from Greenpoint. At once an error was discovered. The engine builders had misset the steam cutoff valves so that the engines could propel her at only three and one half knots. Also, one of the engines driving a blower failed. Consequently, it was late, 7:30 P.M., when the ship finally completed the short trip to the Brooklyn Navy Yard and dropped anchor. The next morning, she was towed into the wharf, but only after the windlass operating the anchor also made trouble. Stimers would take these problems up with Ericsson but did not regard them as serious or insurmountable. On February 25, 1862, the *Monitor* was officially commissioned a fourth-rate ship in the United States Navy.[16]

Opinions among experienced navy men varied as they looked at the newly commissioned ironclad moored at Brooklyn. Commander David D. Porter, sent by the Navy Department to render an expert assessment, pronounced the *Monitor* "a perfect success, and capable of defeating anything that then floated." Dahlgren, looking at her from the dock, thought the ship "a mere speck, like a hat on the surface." What few, if any, realized was the genuine revolution in naval warfare that this ship represented. To be sure, the idea of an ironclad was not new, nor was the concept of a gun turret, or a low freeboard, or heavy, large-bore shell guns, light draft, high maneuverability, steam power, or ventilation systems. All were products of earlier genius. What Ericsson had done, however, and what entitled him to immortal fame, was for the first time to incorporate all these features into one, superbly conceived vessel. Instead of being spread at random through various vessels in the Navy, these advancements combined to produce in the *Monitor* a speedy vessel capable of operating in the shallow southern rivers and harbors, terrible in her offensive power and yet herself presenting such a limited target area, and that almost impervious to enemy shot, that she was practically impregnable. She was a milestone in naval architecture and, even before commissioning, a prototype for the future battleship navies of the world.[17]

But this hardly meant that the *Monitor* was free of defects. The day after her commissioning, she was to have steamed south, but loading her coal—eighty tons of it—and ammunition delayed the start until February 27. Meanwhile, Paymaster Keeler—also in charge of supplies—had to lay in ninety days' provisions for the crew. Finally, however, she got up steam and set out early in the morning. It was snowing heavily as the *Monitor* steamed to the New York City side of the East River. Almost immediately, the man at the wheel found that he could not control the rudder satisfactorily. "We ran first to the New York side then to the Brooklyn & so back & forth across the river, first to one side then to the other, like a drunken man on a side walk," wrote Keeler. Finally, quite unmanageable, the *Monitor* collided with the riverside New York gas works "with a shock that nearly took us from our feet." Seeing the situation hopeless, Worden had the ship towed back to the navy yard.

The commandant at Brooklyn proposed to install a new and better rudder, but Ericsson would have none of that. As coal heaver Ellis heard the conversation, the irate inventor declared: "Put in a new rudder? The Monitor is mine, and I say it shall not be done. They would waste a month in doing it. I will make her steer easily in three days." One of Ericsson's more aggravating points to his associates was that his claims were usually correct. So it was with the rudder. Ericsson, assisted by Stimers, adjusted the apparatus to give the helmsman more control over the vessel's steering, and Stimers estimated that the problem would be easily resolved. Worden disagreed, however, and asked the Navy Department to send a three-man commission to attend the *Monitor*'s next trial trip, on March 3.

It was raining as the ship pulled out into the river for her trial run. The wet iron deck was slippery and uncomfortable to stand on. The crew had set up a circular, tentlike awning on poles atop the turret so that the men and officers could stay reasonably dry, though they still had to run frequently down into the ship in order to escape the cold. They persevered, and fortunately found that the ship's steering was now "in all respects satisfactory," meeting the approval of the visiting officers. It was found, however, that instead of making nine knots as planned by Ericsson, or even eight knots as the contract specified, the ship's engines drove her at a maximum of only seven.

It had been planned to entertain the visiting officers with a handsome luncheon aboard ship while the *Monitor* was steaming about her trials. Everything went well until they all took seats at the table in the now crowded little wardroom. Soup was served by the steward, Daniel Moore. But before they had a chance to finish it, Moore brought out the fish course. He poured their champagne in brandy glasses, and the brandy in champagne glasses. Everything went wrong, and it was not long before they knew the reason why. "To sum it all up in one short sentence," Keeler wrote home, "the Steward, upon whom it all depended, was drunk." Apparently Moore had been testing the wines for some time before serving them, and now he turned the dinner into "a decided failure." The guests bore their hosts' humiliation sympathetically, but poor Moore was slapped in irons for four hours as soon as the *Monitor* returned to the wharf. "He yelled & hollowed & begged & plead, but 'twas of no use," said Keeler. Sober when released, Moore tried to drown his mortification the next morning by taking some liquor from the wardroom stores and getting drunk yet again. Once more he was ironed. Since the ship had no brig for confining offenders under punishment, poor Moore was shut up in a cold, damp locker with only the anchor chain for company.[18]

Despite the difficulties of rudder and rum, the *Monitor* was at last ready for sea on March 4. Weather was a problem now, and Worden would have to wait a day or two for smoother seas before leaving. Then, on March 6, everything was ready. At 4 P.M. she cast off her lines, backed away from the Brooklyn wharf, and steamed down the East River into New York Harbor and off to meet her appointment with history.[19]

Just where was the *Monitor* going? It was a question that had been asked repeatedly almost from the day of her conception in Ericsson's mind. Speculation and request might have destined her for a variety of stations, but from the very first the public and most in the navy just assumed that she would be sent to meet the *Virginia*. What else could stop this Confederate leviathan abuilding at

Norfolk, and what better way to test the *Monitor*'s metal than to send her against it?

Gideon Welles had been receiving progress reports on the *Virginia* almost from the day of her raising. When the Federals abandoned Gosport, the few Union civilians there left with them. One stayed, however. He pretended to sympathize with the South and was thus allowed to remain at work in the navy-yard shops. From his vantage point, he saw every step of the *Virginia*'s construction, and every few days managed to get reports across Hampton Roads to the Union commander at Fort Monroe, Major General John Wool.

Meanwhile, there were other Union sympathizers living in Norfolk, and on June 25, 1861, they got word to the Federals that the *Merrimack* had been raised and put in dry dock, adding (none too accurately) that "her machinery is effectually destroyed." The next day, they reported that Confederate authorities had examined the *Merrimack* and pronounced her "worthless." Better intelligence would come in the months to follow, fortunately. In November, an escaped Union man from Norfolk brought word that the *Virginia* would not likely be completed that winter, and that just then the Confederates were installing the casemate's roof. Much better yet was a December 18 report from W. H. Lyons, Welles's Gosport Navy Yard informant, giving very complete and generally reliable accounts of all of the construction and alterations made to date, including the thickness of her plate, the weight of the ram, and the manufacture of the Brooke rifles. Lyons estimated a completion date of February 1, 1862.

B. S. Osbon, a reporter for the New York *Herald,* actually slipped up the Elizabeth River one very foggy night and came within one hundred yards of the *Virginia*. "I fixed her outlines and proportions in my mind," he later wrote. Withdrawing safely, he eventually returned to his paper an account of his escapade and furnished *Scientific American* a sketch of the vessel drawn from memory. It gave the North its first glimpse of the ironclad it had heard so much of. Though highly inaccurate with regard to the *Virginia*'s submerged fore and after decks, still Osbon's drawing aptly captured the spirit and potential power of the ironclad.

By far the best information that Welles would receive on the enemy vessel came from Master's Mate William A. Abbott, who for a time had been held a prisoner at Norfolk. On January 9, 1862, he reported that the *Virginia* would have port shutters, sloping sides to cause Federal shot to glance off, two engines, a somewhat vulnerable pilothouse, and armor ranging up to two and one half inches in thickness. Much of his information came from a carpenter who had worked on the ship and was later confined with him. The general impression at the navy yard was that the ironclad's ventilation was so poor that her crew could not fight in her long, for want of air. He also warned that the Confederates seemed to place their best hopes with the vessel's ram.

On January 28 came reports that the *Virginia* had left dry dock. Five days later, rumors hit Hampton Roads that she was almost ready to get under steam. About the same time, a tired Negro woman appeared at the Navy Department in Washington and asked to see Welles. She had come from Norfolk, where she watched much of the *Virginia*'s building. It was nearly ready, she said, and even now was receiving its armament. Concealed in her bosom as she came through the lines to the North she carried a letter from a Union sympathizer—probably Lyons—which confirmed her account. Then, this same month, came news that made fears of the *Virginia*'s readiness all but certain. The Norfolk *Day Book* published its account of the ironclad being an utter failure. The ruse was so obvious that Welles knew it was only a matter of days before the vessel made her move.[20]

Several suggestions from officers such as Major General George B. McClellan, commanding the Union's main force in the East, the Army of the Potomac, urged that the *Monitor* be sent to the lower Potomac to combat Confederate batteries there which hindered water traffic from the Chesapeake to Washington, D.C. However, in view of the much more pressing threat of the *Virginia* and what her unknown strength might do at Hampton Roads, Welles was persuaded—if indeed he ever needed any persuasion, having originally planned to test the *Monitor* by sending her to Norfolk—to order the ironclad there instead. Lieutenant Charles Ellet, himself an expert on steam rams, declared that if the *Virginia* left the Elizabeth River, "she will be almost certain to commit great depredations on our armed and unarmed vessels in Hampton Roads." Rear Admiral Louis N. Goldsborough, commanding the North Atlantic Blockading Squadron at Hampton Roads, was particularly anxious to have the *Monitor* there to battle the Rebel ironclad. "I ask therefore if it would not be well to send the Ericsson . . . to contend with that vessel on her own terms," he wrote Welles. "I hope the Dept. will be able to send the Ericsson soon to Hampton Roads to grapple with the Merrimac & lay her out as cold as a wedge."[21]

By February 20 Welles was decided. To Worden, he gave the command: "Proceed with the U.S.S. *Monitor,* under your command, to Hampton Roads, Virginia." By March 6, after all the trials, Worden was ready. Last-minute ammunition and provisions were taken aboard. The steamers *Sachem* and *Currituck* were ordered to accompany the ironclad to the mouth of the Chesapeake, while the steam tugboat *Seth Low* went along to assist. At 4 P.M., March 6, the *Monitor* departed and, in order to make maximum speed, took a line from the *Seth Low* so that she could tow as the *Monitor* steamed. Crowds of men and women lined the banks of the East River. Ellis watched them from the ship's deck as they came "to see us off and to cheer and to shout good-luck and bon voyage."[22]

CHAPTER 6

"I Lived Ten Good Years"

Even as they passed out of the harbor and into the Atlantic, the *Monitor* men were still getting to know their ship and adjusting to the evolving shipboard routine. Because of the mechanics swarming over the vessel right up to the minute of its departure, her crewmen had little opportunity to test the guns, work the turret, or generally familiarize themselves with their new home. For the officers, of course, acclimation to walnut-paneled staterooms and a mess table set with china and specially selected victuals was not too difficult. Indeed, each of them was allowed to bring a manservant along to tend his needs. "I have spent a portion of two or three days in hunting up a contraband," Keeler wrote of his search for a servant, "& finally found a good looking young darkey that came to me well recommended."

Some, such as Keeler, who had never served aboard a warship, "made the discovery that there are some things about it not very romantic." Arising early in the morning to eat breakfast in the wardroom, where the temperature was thirty-five degrees, proved a sobering experience. For Keeler, who "didn't sleep a wink all night, but lay & shivered & shook till I thought the frame work of my berth would be shaken apart" thanks to the cold and his cool linen sheets, the shivering over this frosty morning meal was such that "one can hardly find the way to his mouth." Fortunately, before leaving Brooklyn, the *Monitor*'s wardroom had steam heaters installed, which warmed the surrounding staterooms to more comfortable temperatures. And Keeler wisely substituted warmer, cotton bed sheets for the linen.

The boatswain's whistle sounded every morning at five and with it his loud, hoarse call, "A-l-l hands up hammocks." The officers, though awakened by this, usually slept in until about 8 A.M., when their servants came in with basins of warm water. "8 o'clock Sir," said Keeler's "boy"; "breakfast 'most ready Sir." The officers usually dispensed quickly with their morning toilet, often stepping into the engine room to warm up thoroughly. Then it was into the wardroom for breakfast. "We live well," Keeler determined, "that is we have the best of food provided by our caterer," First Assistant Engineer Isaac Newton.

All the officers ate together in the wardroom, each taking the same seat at every meal. Worden sat at the head, with Keeler to his left and Greene to his right. Newton, the caterer, sat at the opposite end. Newton had been chosen by the others to oversee the purchase and preparation of the officers' food, for which all paid. They also paid for their own dishes, the total cost for everything coming to roughly thirty-five dollars a month apiece—"not very cheap board," thought Keeler.

Following the morning meal, all went about their various tasks. For Keeler, that meant overseeing all provisions, clothing, stationery, small stores such as soap, tobacco, candles, needle and thread, buttons, knives "& all the thousand & one little things a Sailor will stand in need of," as well as managing the ship's money and the men's pay. When off duty, there was little for the officers to do but shut themselves in their staterooms and read or write letters. Such an arrangement called for a good deal of amiability on everyone's part. "As far as I know my fellow officers," Keeler told his wife before the *Monitor* sailed, "I am very well pleased with them & hope everything will pass pleasantly while we are shut up together." Close association produced a quick reaction, however. A few days later the paymaster admitted that "some of the officers as I get better acquainted with them I like better, others not so well." With nothing much to do once under way, they got on each other's nerves, since they dropped into a stateroom to sit and talk about nothing or read a newspaper or pry into affairs of the heart. As a result, nerves were often frayed, and one such interruption after another kept Keeler from reading a letter from home almost an entire day. But these men had to live and fight close together. They could not afford to flare up at each other. Instead, as often as not it was their servants on whom they vented their frustrations. When

Keeler's "contraband" misplaced a letter from home in a well-intentioned attempt to neaten the stateroom, the paymaster "blowed him up."

And in the evenings, after a dinner of bread, butter, beef, cheese, and coffee or tea, when they sat alone in their cabins thinking of home or of what lay ahead, or played games and sipped wines at the mess table, even the quietest conversation filtered into every room through the thin doors. "Every word spoken by the circle around the wardroom table is as audible as if they were seated by my elbow," wrote Keeler. Frequently he found it so distracting that, when writing his wife, he would accidentally write down what was being said in the next room. At 10 P.M. everyone was to be bedded down, or at least quiet, for the night.[1]

So it had been, and so it would be, but not on this trip to Hampton Roads. At first the *Monitor* met smooth seas and fair weather as she steamed south. She floated well atop the waves, little or no water breaking over her deck, which now had all hatches battened down so that the only way in or out of the ship was through the top of the turret and then down to the berth deck. At 9 o'clock that night, March 6, the moon shone brightly on a tranquil scene. The *Currituck* and the *Sachem* steamed peacefully a short distance east of the ironclad, their green running lights casting a dim glow over their nearly deserted decks. Ahead of the *Monitor* some four hundred feet, the *Seth Low* tugged away at the heavy hawser let out from the *Monitor*. On the horizon all around could be seen a number of sailing ships passing in various directions, their white sails glistening in the moonlight. Inside the ironclad, Captain Worden entertained the officers at dinner with stories of his days as a midshipman before the war.

The next morning brought a considerable change of scene. During the night, a light gale had worked up from the west, and the water began breaking over the deck as the waves grew higher and higher. Stimers found that "the sea commenced to wash right across the deck, but if there were no bulwarks to keep the water off, so also there were none to keep it on and when we got into a double reefed topsail gale of wind our lee side was a regular Niagara Falls!"

Here, unfortunately, what had been intended as a safety precaution backfired. Before leaving the navy yard, the *Monitor*'s turret was jacked up slightly and a rough hemp rope was inserted between

1. Confederate Secretary of the Navy Stephen R. Mallory; an unpublished photograph. (Courtesy of the MOLLUS-Mass. Collection, U. S. Army Military History Research Collection, Carlisle Barracks, Pennsylvania.)

2. An unpublished photograph of Lieutenant John M. Brooke, circa 1852, showing him in the uniform of the United States Navy. (Courtesy of George R. Brooke, Lexington, Virginia.)

3. Union Secretary of the Navy Gideon Welles. (Courtesy of the National Archives, Washington, D.C.)

4. John Ericsson, brilliant but egotistical engineer who designed the *Monitor*. (Courtesy of the Naval Photographic Center, Washington, D.C.)

5. The ruins of the Gosport Navy Yard, at Norfolk, May 1862, where the *Merrimack* became the *Virginia*. (Courtesy of the MOLLUS-Mass. Collection, U. S. Army Military History Research Collection, Carlisle Barracks, Pennsylvania.)

6. The USS *Merrimack* before the war. (*Century Illustrated Monthly Magazine*, XXIX, March 1885.)

8. Captain French Forrest, Confederate commandant of the Norfolk Navy Yard. (Author's collection.)

7. Lieutenant Catesby ap R. Jones, who oversaw much of the *Virginia*'s completion and commanded her in the fight with the *Monitor*. (Author's collection.)

9. How people in the North first saw the *Virginia*; a sketch, highly inaccurate, smuggled to Welles by a Norfolk workman, probably W. H. Lyons. (*Harper's Weekly,* November 2, 1861.)

10. A somewhat fanciful depiction of the *Monitor*'s launching; the turret was not placed on the deck until after the hull had been floated. (*Harper's New Monthly Magazine*, XXV, September 1862.)

11. The *Monitor* as the people of the North first saw her; the turret is too tall in proportion to the size of the ship as shown here. (*Harper's Weekly*, March 22, 1862.)

its bottom and the brass ring. It was hoped this would prevent leaks around the turret base in high seas better than letting the turret rest on just the brass. Instead, the rope formed a much more defective seal. As the night passed and the seas grew higher, water began coming through. The sailors on the berth deck underneath were driven from their hammocks in the vain attempt to find a dry sleeping place, and by morning leaks sprang up at almost every hatch, deck light, and other opening on the iron deck, "making it wet & very disagreeable below," thought Keeler.

The paymaster awoke that morning, March 7, to see green waves rolling across his glass deck light. Arising, he found that many on board, including Worden and Surgeon Daniel C. Logue, were suffering from seasickness. Those who were ill were taken to the top of the turret to lie down and get fresh air. Looking over to the accompanying gunboats, they could see that the ships were rolling considerably in the gale. By noon the wind had increased, so that the gun muzzles protruding from the sides of the *Sachem* and the *Currituck* actually dipped into the water as the ships swayed in the gale.

By now the water was coming under the turret "like a waterfall," wrote Greene. "It would strike the pilot-house and go over the turret in beautiful curves, and it came through the narrow eye-holes in the pilot-house with such force as to knock the helmsman completely round from the wheel." Somehow the crew managed to get an afternoon meal down, but the storm outside steadily increased. "Now the top of every sea that breaks against our side rolls unobstructed over our deck dashing & foaming at a terrible rate," wrote Keeler in his leaking cabin. The waves seemed resistless. Soon they were breaking over the six-foot-high smokestacks—specially added for the voyage and removable in action so that nothing would protrude from the deck. The water coming in them threatened to quench the fires at the boilers below. It was also coming in the stacks over the blower intakes.

Everyone was at least reassured by the steady clanking sound of the engines as they continued their work, and by the near presence of the *Seth Low,* still tugging at the hawser. But by 4 P.M. Keeler could see a number of very worried faces atop the turret. Just then he turned to go below, only to meet one of the engineers coming up, black from smoke, weak, barely able to speak or breathe. Keeler started below to get him some brandy when he met some sailors bringing up a fireman and the other three engineers. All appeared to be dead. The deck below had become a nightmarish hell.

What had happened was simple to explain. The water coming down the blower vents wet the drive belts that turned the blowers. This made them loose, to the point that they barely turned the fans. Then a belt broke. With no artificial draft of air, the engines stopped, and carbon dioxide given off by the fires filled the engine room. Engineers Newton and Stimers had raced into the room, followed by several others, and valiantly tried to get the blowers going again. They mended one blower belt while the other barely did its work. But then it, too, snapped. "The fires burned with a sickly blaze," wrote Stimers, "converting all the air in the engine and firerooms into carbonic-acid-gas, a few inhalations of which are sufficient to destroy animal life." The men around him began to stagger and fall. He ordered them all out, and stayed behind himself in a desperate attempt to get a blower going again. "I soon began to find myself getting very limber in the legs," he later recalled, "so I started also for the top of the turret, which I managed to reach just as my strength gave out and I tumbled over upon the turret deck at full length." It was Stimers that Keeler first encountered in trying to go below.

Meanwhile, said Greene, "the water continued to pour through the hawse-hole, and over and down the smoke-stacks and blower-pipes, in such quantities that there was imminent danger that the ship would founder." The steam pumps could not be operated to expel the water from the engine room because they were dependent upon the very same boiler fires that were failing for want of air. In minutes the engine room was uninhabitable, thanks to the gas. And because one of the fleeing engineers had left the engine-room door open, it was spreading throughout the ship.

When Keeler finally went below, he found "the whole between decks filled with steam & gas & Smoke, the Sailors were rushing up stifled with the gas." He started to shut the open door to the engine room, when a sailor said he thought there was still a man left inside. "No time was to be lost," wrote Keeler a few days later, "though by this time almost suffocated myself I rushed in over heaps of coal & ashes & fortunately found the man lying insensible." A sailor helped the paymaster carry the man up to the turret top, where to all appearances he was dying.

Meanwhile, Lieutenant Greene had been doing his best to clear the berth deck of anyone else left below. "I think I lived ten good years," he wrote a week later. Going down to help the men out, "I was nearly suffocated with the gas myself, but got on deck . . . just in time to save myself." He had to admit that at that moment, "times looked rather blue." With the engines stopped and the steam pumps not working, the water was rising in the hull rapidly. Now Greene tried to set up the hand pumps on the berth deck, but between the gas and the pump hose having to reach up through and out of the turret, the men could not exert enough force on the pump to move the water out. This left no recourse but a bucket line to bail out the water. It did little good but, as coal heaver Ellis observed, it did "divert the members of the crew from panic."

Keeler got all of the stricken men from the engine room stretched out on top of the turret, and placed a piece of sail cloth above them as an awning to keep the wind and spray from them. "It was a sorry looking company which crowded the only *habitable* spot on our vessel."

"What to do now we did not know," wrote Greene. They tried running up their flag with the union—the starred, blue portion—down, a sign of distress. But the *Sachem* and the *Currituck* were having such problems of their own that they could give no aid. Almost echoing Greene's words, Keeler wrote his wife that "things for a time looked pretty blue, as though we might have to 'give up the ship.'"

Greene managed to hail the *Seth Low* and order her to pull east, toward land, only a few miles off. The water would be smoother near the shore. It took five hours of perilous towing, the tug succeeding in getting the *Monitor* close enough to shore to enjoy a respite from the rough seas. At about 8 P.M., the gas having cleared from below through the vents and turret, Stimers and the others repaired the blower belts and restarted the ventilation. This in turn allowed them to restart the engines and steam pumps. Happily, Greene found "everything comparatively quiet again." Since Worden had been up all the previous night with seasickness, yet did not want to leave the deck without either himself or Greene being on duty, Greene volunteered to take the first watch, from 8 P.M. to midnight. Worden would relieve him for the four hours to follow, and then Greene would come back on duty. "The first watch passed off very nicely," he was glad to report. Meanwhile, Keeler and Surgeon Logue got all the ill back below to the berth deck, passing a dinner of cheese, crackers, and water to all hands. Since Stimers was the only engineer well enough to go back on duty just yet, Keeler found that "my mechanical genius came in play, as I took charge of the engines till morning."

The relief was unbelievable. The evening turned beautiful. The sea was smooth, the sky clear and moonlit, "and the old tank going along five or six knots very nicely." Greene's only trouble now was staying awake. By midnight, everything looked so good that he told the still-ailing Worden to stay in bed. Greene said he would lie down with his clothes on and turn out himself if anything happened. A grateful Worden agreed, and the executive officer went to his room to take a little nap.

Barely was Greene in his bunk "before I was startled by the most infernal noise I ever heard in my life." The *Monitor* had just passed a shoal when the sea suddenly became very rough, its force directed directly head on to the ironclad. A great wave rushed up through the anchor well, forcing its way through the hawse pipe—the aperture through which the anchor chain was let out of the chain locker—and then shot "in a perfect stream" over the wardroom, clear to the berth deck. The air, rushing through the pipe before the water, made a noise that "resembled the death groans of 20 men & certainly was the most dismal awful sound I ever heard," thought Greene.

Instantly Greene and Worden jumped from their berths and raced to the hawse pipe. Their attempts to stop the torrent of water rushing from it were only partially successful. Then, with no warning at all, huge waves began breaking across the *Monitor* deck again, throwing water down the blower stacks. For a few terrible minutes, they feared a repeat of that afternoon's near disaster. Thanks to the wind blowing directly against the ironclad's bow, the *Seth Low* up ahead could not hear their calls, and there was no other way to signal. Greene found the atmosphere aboard ship as dismal as before, if not worse. "We then commenced to think the *Monitor* would never see daylight."

Anxiously the officers watched the water that came down the

vent stacks. Every few minutes a messenger went down to the fireman in the engine room to see how the blowers were working. Every time came the reply, "slowly," with a warning that they could not go much longer if the water was not stopped. "The sea was washing completely over our decks," wrote Greene, "and it was dangerous for a man to go on them, so we could do nothing to the blowers."

Then, to add to their peril, the wheel ropes—a vital part of the steering apparatus, connecting the helm with the rudder—jumped off the steering wheel and the vessel began sheering back and forth uncontrollably. The strain on the hawser from the *Seth Low* threatened to snap it but, being new, the rope held together. It took half an hour to set the wheel ropes aright, but this still left the urgent problem with the blowers.

Finally, about 3 A.M., March 8, the sea calmed somewhat, though still retaining enough force to send a little water down the stacks occasionally. Still came the same reply to every interrogatory sent to the engine room: "Blowers going slowly but can't go much longer." Fortunately they did. An hour later Greene resumed his watch, and from then until dawn he thought "the longest hour and a half I ever spent. I certainly thought old Sol had stopped in China and never intended to pay us another visit." But visit Sol did, and finally they could again see the sturdy tugboat, still towing ahead of them, and hail her to pull toward land and calmer water.

By 8 A.M. they had reached more pacific surroundings. No one had slept that night, all were hungry. "Breakfast tasted good I assure you," wrote Keeler. The entire berth deck was wet and uncomfortable, cold and slippery. Waves continued to roll across the iron deck, though much less violently, and the water still leaked under the turret and in through the hatches and ports. "It seemed singular," wrote Keeler as he sat in his cabin, "to sit in my room & hear the huge waves roll over my head & look up through the little deck light as the mass of water darkened the few straggling rays."

In stark contrast to the night before, the rest of the day passed rather uneventfully. The men cleaned up as best they could, real damage was found to be slight, the seasick once again sought what recuperation they could find, and the officers went about their regular duties. At noon they passed Cape Charles, at the southernmost tip of the Maryland peninsula, and entered Chesapeake Bay. At 2

P.M. the hawser from the *Seth Low* broke at last but was easily mended. About an hour later, they sighted and passed Cape Henry, on the Virginia side of the Chesapeake's mouth. From here it was less than fifteen miles due west to Fort Monroe and Hampton Roads.

Cape Henry was still in sight when the men on the ironclad heard something to the west. "We imagined we heard heavy firing in the distance," wrote Keeler. As they steamed on, coming closer to Fort Monroe, the men guessed with one another about what was happening up ahead. Keeler stood on top of the turret straining his eyes toward the fort. "As we neared the land, clouds of smoke could be seen hanging over it in the direction of the Fortress, & as we approached still nearer little black spots could occasionally be seen suddenly springing into the air, remaining stationary for a moment or two & then gradually expanding into a large white cloud." What he was seeing were exploding shells bursting in mid-air. "As the darkness increased, the flashes of guns lit up the distant horizon & bursting shells flashed in the air."

When still about ten miles from Fort Monroe, the *Monitor* hailed a passing pilot boat and took the pilot aboard to guide them through the shallows in the approach to Hampton Roads. The officers of the ironclad huddled around him as he came aboard, straining to hear him say what was happening. The *Virginia* had come out of Elizabeth River, he said. She was destroying the fleet in Hampton Roads![2]

The news was startling. But, in moments, surprise turned to resolve. "Oh how we longed to be there," Keeler lamented. The ship seemed to steam toward the fort at a snail's pace, the only sound aboard now the "monotonous clank, clank, of the engine." No dinner was made that evening, nor would anyone have thought to eat it if it had been. All eyes were transfixed by the booming fireworks ahead of them. As they neared the harbor, the shelling seemed to let up in the darkness. All manner of sail and steam ships were running out of Hampton Roads, passing by the *Monitor* "like a covey of frightened quails & their lights danced over the water in all directions." Then, with the firing all but done, something new attracted their eyes. A huge glow glimmered red and yellow in the Roads, fire leaping high into the air around what appeared to be burning masts and spars. A United States frigate of war was engulfed in flames.[3]

Whatever had happened ahead there at Hampton Roads, it had been nearly a year in coming. Upon the evacuation of Norfolk, the remaining United States ships, chief among them the *Cumberland* and the *Minnesota,* had taken up their station in Hampton Roads near Fort Monroe, where they could block the passage in and out of the Roads of any Confederate shipping. These ships, with those supporting them, were incorporated into the Atlantic Blockading Squadron shortly afterward. Welles appointed Captain Silas H. Stringham to its command, but thereafter was continually dissatisfied with Stringham's slowness and reluctance to take any offensive. By September 1861 the Secretary of the Navy would take it no longer. On the eighteenth of that month he ordered Captain Louis M. Goldsborough to relieve Stringham at fleet headquarters in Hampton Roads.

This Goldsborough was a hearty, bluff, intimidating man. Fifty-six years old, a native of Washington, D.C., and a veteran of many years in the Navy, he and his awful temper were known throughout the service. Unbelievably, he had joined the Navy as a midshipman at the age of seven! He left the Navy in the 1830s and commanded a company of foot soldiers during the Seminole War in Florida, later returning to the sea to fight in the war with Mexico. By 1861 he had risen to captain, though he stood rather low in Welles's estimation. "He has wordy pretensions," the Secretary wrote of Goldsborough, "some capacity, but no hard courage. There is a clan of such men in the Navy, varying in shade and degree, who in long years of peace have been students and acquired position, but whose real traits are not generally understood. The Department is compelled to give them commands, and at the same time is held responsible for their weakness, errors, and want of fighting qualities."[4]

Goldsborough steamed to Hampton Roads on the *Congress* and officially relieved Stringham on September 23. He found that he had twenty-nine vessels under his command, spread out from Florida to Washington, D.C. Here at Hampton Roads, of more immediate concern, he had the frigates *Congress* and *Cumberland,* and the *Minnesota.* These were the real power of his fleet. There was also the steamer *Daylight* and the tug *Young America,* as well as one or two steamers in from other stations for coal. Golds-borough immediately began building up his fleet here, adding vessels, switching them with other stations, repairing those which had fallen out of shape. On October 12 the Atlantic Blockading Squadron was divided in two, north and south. The South Atlantic Blockading Squadron went to Captain Samuel F. Du Pont. The North Atlantic Blockading Squadron, still headquartered at Hampton Roads, remained with Goldsborough.

By February 1862 he had built up quite a fleet, stationed off Fort Monroe. In addition to the *Congress,* the *Cumberland,* and the *Minnesota,* he also had the frigate *Roanoke,* the steamer *Cambridge,* the storeship *Brandywine,* three coal ships, a hospital ship, five tugboats, a side-wheel steamer, and a sailing bark. In all, his station numbered nearly two thousand seamen and 188 guns, a formidable force to meet whatever the Confederates might send.[5]

Commanding the most interest, of course, were the steam frigates. The *Congress,* with fifty guns, was easily the most imposing. She was twenty years old now, an 1869-ton screw frigate armed with ten 8-inch smoothbore cannon and forty 32-pounder guns. A single broadside from her could hurl nearly half a ton of iron and shell at an enemy. Commander William Smith was in charge of her. "The 'Congress' was a fine, large, roomy and comfortable frigate," wrote a man serving aboard her, "and had been a model in her day." This model was having her problems as the spring of 1862 approached, however. For one thing, Commander Smith was worried by the fact that none of her guns was rifled. Rifled cannon could throw a shell considerably farther than smoothbores, and he feared that an enemy vessel could stand off a sufficient distance from him so that "we should only be a good target for them, as none of our guns could throw a shot to them."

There was also a serious shortage of crewmen. The terms of enlistment for almost her entire crew expired on January 13, 1862, and Smith could get few new replacements, thanks to the high demand for naval enlisted men at other stations. Finally he managed to pull 267 men together from among the several other, fully manned ships in Hampton Roads, but still he was a third understrength. Among those on board were Captain William J. McIntire and 88 men of the 99th New York Infantry, on loan from General Wool at Fort Monroe. They were acting as gunners, and for some time had been practicing at the *Congress'* broadside guns. For some time, indeed since January, Welles had wanted to send the ship north, first to Boston, and then, on March 7, to the Potomac, both to ship a new crew and refit, and to protect the capital. A matter of some interest to a number of people was the fact that the *Congress'* paymaster was McKean Buchanan, brother of the Confederate commander of the James River defenses, Franklin Buchanan.[6]

Next in number of guns, though actually mounting a more effective armament than *Congress,* was the six-year-old *Minnesota*. Interestingly enough, she was a sister ship of the *Roanoke* and, ironically, of the former *Merrimack*. A screw frigate like the *Congress,* she displaced almost twice that ship's tonnage. Her battery consisted of one 10-inch and twenty-eight 9-inch Dahlgren smoothbores, fourteen 8-inch guns, two 24-pounders, and two extra-heavy 12-pounders. She had already seen some war service in an expedition against Hatteras Inlet, North Carolina, in late August 1861. Though Goldsborough was using her as his flagship, *Minnesota's* actual commander was Captain Gershom J. Van Brunt. Back in November 1861, one of Van Brunt's lieutenants aboard the ship had been a recently released prisoner, John Worden.[7]

The sister ship *Roanoke* was a sad case. Launched just twelve days after the *Minnesota,* she weighed slightly more but mounted only forty-six guns, almost identical in number and type to Van Brunt's ship. She had come to Hampton Roads in November 1861 in a disabled condition, one of her engine crankshafts useless. Yet she was allowed to sit without repairs for four months. Since there was nothing wrong with her guns, it was felt she could still be useful against the *Virginia* if she attacked the fleet, but *Roanoke's* commander, Captain John Marston, would still complain in February 1862 that "when I think of this ship's crippled condition—no engine and 180 of her crew deficient—it makes me sick at heart." The seeming negligence baffled the crewmen as well. "We sailors couldn't understand why the government should leave such a powerful ship in a condition like that," one of them wrote.[8]

This left the *Cumberland.* Just nine years old, she had at one time been a magnificent forty-four-gun screw frigate, the flagship of Commodore Joseph Smith's Mediterranean squadron, and of the African squadron as well. In 1856 she had been "razeed"—cut down a deck, making her into a sloop of war mounting twenty-four guns, twenty-two 9-inch smoothbores, one 10-inch smoothbore, and one formidable 70-pounder rifle. Serving as the flagship of the Home Squadron in 1860, *Cumberland* cruised off Veracruz until early 1861, when threats of war at home called her back to Hampton Roads. Anchored off Norfolk at the suggestion of officers who later went over to the Confederacy, she was intended to play a part in blocking up the Elizabeth River to prevent herself and other valuable ships, such as the *Merrimack,* from getting out. In the panic to evacuate the navy yard in April, she was saved from the torch and taken across Hampton Roads to anchor near Fort Monroe. There followed a brief refitting trip to the North, and subsequently participation in the Hatteras Inlet operations, where she was reputedly the last American frigate to go into battle under sail. Then it was back to Hampton Roads, in November 1861, to spend the following winter blockading off the mouth of the James River. Captain William Radford was her commander in March 1862, but he being absent on court-martial duty, his executive officer, Lieutenant George Morris, was in charge of the ship.[9]

These were the mighty warships that the Union trusted to blockade Confederate shipping on three rivers, protect and support several nearby army installations, and keep the dreaded *Virginia* bottled up at Gosport.

The arena in which Goldsborough's fleet operated was unique. More than once, Hampton Roads had been compared to a great marine theater, a grand stage for some epochal drama to play. It was formed by the confluence of the James River flowing southeast from Richmond, the Nansemond running up from the southwest, and the Elizabeth River from the south. Where they came together they formed a sort of water corridor roughly eight miles long running to Chesapeake Bay. On the north, this corridor, Hampton Roads, was bordered by "the Peninsula," between the York and James rivers. At its easternmost corner, Old Point Comfort, sat Fort Monroe, a mighty casemated bastion whose guns commanded all approaches to Hampton Roads. The only major army installation in Virginia that did not fall to the Confederates, it was the headquarters of the Union Department of Virginia, commanded by Major General John Wool. In addition to the troops stationed at the fort—ten regiments of infantry and four artillery batteries—there were others at Camp Hamilton, two miles east of the fort, and seven regiments and one battery at Newport News' Camp Butler, on the western corner of the Peninsula, by the mouth of the James.

Just over a mile south of Fort Monroe, midway between it and Willoughby's Point, the southern edge of the Roads' entrance, the Federals had constructed a small artificial stone island called Rip Raps. Here they placed a battery. Since the main channel into or out of Hampton Roads lay between Rip Raps and Fort Monroe, the guns of the two could combine to deliver a murderous cross fire on any enemy vessel foolhardy enough to attempt the passage. Between Rip Raps and Willoughby's Point the water was at the most eighteen feet deep, too shallow for most vessels to chance.

Two miles west of Willoughby's, at the mouth of the Elizabeth River, sat a line of Confederate batteries on Sewell's Point. The guns effectively commanded the channel in the Elizabeth along which all shipping must pass, but their range was not sufficient to interfere with Federal vessels out in the Roads. Nearly five miles southwest of Sewell's sat Craney Island, the western lip of the Elizabeth's mouth. Here, too, Confederate batteries guarded the entrance. And another five miles west sat the batteries at Pig Point, guarding the entrance to the Nansemond.

Thus the forces stood arrayed, the Federals controlling the entire northern shore of Hampton Roads and the entrance to the James, and the Confederates effectively guarding the southern banks, the Nansemond, the Elizabeth, and thereby Norfolk and Gosport. The requisite tasks of the contending parties were obvious and clear-cut. For the Confederates, the *Virginia* and the other little warships at Norfolk were of no use at all unless they could be taken out of the Elizabeth and up the James to defend Richmond, or else pass Fort Monroe and escape to relieve the blockade elsewhere or threaten northern ports. In either case, Buchanan would have to face Goldsborough's fleet. For the Federals it was equally clear. They must hold Hampton Roads and thereby keep the three rivers bottled up. And, sooner or later, they must face the *Virginia*.

This last had been on the mind of Goldsborough and his command for a long time. He was an early advocate of ironclads. Back in September 1861 Goldsborough had urged the government to construct a fleet of thirty armored warships. Do so, he said, and "you will have the enemy thrown upon his knees." General-in-

Chief Winfield Scott sneered contemptuously at the idea, and even when Goldsborough did manage to get a project going to produce eighteen ironclads, it fell through.

With this background, it was no wonder Goldsborough turned such an attentive ear to all reports on the *Virginia*'s progress. He had been in command at Hampton Roads less than two weeks before he began sending almost daily reports on her to Welles, and from the first he believed that the Rebel ironclad would come to battle with him. At first it was thought the *Virginia* and her consort ships would try to run past Fort Monroe to reach the sea. This came from Wool, whom Goldsborough regarded as "that inflated fool." But Wool's character hardly controverted the seriousness of an anticipated attack. "Unless her stability be compromitted by her heavy topworks of wood and iron and her weight of batteries," Goldsborough wrote of the *Virginia* in October 1861, "she will, in all probability, prove to be exceedingly formidable." Anticipating that the ironclad, on emerging from the Elizabeth River, would naturally pass Sewell's Point before turning west toward Newport News and the James, Goldsborough placed the *Congress* and the *Cumberland* off the latter place. When they had engaged the *Virginia*, he would move against her from Fort Monroe in the *Minnesota,* and with "everything else that may be on hand at the time." Thereby he hoped to catch the ironclad in a cross fire while, at the same time, cutting off her line of retreat. "Nothing, I think, but very close work can possibly be of service in accomplishing the destruction of the *Merrimack,*" he wrote Welles, "and even of that a great deal may be necessary."

The *Virginia* did not appear as expected, though reports of her anticipated coming continued to filter across Hampton Roads. By December 1861, as Goldsborough prepared to leave Hampton Roads to direct an attack on Roanoke Island, North Carolina, his fears had not diminished in the least. To command in his absence he would leave Captain John Marston, and with him he left complete instructions on what should be done if the *Virginia* made an appearance. The tugboats *Zouave* and *Dragon* were detailed particularly to tow *Congress* and *Cumberland* wherever necessary should the former not have time to get up steam or the latter find no wind for her sails. Still the ironclad did not appear. By February 1862, with reports still coming in of an impending attack, Marston could say confidently, "I am anxiously expecting her and believe I am ready."

In the middle of this month, an Irishman presented himself at Fort Monroe and demanded to see General Wool. He was referred to Wool's chief of staff, Colonel Le Grand B. Cannon. "I want to see the General," said the Irishman. Cannon resisted, asking the man's business, but to no avail. Finally the colonel threatened to have the man arrested, and this produced results. After the room was cleared of all but these two men, the Irishman had Cannon slit the lining of his jacket. "I cut the cloth as he indicated," Cannon remembered, "and found, on a piece of cotton cloth sewed inside the lining, a communication from the loyal workman in the Norfolk Navy Yard." Undoubtedly this was another message from William Lyons. The *Virginia* would be out in less than a month, he said. Then it was the Confederates' intention to attack *Congress* and *Cumberland* with her, while Major General John B. Magruder's little army at Yorktown would attack Newport News from the land.

Wool immediately sent Cannon to Washington with dispatches to inform the War Department of the intended attack. After no little difficulty, Cannon met with Secretary of War Edwin McM. Stanton, who in turn directed that the matter be brought before the President. According to Cannon, Lincoln then called a cabinet meeting before which the colonel presented his story. Cannon would claim that Assistant Secretary Fox was almost scornful of the report of the *Virginia,* saying, "Mr. President, you need not give yourself any trouble whatever about that vessel." Thereupon, says Cannon, the whole matter was dismissed. Knowing the concern felt by Welles and Fox over the Rebel ironclad, Cannon's recollection is a little suspect, but it does point up the possibility that the Federals had heard so many times that the *Virginia* was coming that they now tended not to be too much on their guard when a new report appeared.[10]

Indeed, many were simply sick of hearing about the *Virginia.* Marston lamented to Welles that the *Congress* and other ships badly in need of refitting could not be sent north "as long as the *Merrimack* is held as a rod over us." Van Brunt agreed. Hearing on February 23 that the ironclad had finally been launched, he told the Navy Department that "the sooner she gives us the opportunity to test her strength the better." The waiting and the rumors were irksome. "Report says she is ready to come out," he wrote, "I sincerely wish she would, I am quite tired of hearing of her." This did not mean, however, that Van Brunt and the others were not interested in getting further reports on the ironclad's progress. Standing off Fort Monroe were ships of British and French observers, neutrals who had almost daily intercourse with the Confederates at Norfolk. Frequently the Federals tried to get information from these visitors as they returned to their ships under flag of truce, but to no avail.

Even without information from the foreigners, however, by the end of the first week of March 1862, Van Brunt and Wool knew that it was now a matter only of days before the *Virginia,* too, kept her appointment with history. Gustavus Fox, expecting that the *Monitor* would reach Hampton Roads by Sunday, March 9, determined to go there himself to see her. He seemed to sense that something was about to happen, and he wanted to be there.[11]

The men in the ranks at Hampton Roads knew it was coming, too. It had been a dull, unexciting winter for them so far, and a cold one. "The winter was a severe one," wrote Lieutenant Thomas O. Selfridge, Jr., of the *Cumberland,* "no fires were allowed, and our enforced idleness became extremely irksome, and we all looked forward to a relief in the spring, and a chance for active operations." Anchored off Newport News with the *Congress,* Selfridge's ship passed January and February in constant drill. One watch always slept at the guns, anticipating a night attack, and the ship was always kept cleared for action. Small arms stood within easy reach, the shot racks on the decks next to the guns were filled, and the crewmen drilled "until every man knew not only the duties of his own station at quarters, but those of every station as well," recalled Master Moses S. Stuyvesant. Meanwhile, the men were always interested in news of the *Virginia,* though "in fact," Selfridge would recall, "rumors of her expected appearance came so often, that at last it became a standing joke with the ship's company."

Aboard the little *Dragon,* too, the men wondered. Hoping to get some inkling of Confederate progress, this little steamer bravely moved in toward Sewell's Point every night, getting as close to the fort as possible. One night, in a dense fog, she got so close that dogs in the Confederate barracks could be heard barking. Then about March 1 the *Dragon* got what many thought was real, concrete news. Frequently, Confederate signal boats would come out under flag of truce to transfer people from Norfolk who wished to go to the North. The *Dragon* would meet the boats, make fast to them, and transfer the civilians. Meanwhile, the officers on both sides bantered and gossiped, exchanging trinkets and newspapers. On this day, the *Dragon*'s engineer called over to the engineer of the Confederate boat, "How about this old *Merrimack?*"

"Oh," came the reply, "she's all right. Didn't you hear the guns the other day when we tested her?" They had indeed. "You look out," he continued. "She may be out in about a week." That would make her appearance March 8, 1862.

On Friday, March 7, the flag-of-truce boats shuttled the foreign officers out to their boats as usual and, as usual, the observers would tell nothing of Confederate doings at Norfolk. That evening, since the weather had taken a sudden change for the better, the men of the *Cumberland* held a party aboard ship. The night passed peacefully, promising a beautiful Saturday to follow.

In the early dawn hours of March 8, the signal officer at Fort Monroe noted something peculiar. No notice had been given by the French corvettes standing off the fort that they intended to put out to sea. Such would have been customary, in order that the fort could fire a parting salute. But now the signalman clearly saw the corvettes getting up steam. They did not move as yet, but the fact did not escape Cannon and others that if the *Virginia* were to come out and battle the fort, the French ships might find themselves in the line of fire. Immediately, word was sent to Brigadier General Joseph K. F. Mansfield, commanding the troops at Newport News. As the sun rose higher above the Atlantic horizon, Cannon and others could only wonder what the Frenchmen had learned in Norfolk the day before. Why were they preparing to steam away unannounced, and from what?[12]

CHAPTER 7

"That Thing Is A-comin'"

Even before Franklin Buchanan took command of the James River defenses, and thereby of the *Virginia,* preparations had been made for the ironclad's appearance in Hampton Roads. Early in 1861, obstructions had been sunk in the main channel of the Elizabeth to prevent Federal warships from coming up it to Norfolk. In December, French Forrest ordered that, "as the period is fast approaching when it is presumed that the *Merrimack* will be in readiness to proceed down to Hampton Roads," the obstructions should be removed. On February 8, 1862, Buchanan, still in Richmond, ordered that the James River Squadron vessels *Patrick Henry* and *Jamestown* be held ready to co-operate with the *Virginia* when she should be ready for service.

Even before seeing the ship, Buchanan had formulated somewhat his plan of attack. It would be simply to let the *Virginia* do the fighting, while these other two ships stayed out of the line of fire, ready however to come into action if so ordered. To provide for an emergency, he had Forrest order Porter to install two lifeboats aboard the ironclad, preferably on her stern. On February 16, Forrest suggested that all flag-of-truce communication with the enemy be cut off "until the great experiment we have in contemplation has been submitted to the test." He was not too successful in this, as the *Dragon*'s engineer could testify.

Preparations went swiftly now. On February 17, the crew was ordered aboard the ironclad and she was commissioned. Already the oil necessary for her machinery had been obtained, and the Navy Department had been hard at work procuring ammunition. The ironclad was loaded as she sat at dockside at Gosport. "Every pound of powder that could be procured has been sent to Norfolk for the *Virginia,"* the department claimed. Nearly eighteen thousand pounds of it was needed, and to obtain it Buchanan and Forrest depleted the stores of several other ships at the navy yard, appealed to Major General Benjamin Huger, commanding Confederate Army forces at Norfolk, and literally begged everywhere possible. By March 4, they had much of what was needed, but the ironclad's magazine was not sufficiently filled until March 7.

Meanwhile, there were matters of ruse and deception to consider. The spurious report of the *Virginia's* failure was placed in the Norfolk *Day Book.* Then, fearing that loyal Union men in the area might try to signal information on the vessel to the enemy, Forrest gave orders that any time signal rockets were seen, all the Confederate batteries in the area were to send up similar rockets, hoping to make the Federals believe that the Rebels were only signaling among themselves.[1]

While readying the *Virginia* for action, Buchanan had been planning his attack for some time. What he conceived of originally was a joint army and navy enterprise. While he attacked the frigates in Hampton Roads, he wanted General Magruder's little army to move on Newport News by land. Magruder was at first amenable to the idea but by late February had changed his mind. There were rumors of Federal build-ups at Newport News. Late-winter rains were making the roads difficult for infantry and almost impassable for artillery. By February 25, for these and other reasons, Magruder had changed his mind. "I do not think the movement advisable," he notified the War Department, leaving it to them to notify Buchanan.

Faced with this, Buchanan nevertheless went ahead with his own plans, and did so in almost absolute secrecy. Only Mallory, Magruder, Commander John R. Tucker commanding three small ships in the James, and apparently Lieutenant Jones, knew his intentions. Buchanan hoped to slip quietly down the Elizabeth after dark on Thursday, March 6, taking a position a short distance off Newport News. At dawn, he would surprise the *Congress* and the *Cumberland,* destroy them, and then shell the batteries on shore.

As is often the case, weather and human frailty conspired against Buchanan. Preparations were made carefully. All the obstructions in the Elizabeth's channel were marked with lights so the

Virginia might steer clear of them. A thick coating of tallow was spread over the sides and top of the casemate, supposing, as Jones said, "that it would increase the tendency of the projectiles to glance." The men and officers came aboard and the ship was readied. But the weather was too inclement—perhaps the same storm that within a few hours would threaten the little *Monitor* as she steamed south from New York. Buchanan had no choice but to postpone his departure. At this point he might have hoped to try again the next night, March 7, should the weather improve, but now he learned that all five of the pilots who were to guide him stood agreed that they could not take the ship out at night. With no buoys, no running lights, and a heavy, untested ship that might be terribly slow to steer in avoiding obstacles, they would not risk the passage. Buchanan had no choice but to wait.[2]

Even as he waited, on March 7 the *Virginia* finally took on the last of her preciously needed powder. This day also, there came from Mallory a confidential letter which, better than anything else, expressed his ultimate hopes for the ironclad. Back in November 1861, the Secretary of the Navy had suggested that if the *Virginia* could prove successful in Hampton Roads, she might then steam up the Chesapeake to the Potomac and then proceed to Washington, D.C., to shell the navy yard there and destroy the bridges connecting the Federal capital with Virginia. Now Mallory developed his vision even more. "I submit for your consideration the attack of New York by the *Virginia*," he wrote. Surely she could pass Old Point Comfort safely and, in a smooth sea, make the passage to New York. "Once in the bay, she could shell and burn the city and the shipping. Such an event would eclipse all the glories of the combats of the sea." After such a bold stroke, thought the Secretary, "peace would inevitably follow. Bankers would withdraw their capital from the city. The Brooklyn navy yard and its magazines and all the lower part of the city would be destroyed, and such an event, by a single ship, would do more to achieve our immediate independence than would the results of many campaigns." Here, then, was Mallory's idea of the true potential of this leviathan. He was a man of vision, to be sure, one with a grasp for the bold, the daring. What this ship might achieve for the Confederacy, however, was now beyond his hands. It must all depend upon the boldness and daring of Franklin Buchanan and his untrained and untried crew, in an untested vessel, pitted against the undoubted mettle of a Federal fleet in Hampton Roads.[3]

Morning, March 8, 1862, came, and with it an abrupt change in the weather, and for the better. Buchanan was decided; now the *Virginia* would move. Once again her casemate was covered with tallow, or "ship's grease," spread on as thick as would hold. Then, at 11 A.M. crewmen cast off all lines and the ironclad steamed away from Gosport Navy Yard, heading north, down the Elizabeth River, toward the Federal fleet. Workmen at their tasks crowded the vessel right up to the minute of her departure. The last mechanics only jumped off onto the dock as she was pulling away into the channel.

All along both sides of the river, the people of Portsmouth and Norfolk lined the banks. No one knew what was coming, but thousands were curious about this vessel making its first voyage. The *Virginia*'s surgeon, Dinwiddie B. Phillips, found that "everything was quiet and calm, and nothing indicated any departure from the usual routine of affairs except that the shores and landings on either side of us were thronged with people, most of them, perhaps, attracted by our novel appearance, and desirous of witnessing our movements through the water." He feared, however, that many others were there only to see her fail. "Few, if any, entertained an exalted idea of our efficiency, and many predicted a total failure." Midshipman Littlepage saw even-more-forthright signs of foreboding. "As we passed along we found the wharves crowded with people, men and women, the women cheering us on our way, and many of the men with serious countenances. One man, I remember, called out to us, 'Go on with your old metallic coffin! She will never amount to anything else!' "[4]

Up to this time, the only men on board who knew the *Virginia*'s true mission were Buchanan and Jones. Lieutenant John R. Eggleston recalled that "we thought we were going upon an ordinary trial trip." Lieutenant Wood agreed, but there were some who by rumor or intuition felt that something more than a trial was at hand. Shortly before the *Virginia* embarked, a number of her lieutenants attended church for the first time since they came here, taking the Holy Sacrament. Even now, as the vessel steamed down the river, wives and children in Norfolk and Portsmouth were in their churches, praying.[5]

A mile and one half brought the *Virginia* abreast of Norfolk. The ship was moving slowly. Realizing that it would be some time yet before she got out of the river, Buchanan had the boatswain pipe all hands to "dinner"—as the noon meal was then called. Meanwhile, he summoned Chief Engineer Ramsay to him. Ramsay had been running the engines slow thus far, "to guard against any accident." Still, it had already become obvious to all aboard that the ship was neither speedy nor maneuverable. "From the start we saw that she was slow, not over five knots," said Wood. "She steered so badly that, with her great length, it took from thirty to forty minutes to turn. . . . She was as unmanageable as a water-logged vessel."

Before the *Virginia* left dock, Buchanan had called on Ramsay. "Ramsay," he asked, "what would happen to your engines and boilers, if there should be a collision?"

They were braced tightly, replied the engineer. No collision would harm them.

"I am going to ram the *Cumberland*," announced Buchanan. "I'm told she has the new rifled guns [she had one 70-pounder rifle], the only ones in their whole fleet we have cause to fear. The moment we are out in the Roads I'm going to make right for her and ram her." Buchanan wanted to know if a trial trip for the engines was necessary, but Ramsay then told him that the ten-mile trip necessary to reach the Federal ships would be trial enough. If any trouble developed with the engines, there would be plenty of time to turn back. Now, as Ramsay reported to Buchanan on the *Virginia*'s top deck, he was happy to report that "the machinery is all right, sir." Indeed, one of the pilots estimated that she was making eight or nine knots.

Just then, the ship's caterer sent Ramsay a message to come to the wardroom to eat, cheerfully saying, "Better get your lunch now, Mr. Ramsay. It will be your last chance. The galley-fires must be put out when the magazines are opened." The planned attack seemed not to be such a tightly held secret after all, if the caterer's statement is genuine and what Ramsay saw on his way to the wardroom confirms the fact. "Passing along the gun-deck I saw the pale and determined countenances of the guns' crews, as they stood motionless at their posts, with set lips unsmiling. . . . This was the real thing." In the wardroom Ramsay found a number of officers seated at the table "daintily partaking of cold tongue and biscuit."

At one end, however, sat Assistant Surgeon Algernon S. Garnett looking over a case of surgical instruments and laying out lint for bandages. "The sight took away my appetite."[6]

While the *Virginia's* crew ate or tended to their tasks, the two small steamers *Raleigh* and *Beaufort* accompanied her down the Elizabeth. Buchanan had designated them her consorts for the coming fight. The evening of March 7 he sent for their commanders, Lieutenant Joseph W. Alexander and Lieutenant William H. Parker respectively, and informed them of his intentions. Their pilots were assigned, and Buchanan told them to watch for a new signal he might fly. "Sink before you surrender," it said, meaning they were to fight their ships to the bottom before giving up. The next morning, they left in company with the ironclad. Parker, aboard the *Beaufort,* eloquently characterized what he saw: "A great stillness came over the land," he said, despite the number of smaller craft that were moving down the river with them. "Everything that would float, from the army tug-boat to the oysterman's skiff, was on its way down to the same point loaded to the water's edge with spectators." Captain Forrest was aboard one of them. Yet, despite this following, "no voice broke the silence of the scene; hearts were too full for utterance; an attempt at cheering would have ended in tears, for all realized the fact that here was to be tried the great experiment of the ram and iron-clad in naval warfare." The men on the *Virginia* were the most calm, Parker thought, while on his own ship he found the crew exhibiting a "careless *insouciance.*"[7]

Those people on the shore had been gathering for hours, ever since they heard the signal gun at 11 A.M. that announced the *Virginia's* departure. Private James Keenan of the 2nd Georgia Infantry Battalion, stationed in Norfolk, heard it. "In an instant the whole city was in an uproar, women, children, men on horseback and on foot were running down towards the river from every conceivable direction shouting 'the Merrimac is going down' . . . I saw the huge monster swing loose from her moorings and making her way down the river. . . . A good portion of her crew were on top and received the enthusiastic cheers from the excited populace without a single response. Everything betokened serious business." Indeed, from as far as twelve miles away, Confederate soldiers and officers were riding down to the riverbanks in response to the message passed from mouth to mouth: "The *Virginia* is coming up the river."[8]

At about twelve-thirty, the *Virginia* took a towline from the *Beaufort*. It was a measure to assist in steering the ironclad, since, her keel running very close to the bottom now, the ship's rudder was having little effect in turning her. Rounding a point two miles north of Norfolk, the Confederates could see, several miles ahead through the mouth of the Elizabeth, Sewell's Point and Fort Monroe. A few points of the compass to port—the left—was Craney Island and, in the distance behind it, Newport News and the anchored *Congress* and *Cumberland*. Buchanan's sailors could see that the frigates' lifeboats were hanging from lowered booms, ready for people to come and go ashore. In their rigging the Yankee seamen had hung their Saturday washing, according to custom placing their white garments on the starboard rigging and their blues on the port. "Nothing indicated that we were expected," mused Lieutenant Wood.

It was a curious moment for some aboard the *Virginia*. Surgeon Phillips, looking out at the frigates, recalled the time six years before when he had served aboard the *Cumberland* in the Mediterranean. Lieutenant Eggleston, too, could recall serving as a midshipman aboard both *Cumberland* and *Congress*. Looking now at the latter, "my floating home for nearly three years," Eggleston lamented that "little did I think then that I should ever lift a hand for her destruction."[9]

Nothing seemed to happen, at first. "As we gradually drew nearer and nearer to them," Phillips wrote of the Federal frigates, "the curiosity of the *men* seemed to be somewhat aroused, and some of them collected together at the port-holes and on the forecastles to look at us, but for a long time no official notice was taken of us." But at the same time, a host of smaller sailing craft and tugboats in the Roads scurried, said Ramsay, "to the far shore like chickens on the approach of a hovering hawk." Before long, Ramsay could see signal flags running up the masts of the frigates. "The Merrimac has come down," he thought they said. Then the clotheslines came in, the boats were pulled up or sent to shore, and "suddenly huge volumes of smoke began to pour from the funnels of the frigates *Minnesota* and *Roanoke* at Old Point [Comfort]." Topsails were shaken out aboard the *Cumberland* and the *Con-*

gress, and drums and fifes called the men to their battle stations.[10]
Observing all this from the top deck of the *Virginia,* Buchanan
now stepped down to the gun deck and called all hands around him.
Finally he told them that this was no trial, though by now all surely
knew it. Buchanan's speech to them was short and to the point.
"Sailors," he reportedly said, "in a few minutes you will have the
long-expected opportunity to show your devotion to your country
and our cause. Remember that you are about to strike for your
country and your homes, your wives and your children." The eyes
of the whole world were upon them, he said. In the name of their
beloved Virginia, let every man do his duty. Then came the order:
"Beat to quarters."

The men went to their stations quietly, secured the guns for action, and stood at the ready. They had passed Craney Island and
were now coming abreast of Sewell's Point. The men at the Confederate batteries along both banks of the Elizabeth had been cheering
them lustily, filling the air with their caps thrown up in the huzza.
Buchanan spoke to his officers, explaining the situation before them
more fully and telling them that they would have to dispose of *Cumberland* and *Congress* first, before *Minnesota* and *Roanoke* could
come up from Fort Monroe. He intended, he said, to head directly
for the *Cumberland* to ram her.

Once out of the Elizabeth's channel and fairly into the Roads,
Buchanan turned the *Virginia* west, toward Newport News. It was
about one-thirty now, and the *Beaufort* took back in her towline
from the ironclad. Both the *Beaufort* and the *Raleigh* steamed along
on the port side of the *Virginia,* shielded by her, somewhat, from
the enemy. There had been rumors in Norfolk for some time that
the Federals had placed "torpedoes"—explosive mines—in the channel at Hampton Roads, and the Confederates now watched anxiously for them. To everyone's relief, none were found.

Amid the mounting tension on the ironclad, a powder boy from
North Carolina gave his money purse to the commander of his gun,
Midshipman Henry H. Marmaduke—son of a former governor of
Missouri. "Mr. Marmaduke," he said, "I'm likely to be killed in this
fight. If I am, will you send my money to my father?" Marmaduke
took the purse, then looked to his gun. It was two o'clock now, and
Lieutenant Charles C. Simms, commanding the ship's bow pivot
gun, one of Brooke's rifles, was ready. The *Cumberland* was less

than a mile away, easily within range. At a signal from Buchanan, Simms yanked the rifle's lanyard and, amid a deafening roar as the cannon's blast reverberated inside the casemate, sent a shell screaming toward the enemy. The long-awaited battle had begun.[11]

The Confederates were in large part correct in thinking they had surprised the Federal fleet. The repeated failure of rumors to materialize had somewhat lulled the Yankees' watchfulness. Instead, they were enjoying the magnificent break in what had been, until that morning, miserable weather. "Never has a brighter day smiled upon Old Virginia than last Saturday," wrote a correspondent for the Boston *Journal* a few days later. "The hours crept lazily along, and sea and shore in this region saw nothing to vary the monotony of the scene. Now and then a soldier might be heard complaining that this detachment of the loyal army was having no part in the glorious victories which everywhere else are crowning American valor with such brilliant success, or a sailor might be noted, on shipboard, telling how much he hoped the Merrimac would show herself, and how certainly she would be sunk by our war vessels." The men were doing their washing, cleaning camps ashore, playing games, and generally delighting in the splendid sunshine. Signal boats were out in Hampton Roads patrolling, but there was no reason to expect that anything would happen.[12]

At about noon, the lookouts at Fort Monroe first saw something under steam coming down the Elizabeth River. General Wool shortly sent word to Mansfield at Newport News to gather his troops together in case of an attack from Magruder's Confederates. By this time, the lookouts on the *Roanoke* and the *Minnesota* had seen the coming threat as well. At 1:08 P.M., a lookout vessel raised signal number 551, reporting the enemy approaching, and Marston, aboard *Roanoke,* went to work at once. He ordered the *Minnesota* to get under way and then called for the tugs to tow his own, disabled ship into the Roads to meet the *Virginia.* "My, didn't orders ring out sharp, and men jump lively," wrote a man aboard the tug *Dragon* as she sped to *Roanoke*'s side. At one-ten, the enemy ironclad actually came in sight. "Pretty soon that great black thing, different from any vessel ever seen before, poked her nose around Sewall's [sic] Point." Within minutes, the *Roanoke* had upped anchor and was under tow, though moving with agonizing slowness.

12. Captain Franklin Buchanan, commanding naval defenses of the James River, made the *Virginia* his flagship and with her attacked the Federal fleet. (Courtesy of the Naval Photographic Center, Washington, D.C.)

13. Lieutenant John Taylor Wood, in charge of the *Virginia*'s stern pivot gun. (*Century Illustrated Monthly Magazine,* LVI, July 1898.)

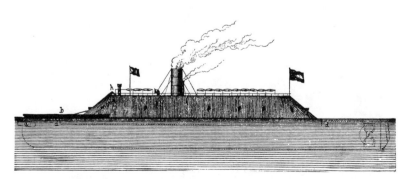

14. An outline of the *Virginia* as she looked on March 7, 1862. (*Century Illustrated Monthly Magazine,* XXIX, March 1885.)

15. Lieutenant John L. Worden, an unpublished photo of the *Monitor*'s first commander. (Courtesy of the MOLLUS-Mass. Collection, U. S. Army Military History Research Collection, Carlisle Barracks, Pennsylvania.)

16. Chief Engineer Alban C. Stimers, who oversaw much of the *Monitor*'s construction and served her well at Hampton Roads. (Courtesy of the Naval Photographic Center, Washington, D.C.)

17. The ships the *Monitor* was coming to save: the USS *Congress* at left and the USS *Cumberland* at right, lying off a Newport News battery. (*Harper's Weekly,* March 22, 1862.)

18. Bluff, much-disliked Commodore Louis M. Goldsborough, commanding the South Atlantic Blockading Squadron, headquartered at Hampton Roads. (Courtesy of Library of Congress.)

19. Major General John E. Wool, commanding at Fort Monroe. (Author's collection.)

20. A bird's-eye view of Hampton Roads, Fort Monroe in the foreground; above Rip Raps (5) are the Elizabeth River, Norfolk (10), and Portsmouth (11); Newport News (17) is at the right. (Courtesy of the MOLLUS-Mass. Collection, U. S. Army Military History Research Collection, Carlisle Barracks, Pennsylvania.)

21. The USS *Cumberland*. (From the *Official Records, Navies.*)

22. The USS *Congress* while under attack. (*Century Illustrated Monthly Magazine*, XXIX, March 1885.)

The *Minnesota,* by this time, was well under way. Her lookout had spotted the *Virginia* at the same time as, or earlier than, *Roanoke's,* but she did not move until orders came from Marston. Below decks, a number of the frigate's engineers were playing a quiet game of chess when a midshipman came down and informed them that the enemy ironclad was coming. Refusing to believe what was assumed to be another rumor, the players "complimented him on his command of countenance, but refused to be sold [fooled] again, and went on with our game." Then an order came down for them to report to the engine room. "This looked like work," wrote one of them. Carefully setting their game aside without moving the pieces, the engineers went to their station. It took Van Brunt only eight minutes to get his ship moving, but it would take him an hour at least to reach Sewell's Point, and considerably longer to get to Newport News, where the *Virginia* seemed to be heading. There was no assurance at all that either he or Marston could get there in time.[13]

It was about 12:40 P.M. that the Federals at Newport News first saw the enemy coming out from Norfolk. A few minutes later, the "long roll" was sounded ashore, calling Mansfield's men to assemble, while the cry "The 'Merrimac' is coming" ran through his camps. Meanwhile, Mansfield immediately dispatched word by telegram to Wool, who was already aware of the *Virginia's* coming.

For the *Congress,* too, it had been a quiet morning, the men busy in preparing the ship for the next day's inspection. Gunner Frederick Curtis was summoned to Lieutenant Joseph B. Smith's cabin to do some repairs, and while there, engaged in a pleasant conversation with the affable officer. Smith, the son of Commodore Smith, had taken over command from Captain William Smith. Outside, the ship's quartermaster was looking over the sunlit Roads through his spyglass when suddenly, at twelve forty-five, he saw a column of heavy black smoke over toward Sewell's Point. "I wish you would take the glass and have a look over there, Sir," he said to a nearby officer, "I believe *that thing* is a-comin' down at last." Smith waited twenty minutes or more to confirm that it was the *Virginia,* however, before he ordered the ship's guns run out their ports and the decks cleared for action.[14]

The *Cumberland* lay anchored two hundred yards north of the *Congress* and about three hundred yards off Newport News, with

Lieutenant George N. Morris, executive officer, in charge. The crew were just finishing their noonday meal, at twelve-forty, when heavy black smoke was sighted off Craney Island. "Soon after the hull of a large vessel shaped like the roof of a house, with one smokestack, appeared in sight," recalled Acting Master's Mate Charles O'Neil. Lieutenant Selfridge had been the first to spot it. Because of the distance involved—nearly seven miles—there was a slight mirage effect, so that Selfridge could not at first tell if the ironclad was really coming out. Soon, though, there was no doubt.

Immediately, the *Cumberland*'s sails were furled, the drying wash was pulled in, and "beat to quarters" was sounded on the drum. The ship was then swung, or pivoted, on her anchor so that she lay directly across the James River channel, with her broadside toward the *Virginia*'s line of approach. The guns were double-charged with powder, and sand was spread on the gun deck. In battle it would soak up the blood and keep the gunners from slipping and sliding in their comrades' gore.[15]

One of the *Cumberland*'s tenders was the tugboat *Zouave,* an old Hudson River tug bought, crew and all, by the government. She performed picket duty for the fleet here at night, and assisted the warships in the day. This morning, coming in from her nightly assignment, the *Zouave*'s commander, Acting Master Henry Reaney, picked up the mail from the *Cumberland* and the *Congress* and delivered it to Fort Monroe. Picking up mail there from a northern steamer, he returned to Newport News, delivered it, and then put in to the wharf for lunch.

At about twelve-thirty, Reaney's quartermaster saw the *Virginia*'s smoke in the distance, and, at the same time, the *Cumberland* signaled for Reaney to come alongside. There the *Zouave* was ordered to steam toward Pig Point, at the mouth of the Nansemond, to see what it was that was coming. "It did not take us long to find out," Reaney later recalled, "for we had not gone over two miles when we saw what to all appearances looked like the roof of a very big barn belching forth smoke as from a chimney on fire." Making out the Confederate flag, Reaney knew it was the *Virginia*. Immediately, he had the *Zouave*'s forward gun, a 30-pounder Parrott rifle—much similar to the Brooke rifle in design—loaded and fired, the first Federal shot of the day. Five more rounds were sent at the oncoming ironclad before *Cumberland* signaled for Reaney to come back to her assistance.[16]

The *Virginia* did not answer Reaney's shots, nor did she reply to any of the shot and shell fired at her by shore batteries at Newport News or by the *Congress* and the *Cumberland,* even though their fire became increasingly brisk. The first Confederate shot of the day was actually fired from Parker's *Beaufort,* a canal boat before the war and now armed with a 32-pounder rifle and a 24-pounder carronade (a sort of mortar). At 2 P.M., without orders, Parker fired his rifle at the *Congress.* At the same time, he ran up the flag he had flown in the fight at Roanoke Island, a pennant somewhat resembling the French flag, and which Marston aboard the *Roanoke* mistook for that nation's colors. Then, looking over at *Virginia,* Parker saw Buchanan send up the signal to "close action"—move in and fight. It was the last battle signal the ironclad would fly that day.[17]

Buchanan waited until he was within easy range of the *Cumberland* before he ordered Lieutenant Simms to fire the 7-inch Brooke-rifle bow gun. The shell screamed across the Roads and hit the enemy warship squarely, passing through the starboard-quarter rail, scattering flying splinters, which wounded several marines nearby. "The groans of these men," wrote Selfridge, "the first to fall, as they were carried below, was something new" to the rest of the gunners aboard.

Quickly, the crew at one of the *Cumberland*'s forward guns loaded and ran the gun out. Their shot missed the mark and, as they were reloading for another, Simms fired his Brooke rifle again. The Confederate shell burst in the very midst of the crew reloading the *Cumberland*'s cannon. It killed every man there except the powder boy and the gun captain, who, while holding a handspike to guide the gun's aiming, had both arms taken off at the shoulder. Without uttering a groan he was taken below, while his gun lay completely disabled.

"Our firing became at once very rapid from the few guns we could bring to bear as she approached slowly," wrote Stuyvesant, commanding *Cumberland*'s after gun division. Selfridge, in charge of the forward gun division, found that "events followed too fast to record them." The dead, as they fell, were thrown to the port side of the deck, out of the way, while the wounded were sent below. "No one flinched, but went on loading and firing, taking the place of

some comrade, killed or wounded, as they had been told to do."
More men were falling from wounds due to the flying splinters than
from exploding shells. The first and second captains of every forward gun were either killed or wounded. Selfridge, with a box of
cannon primers in his pocket, went hurriedly from gun to gun, placing the primers in the breech vents and firing the cannon "as fast as
the decimated crews could load them."[18]

By now, though still three or four hundred yards from the
Cumberland, the *Virginia*'s advance brought her abreast of the
Congress, which had been firing on her for some time. "The 'Merrimac' was steaming slowly towards us," wrote a man aboard the
frigate, "and every eye on the vessel was on her. Not a word was
spoken, and the silence that prevailed was awful. The time seemed
hours before she reached us." At about two-thirty or shortly thereafter, the ships were only three hundred yards apart and the
Congress sent a starboard broadside at the ironclad. It had no effect
at all upon her plated sides.

Aboard the *Virginia,* her starboard battery of four guns was
trained on the *Congress* as that ship fired its broadside. Lieutenant
Eggleston had been looking out one of the gun ports a few moments
before, seeing nothing but water until the *Congress* came into view,
framed in the port. Immediately, he saw the flash of her broadside
and jumped back. His first thought was how fortunate it was that
none of the Federal projectiles hit an open port on the ironclad. The
result could have been disastrous.

Quickly, Eggleston loaded the two guns under his command.
They were "hot shot" guns, for firing balls heated almost red hot in
the furnace below them. The glowing shot was hauled up in an iron
bucket and then placed in the gun muzzle by means of tongs grip-
ping "tugs," or holes in the ball. Once in the muzzle, the ball was
rolled back against a water-soaked wad, which separated it from the
powder charge. Then another wad was rammed in after the ball and
the cannon was ready to fire.

At the command, the *Virginia*'s broadside belched flame and
glowing shot at the *Congress.* The effect was terrible. "All I remember about that broadside," wrote a gunner on the *Congress,*
"was of feeling something warm, and the next instant I found myself lying on the deck beside a number of my shipmates." One of the
Virginia's shells came in through the porthole of gun number seven,

struck the carriage and dismounted the gun, and killed or wounded the entire crew, "sweeping the men about it back into a heap, bruised and bleeding." Meanwhile, one of Eggleston's hot shot cut through the ship to a cabin on the port side, starting a fire that the ship's fire hose could not put out. At the same time, the other hot shot started a fire near the after magazine, threatening to reach the ship's powder. As the *Virginia* continued on her course toward the *Cumberland*, she and *Congress* would continue to trade shots, but already the latter was seriously injured and fighting at a heavy disadvantage.[19]

Still, the ironclad did not swerve from her intended victim, the *Cumberland*. Northern correspondents at Newport News and Fort Monroe vividly described the scene: "Now she nears the *Cumberland* sloop of war," wrote one, "silent and still, wierd [sic] and mysterious, like some devilish and superhuman monster, or the horrid creation of a nightmare. Now, but a biscuit toss from the ship, and from the sides of both pour out a living tide of fire and smoke, of solid shot and heavy shell. We see from the ship's scuppers running streams of crimson gore." The Federal ship fired bravely, but her shots "struck and glanced off, having no more effect than peas from a pop-gun" on the *Virginia*.

Aboard the *Cumberland,* even as they worked the guns, the men watched the approaching monster. "As she came ploughing through the water right onward toward our port-bow," said the *Cumberland*'s pilot, A. B. Smith, "she looked like a huge half-submerged crocodile. . . . At her prow I could see the iron ram projecting, straight forward, somewhat above the water's edge, and apparently a mass of iron." The Federals fired as best they could, only to see their projectiles "bouncing upon her mailed sides like India-rubber, apparently making not the least impression." They did, however, shoot away the ironclad's flagstaff. But on she came. Pilot Smith lamented that "it was impossible for our vessel to get out of her way."[20]

Aboard the *Virginia* the excitement mounted as she drew ever closer to the *Cumberland*. The din inside the casemate as the enemy projectiles struck her sides was terrible, but the ship remained undamaged. "They struck our sloping sides," wrote Ramsay, "were deflected upward to burst harmlessly in the air, or rolled down and fell hissing into the water, dashing the spray up into our ports." Buchanan was standing where he had been since the action commenced, in an open hatch on the top deck, foolishly exposed but, miraculously, unhurt. According to some, he now called out to the *Cumberland* to surrender, to which Lieutenant Morris replied, "Never!"

Buchanan stepped down into the pilothouse and called Ramsay. As soon as the ironclad rammed the enemy ship, Ramsay was to reverse the *Virginia*'s engines without waiting for orders to do so. Back Ramsay went to the engine room. Then he heard two rings of the signal gong, meaning stop engines. Then came three gongs, the signal to reverse engines. Either Buchanan had gotten excited and ordered the engines reversed too soon, or else he hoped to have them already reversed before striking the *Cumberland* so that the ironclad might back away all the sooner. Ramsay followed his orders. Then, he said, there was an "awful pause."

On the gun deck, Eggleston was trying to see through the smoke from his guns but could make out very little of the ironclad's progress toward the *Cumberland*. Then he felt a slight jar, as if the ship had gone aground. He did not know what it was at first, until Lieutenant Robert Minor came running along the deck waving his cap and yelling, "We've sunk the Cumberland."[21]

The *Virginia*'s prow had broken through a ring of timbers surrounding the enemy ship, placed there to prevent floating torpedoes from striking her sides. The crash of the timbers was audible to Lieutenant Jones above the din of battle, but not to others aboard the ironclad. Then the *Virginia*'s formidable iron ram, backed by several hundred tons of ironclad propelled at about six knots, tore into the *Cumberland*'s starboard side below the water line, striking her near the bow. The impact was barely felt by many on the ironclad, but Ramsay, at the engines, was nearly knocked from his feet. At the same instant, Simms fired another shell, into the very heart of the rammed ship.

"The crash into the *Cumberland* was terrific in its results," Minor would write in a few days. "Our cleaver fairly opened her side." Wood thought that the *Virginia* opened a hole in her wide enough to "drive in a horse and cart." In fact, though no one could see the hole very well since it was below the water line, it appears to have been about seven feet wide. The water rushed in with irresistible force, almost instantly flooding the *Cumberland*'s hold. And now it became painfully evident just why Buchanan had wanted to have the engines reversed as soon as possible. The *Virginia* had opened such a hole in her adversary that the sloop immediately began to list to starboard as the water filled her. In doing so, she bore down on the ironclad's ram, still inside her, and began forcing the *Virginia* down by the bow. Unless Buchanan could get his ship backed out quickly, the sinking *Cumberland* could hold her trapped in this position, perhaps even taking the ironclad down with her.[22]

The scene aboard the *Cumberland* was surprisingly calm, perhaps because the men at the guns knew from the first that there was no possibility of their getting out of the *Virginia*'s way. The men worked their guns right up to the moment of impact. "The shock of the collision was, of course, perceptible," wrote Stuyvesant, "but was not violent." Instantly came reports from below decks that large quantities of water were coming through the hole, and to most it was immediately evident that the *Cumberland* must sink. Still her men stood bravely by the guns, delivering shot after ineffective shot point-blank against the ironclad's casemate.

At this moment, as the sloop had the *Virginia*'s prow trapped within her hold, a fleeting opportunity came and was lost. The ironclad was directly beneath the sloop's starboard anchor. Had someone thought to let the anchor drop, it could have held fast to the *Virginia* and pulled her down as the *Cumberland* sank. But the chance passed almost as soon as it came, for shortly the Yankee sailors saw the *Virginia* slowly pivot by her trapped bow until the ships were nearly parallel. And then the ironclad broke free.[23]

What had happened was a godsend to the Confederates. As soon as he felt the crash, Ramsay started looking to see that the *Virginia*'s engines pulled her back out of the enemy ship. "The engines labored," he wrote, "the vessel was shaken in every fiber," but the ironclad did not move. Instead, he noticed that she was starting to depress visibly at the bow as the sinking *Cumberland* pulled her down. Then he heard a terrific explosion that seemed to come from the boiler room. Fearing that the boilers had burst, Ramsay was relieved to find that it was only an enemy shell exploding in the smokestack, its spent iron fragments raining down on the floor in the boiler room. Then the force of the tidal current began to pivot the stalled *Virginia* until her starboard side nearly faced the *Cumberland*'s. A fortunate wave rolled the Federal sloop slightly in its swell and, the tension on her bow relieved slightly, the *Virginia* finally backed out. She did not withdraw without injury, however. Littlepage had noticed, weeks before, that a flange was cracked when the ironclad's ram was installed. The strain inside the *Cumberland*'s hold now worked on this defect, breaking the ram entirely loose before the ironclad backed out. "Like the wasp," wrote Ramsay, "we could sting but once, leaving the sting in the wound."[24]

To the thousands of spectators lining the shores of Hampton Roads, the battle thus far had seemed like a gigantic staged extravaganza. Henry Wise and his sons John and Richard had ridden furiously to reach Sewell's Point to witness the fight. "The scene was truly inspiring," John Wise would recall, though lamenting that the fight was taking place so far away, off Newport News. "For the details, we who had no glasses were dependent upon those who had." They could see "a great puff of smoke roll up and float off from the Merrimac," as Simms first fired the bow pivot gun. A moment later came the flashes of the broadsides from the *Congress* and the *Cumberland,* and then, delayed by twenty seconds or so, came the sound of the guns' reports. A nearby officer with field glasses gave a running commentary on the action. "She is heading direct for the Cumberland," he said, and a moment later, "she has rammed the Cumberland!" "The Cumberland is sinking," he cried finally, all to the cheers of the spectators.

This same scene was enacted in a host of places. Raleigh Colston had a much better view, from Ragged Island, across the James from Newport News, and within only three or four miles of the fight. Curiously, though, thanks to some atmospheric inversion, they could see every bit of the action but could hear nothing. "We could see every flash of the guns and the clouds of white smoke, but not a single report was audible," he recalled. It could not detract from the splendor of the scene as the *Virginia* rammed the enemy ships. "I could hardly believe my eyes when I saw the masts of the *Cumberland* begin to sway wildly." A Confederate soldier watching, Private Keenan, marveled that "the Merrimac never halted nor fired a gun in reply to the Cumberland which was firing away with desperation. You may be able to partly imagine the great anxiety which prevailed along the shore now lined with thousands of anxious spectators. Every one said, 'why don't the Merrimac fire, the Cumberland will sink her.'" But finally Keenan was rewarded with the sight of the rammed sloop going down. For those observing from the northern side of the Roads, the scene was no less imposing, though dismaying as the destruction being wrought on the Federal ships became evident. "Now the ram has taken her position bow on," a reporter said in describing the action, "and slowly she moves and horribly upon the doomed vessel. Like a rhinoceros she sinks down her head and frightful horn, and with a dead, soul-rendering crunch she pierces her on the starboard bow, lifting her up as a man does a toy."[25]

Understandably, the men aboard the contending ships were wholly oblivious of the spectators ashore. Once the *Virginia* pulled free of the sinking *Cumberland,* she pulled back to a position parallel with the enemy and only about twenty feet away. Here the two warships hurled tons of iron at each other in a furious fusilade that enshrouded both in smoke and flame. Some men on the *Virginia* believed that they heard the screams of women aboard the other ship, perhaps some ladies having remained from the party the night before. There is no evidence to support the claim, but then, in the confusion, few were certain of what was happening. Some believed that the *Virginia* rammed the sloop a second time, though in fact she did not.

Only the terrible, raging battle between the two was certain fact. "The shot and shell from the *Merrimack* crashed through the wooden sides of the *Cumberland* as if they had been made of paper, carrying huge splinters with them and dealing death and destruction on every hand," wrote O'Neil. "Several shot and shell entered on one side and passed out through the other carrying everything before them." A gunner had both legs shot away, yet took three steps on the bleeding stumps to fire a final shot before falling dead. Another man lost both arms; yet, before he died, managed to urge his comrades to "Give 'em fits."

For nearly half an hour the *Cumberland* took and returned the *Virginia*'s fire. Aboard the sloop, Stuyvesant saw "a scene of carnage and destruction never to be recalled without horror." "The once clean and beautiful deck was slippery with blood, blackened with powder and looked like a slaughter house," wrote O'Neil. Meanwhile, the water kept pouring into her hold as the bow slowly went down. Soon the water was up to the forward gun deck, having flooded the forward powder magazine and drowned most of the wounded, who had gone below. Acting Master William Kennison bravely continued to man the forward pivot gun with crew, even though they were knee-deep in the water. With the deck torn up all around them, Kennison's gunners kept firing until their gun's muzzle went under, before they abandoned ship.

Soon the berth deck was flooded, and any remaining wounded who had gone below were drowned. The rest of them were sprawled out on the main deck, many of them crying pitiably as they saw a watery grave slowly approach. Fire broke out but was soon extinguished. Now the water was coming into the *Cumberland*'s bow ports as they went below the surface, making any further use of her pumps a waste of time. Some powder had been saved before the forward magazine went under, and now the gunners had to start using that from the after powder room to keep the *Cumberland*'s guns blazing.

Lieutenant Morris made at least an attempt to have the ship swing around on her anchor cable in order to bring the fresh guns on the other side to bear, or else to up anchor and try to get to shore. O'Neil and Master's Mate John M. Harrington went to see to the matter when a shell tore past, taking away Harrington's head and leaving four of their assistants "spattered with the blood and brains of that unfortunate officer." And by now the sloop was so waterlogged that any hope of moving her had vanished.

Frantically, Selfridge and Stuyvesant kept their gun crews firing, though with no apparent effect on the ironclad. "I was fighting mad when I saw the shells from my guns were producing no effect upon the iron sides of the *Merrimac*," Selfridge later recalled. He gathered the remnant of his forward gun division, about thirty men, and with them hauled a gun that was about to go under back to an open port. They barely got it in place when a shell burst among them, killing or wounding almost every one. "There was no one left in the first division," he wrote, "not a gun's crew could be mustered." All about him lay the blood and mangled corpses of his comrades. Some of the guns were run in where they had last been fired, many of them spattered with blood. The rammers, sponges, buckets, and all the accouterments of the cannon lay broken and scattered about the splintered deck.

Wood, watching from the *Virginia,* declared of the Federal sloop that "no ship was ever fought more gallantly." But it was of no use.

As the few remaining men at the stern guns kept up their fire, the *Cumberland* suddenly lurched to port as her berth deck went completely under. One gun broke loose from its tackle on the starboard rail and rolled down across the sloping deck, crushing a sailor against the port rail. By now, it was about 3:35 P.M., and Morris could not expect his men to hold out longer. He gave the order to abandon ship. Everyone jumped over the side, those wounded who could walk coming with them. Selfridge was among the last to leave, on his way helping the ship's fat drummer boy over the side, where he used his drum as a buoy. Out in the water, the men frantically swam for the shore at Newport News, while a number of small cutters put out from the beach to pick them up. Morris himself could not swim, and was only saved when O'Neil threw him a line from one of the rescue boats. Behind them, as the *Cumberland* finally went under by the bow with a great hiss and boiling from air escaping the hold, the survivors could still see a few men clinging to the ship's rigging. Possibly, since the ship's masts would still protrude from the water some distance once her hull settled on the bottom, these men might be rescued later. If the Federals could take any consolation at all from the heartbreaking scene of their ship going down, it was that her flag still waved at her top. "She went down bravely, with her colors flying," wrote the *Virginia*'s Jones. Those colors would continue to fly through the remainder of the battle.[26]

It might have soothed the Yankee sailors' feelings a little to know that they had made the ironclad pay a bit for her victory over the *Cumberland*. The fire they delivered to the Confederate ship was terrible. The heat from the guns' flash set the grease on the *Virginia*'s casemate popping and crackling. "It seemed that she was literally frying from one end to the other," thought Littlepage. The smoke from the burning grease blew in through the ironclad's ports and mixed with the powder smoke inside, "making it so dense that we could hardly breathe." One of Littlepage's gunners, Seaman John Hunt, turned to Seaman James "Jack" Cronin, at one of Eggleston's guns, and cried out, "Jack, don't this smell like hell?" "It certainly does," Cronin called back, "and I think we'll all be there in a few minutes!"

Shortly after ramming the enemy sloop, and before the ironclad backed free of her, Simms fired his bow gun again. The gun's sponger, Charles Dunbar, got so caught up in the fight that, immediately, he leaped to the porthole to swab the gun for another round. A shell from the *Cumberland* cut him in half. Once the ironclad pulled out of the sloop, the Federal ship did her even more damage. The Yankee gunners tried their best to aim their guns at the *Virginia*'s ports, hoping to put a shot inside her. As the ironclad was backing out, one of Stuyvesant's guns found its mark. A shell hit Marmaduke's forward port broadside gun and exploded, breaking off more than a foot of its muzzle, and killing one man and wounding or stunning the rest of its crew. Marmaduke was knocked to the deck bleeding from a painful arm wound. Just then, the boy who, before the fight, had entrusted his purse to the midshipman, now came to him and said, "Oh, Mr. Marmaduke, you're going to die. Give me back my money." Soon thereafter, one of the hot-shot guns aft of Marmaduke's was loaded and ready for firing when it, too, was hit in the muzzle. The exploding shell knocked almost two feet off the front of the gun, while at the same time causing the cannon to go off, sending its sizzling iron into the *Cumberland*. Neither of the *Virginia*'s two shortened guns could be fired thereafter without their muzzle flames setting fire to the wooden backing inside the casemate. Another Federal shot soon parted the ironclad's anchor chain, sending it flying back into the ship to injure a few men. Meanwhile, everything on the outside of the casemate, boats, a small guard howitzer, top-deck railings, were swept away. Jones actually believed that if the Federal gunners had depressed the muzzles of their cannon to aim at the *Virginia*'s water line, they might have put a shot or two under her barely submerged iron eaves. If so, he felt, "we would have been seriously hurt, if not sunk."[27]

The scene along the gun deck of the ironclad was only slightly less confused than that on her adversary, the single thought being to send more and more iron into the sinking sloop. Ramsay caught the action in words:

> On our gun-deck the men were fighting like demons. There was no thought or time for the wounded and dying as they tugged away at their guns, training and sighting their pieces while the orders rang out: "Sponge, load, fire."
> "The muzzle of our gun has been shot away," cried one of the gunners.

"No matter, keep on loading and firing—do the best you can with it," replied Lieutenant Jones.

"Keep away from the side ports, don't lean against the shield, look out for the sharpshooters," rang the warnings. Some of our men who failed to heed them and leaned back against the shield were stunned and carried below, bleeding at the ears. All were in high courage and worked with a will; they were so begrimed with powder that they looked like negroes.

"Pass along the cartridges."

"More powder."

"A shell for number six."

"A wet wad for the hot-shot gun."

"Put out that pipe and don't light it again on peril of your life."[28]

The ironclad was entirely enshrouded in the smoke from the battle. Few aboard could see anything of what was happening on the *Cumberland,* but Buchanan knew that she was sinking and felt that now it was time to turn to the *Congress.* To do so required that the ironclad turn around, as she was facing up the James River channel. Because of the ship's slow speed and sluggish steering, made worse by the shallowness of the channel here, Buchanan had to run her up the river some distance and then begin a wide, slow turn. Her keel dragged in the mud throughout. As she turned, the vessel came in for fire from Federal batteries at Newport News, and replied in kind, with little damage done on either side. The men aboard the *Congress,* thinking that the *Virginia* was withdrawing from the fight by pulling up the James, began cheering wildly. They stopped abruptly when the ironclad slowly turned back toward the Roads. Buchanan, meanwhile, was heartily cheered when, in looking up the James, he saw Commander John R. Tucker bringing the James River Squadron down to his assistance. Before the fight, Buchanan had advised Tucker to come down the river and run past the enemy batteries at Newport News if he heard firing in Hampton Roads. Now Tucker appeared with the gunboats *Patrick Henry, Teaser,* and *Jamestown.* The latter two successfully ran the batteries, but *Patrick Henry* took a shot in her boiler and had to be towed out of the action until it was repaired. The others stayed behind the *Virginia,* ready to obey Buchanan's orders.[29]

While the ironclad turned, Parker's *Beaufort* kept up the fire it had trained on the *Congress* since the action began. Parker was aided for a time by the *Raleigh,* but soon that ship's one and only gun was temporarily disabled and it had to pull out of the action. Meanwhile, Parker maintained his fire, though he failed to do the *Congress* much damage. Encouraging as this was to the Federals on board, they were even more heartened to see the *Roanoke,* the *Minnesota,* and now the *St. Lawrence* steaming to their aid. But the already ailing *Roanoke* barely got past Sewell's Point before she ran aground. The *Minnesota,* meanwhile, advanced considerably farther before she, too, ran aground on what was called the "middle ground"—a shallows in the middle of the Roads that divided it into north and south channels. Van Brunt had hoped he could force the ship over, but found himself stuck fast. The frigate *St. Lawrence,* a fifty-two-gun giant commanded by Captain H. Y. Purviance, had come to the Chesapeake two days before to relieve the *Congress.* She did not learn of what was happening in Hampton Roads until two-thirty, and came in considerably behind the other two frigates. Yet she, too, would eventually ground—not far from the *Minnesota.* They opened on the *Virginia* with whatever guns they could bring to bear, but the range was too great to have any effect. At the same time, the Federal frigates were constantly under fire from the Confederate batteries on Sewell's Point and from sharpshooters along the shore, some of whom waded out into the water to fire their rifles.[30]

The fight now would be for the *Congress.* Upon seeing the fate of the *Cumberland,* Lieutenant Joseph Smith ordered the sails set on his ship and signaled for Reaney's *Zouave* to leave the sinking sloop and come to his aid. "It seemed to me cruel to leave her," Reaney felt as he steamed away from Morris' ship, "but I had to obey orders." Coming alongside the *Congress,* he sent lines up to the frigate's bow and made them fast. The warship was on fire still, and the confusion caused by this delayed for precious minutes the fastening of the lines. "The cries of the wounded were terrible," Reaney recalled. Finally, the lines secured, Smith ordered the *Zouave* to tow them toward the shore at Newport News. Assisted by a light breeze in his sails, Smith hoped to save his ship by beaching her in water too shallow for the heavy-draft *Virginia.* This, at least, would protect her from ramming.

The *Congress* was well under way toward the shore by the time the *Virginia* completed her turn and took a position off her stern, a few minutes before 4 P.M. But already the ironclad had begun to exact a terrible toll from the frigate. Lieutenant Wood, commanding the after pivot rifle, had not had an opportunity to fire his gun during the fight with the *Cumberland*, since he could not bring it to bear through any of its three ports. But as the ironclad steamed away from the sinking sloop, the *Congress* came in sight through the stern port, and Wood sent three shells in rapid succession toward the frigate. The first shot dismounted the *Congress'* starboard stern 32-pounder and knocked the muzzle off. Wood's second shell hit her astern, passing through the wardroom and steerage and out onto the berth deck, killing or wounding several before it exploded amid a line of cooks and ship's boys passing powder forward from the after magazine. The third shot apparently dismounted the only other stern gun aboard the frigate.

Now, as the *Virginia* stood barely two hundred yards off the *Congress'* retreating stern, her broadsides were murderous. The little *Zouave* took some of the fire. Her pilothouse and figurehead were carried away, while blood from the frigate's deck ran "onto our deck like water on a wash-deck morning." But the frigate took the worst of it. Lieutenant Smith, moving from the quarterdeck to the main deck, was struck at about four-twenty by a shell fragment that carried away his head and a portion of his shoulder, sending his shoulder strap—his insigne of rank—flying to the deck. Even though the ship's former commander, William Smith, was aboard, he was no longer attached to her, and the command now devolved upon Lieutenant Austin Pendergrast.

Within another ten minutes, the stern of the frigate was demolished by the ironclad's shots. There were several fires blazing aboard her now, and with her two stern guns out of action, the *Congress* could not fight back. Soon she ran aground, but still under the guns of the *Virginia*. Pendergrast started getting the ship's wounded up from the sick bay to the main deck to put them on boats going ashore, but the operation had only started when the *Beaufort*, the *Jamestown*, and the repaired *Patrick Henry* began adding their fire to that of the ironclad. Some wounded men jumped overboard, only to drown; others were killed in the firing. Another shell put the remainder of the powder-passing line out of

action, Paymaster McKean Buchanan being one of the few to survive the fire from his brother's ship. Water being thrown over burning deck planks fell on the wounded and dying. Axmen were busy
hacking down bulkheads to pass fire hoses to threatened areas.
The entire midships was a scene of confused desolation. The main
deck, thought Reaney, was "literally reeking with slaughter."[31]

Seeing that help from the grounded *Minnesota* was impossible,
and viewing the awful carnage aboard the *Congress,* Pendergrast
consulted with Commander Smith on the propriety of surrender.
Both agreed that it was the only alternative to annihilation. After
taking the *Virginia*'s fire for nearly an hour, the Federal frigate
hauled down her colors at about four forty-five, and soon thereafter
ran up a white flag. At the same time, the crew threw overboard
what powder they could and disabled the remaining guns by driving
spikes into their breech vents. Reaney called up to Pendergrast to
see if he was needed any more. The lieutenant told him to take care
of himself, and so the *Zouave* cut her lines and backed into the
channel, slipping past the *Virginia* to go to the assistance of the
Minnesota, but not before a Rebel shell knocked away her rudder
post. The boats aboard which Pendergrast hoped to save his
wounded did not fare so well. Most had been shot away during
the fight, and now others swamped when overloaded.[32]

When he saw the white flag ride above the *Congress,* Buchanan
stepped out on the top deck of the *Virginia* for a better look. He ordered his gunners to cease firing, and then signaled for Parker, in
the *Beaufort,* to come within hailing distance. Yelling across the
water, Buchanan told Parker to take his ship and the *Raleigh* alongside the *Congress* to receive her surrender. He was to take all the
Federal officers prisoner, allow their crew to go ashore, and then
burn the frigate where she stood.

Parker steamed across the now quiet waters to the side of the
grounded warship, stopping at her port gangway. First he sent a
midshipman aboard to tell Pendergrast to report to the *Beaufort*'s
deck, and then ordered a number of his men to board the frigate
and help with unloading the Federal wounded. Shortly Pendergrast
and Commander Smith came down the *Congress*' side and presented themselves to Parker. Now Parker learned that Joseph
Smith, his former friend and classmate at the Naval Academy at
Annapolis, was dead. The Federals officially surrendered the ship,

but found that they did not have their personal side arms to surrender as well, as was the custom. Pendergrast did symbolically hand over a seaman's cutlass that he had picked up, but Parker sent them back aboard their ship for their regular arms. At the same time, he told them his orders, but Pendergrast explained that many of his wounded could not be moved quickly and begged Parker not to fire the ship. But Parker had his instructions. About the same time, as he surveyed the terrible damage done by the *Virginia's* broadsides, he commented in tones loud enough for a Federal prisoner to hear: "My God, this is terrible. I wish this war was over."

In the next few minutes the war almost did end for Parker. Pendergrast and Smith had gone back aboard the *Congress* for their side arms and to help with the wounded. Parker had sent the *Raleigh* around to the other side of the frigate to help take on prisoners, while a number of Yankees had already come aboard the *Beaufort.* "I had scarcely given him the order," Parker said of the *Raleigh's* captain, "when a tremendous fire was opened on us from the shore." Immediately, two officers aboard the *Raleigh* were killed, while, on the *Beaufort,* every man on the hurricane deck was either killed or wounded. Parker himself was hit slightly in the knee, while another bullet took away part of his cap and his spyglass. Two others passed through his clothes without injuring him.[33]

What had happened was totally unexpected by the Confederates. Throughout the day so far, the *Virginia* had sent an occasional shell toward the Federal camps at Newport News as opportunity permitted. Very little damage or injury was done except to General Mansfield's headquarters. A shell passed through his room, disrupted it entirely, and covered the general with splinters. Only its failure to explode spared his life. This hardly put him in a friendly mood, and he renewed his urgings to his sharpshooters on the shore line to do their best. The men, mostly members of the 20th Indiana Infantry, were too far from the *Virginia* to do her crew much harm. However, when the *Congress* surrendered and the two Confederate steamers came alongside her, Mansfield saw his chance. He ordered the two rifle companies of the 20th Indiana to turn their fire on Parker to prevent his taking the frigate. When a captain reminded Mansfield that, since the ship had surrendered, the Confederates had the right to take possession of her, the general howled back, "I know the d——d ship has surrendered, but *we* haven't." As the men of the 20th opened fire, three rifled cannon on the beach also opened—with grapeshot. Ironically, one of the guns was manned by Master Stuyvesant and fourteen men of the *Cumberland* who had escaped and now were bent on revenge.[34]

Their vengeance backfired somewhat. While the fire from shore was most effective against Parker's command, it also killed and wounded several prisoners from the *Congress*. Pendergrast begged Parker himself to run up a white flag to stop the firing, but he refused. "Make haste," Parker told the men moving off the wounded; "those scoundrels on shore are firing at me now." Pendergrast asked permission to go back aboard his ship to assist the wounded, and Smith accompanied him. Now Parker blew the *Beaufort*'s whistle. The fire from shore was too hot, and he had to get away. His men came tumbling back aboard, but there was no sign of Pendergrast or Smith, who apparently had taken this opportunity to avoid being captured. Parker was forced to put off without them. Then a few men aboard the *Congress* opened fire on him, despite the fact that they were technically surrendered. At once, Parker steamed off toward Sewell's Point to unload his prisoners and wounded.[35]

Buchanan did not care for Parker. "In my opinion," he would write Mallory in a few days, "Lt. Commdg. W. H. Parker is unfit to command." He "wants judgement and discretion," Buchanan would complain. Already today the captain was angry that Parker had opened the action by firing from the *Beaufort* before the *Virginia*. Worse, Parker now did not bother to report to Buchanan the reason why he failed in his assignment. From his position aboard the *Virginia*, Buchanan could not see that the firing from the shore had any effect on Parker and, after waiting a few minutes to see if the *Congress* would break out in flames as he expected, he became furious that the *Beaufort*'s mission was unfulfilled. "The old gentleman became very anxious to destroy her," wrote Minor a few days later. Already Minor had once volunteered to go and burn the *Congress*, but Buchanan had sent Parker. Now Minor asked again, and the captain accepted.

Taking eight men with him, Minor put off in the ironclad's only remaining boat and pulled at the oars toward the *Congress*. During the action between the *Virginia* and the frigate, the James River steamers had been engaging the grounded *Minnesota*, and now Buchanan signaled for the *Teaser* to break away and cover Minor's approach to the *Congress.* "I did not think the Yankees on shore would fire at me on my errand to the *Congress,*" Minor would write to Brooke three days later, "but when in about two hundred and fifty yards of her they opened fire on me from the shore . . . and the way the balls danced around my little boat and crew was lively beyond all measure." Two of Minor's men were hit, and then a bullet struck him in a rib, glanced, and came out near his heart. "It knocked me down for a second or so, but I got up and cheered my men." Immediately, Minor turned his boat toward the approaching *Teaser,* which soon came alongside and took them all aboard and back to safety.[36]

When the *Teaser* signaled what had happened, Buchanan became livid with rage. "Destroy that —— ship!" Eggleston heard him exclaim. At once, the *Virginia* got under way again and backed up close astern of the *Congress.* A torrent of hot shot and incendiary shell poured forth from her broadside, ripping the frigate unmercifully and setting her afire in a host of places. Buchanan, fuming in his anger, called for a rifle from below and, standing fully exposed on the top deck, fired back at the sharpshooters on shore. His firing did not go unnoticed. "About 50 Men all sharpshooters went down on the Bank of the river and when ever a man came up on top of the Mermick wee shott at him all together," wrote a corporal of the 1st New York Mounted Rifles. Shortly, one of those shots hit Buchanan's left thigh, disabling him. He was carried below and placed in his cabin with the wounded Minor, who had been taken off the *Teaser.* Meanwhile, the firing on the *Congress* continued for a few minutes more. "Dearly did they pay for their unparalleled treachery," wrote Eggleston. "We raked her fore and aft with hot shot and shell."[37]

It was after 5 P.M. now, and already the sun was nearing the horizon. When Buchanan was wounded, he ordered Lieutenant Jones to take command and fight as long as the men and light lasted. "Brave, cool, determined old Jones fought the action out in his quiet way, giving them thunder all the time," wrote the wounded Minor. With the *Congress* ablaze, he now turned his attention to the grounded *Minnesota.* The *St. Lawrence* and the *Roanoke* had by this time freed themselves and moved back toward Old Point Comfort, sending their tugboats to help the stranded frigate on the "middle ground." The *Jamestown* and the *Patrick Henry* were doing a good deal of damage to the *Minnesota* as the *Virginia* approached. Several were killed and wounded as Van Brunt fought to get afloat once more. Engineer Thomas Rae found that "one's feelings at such a time are a marvel. I appreciated the danger, and was much cooler than I have been thinking it over since, but it did not seem more exciting than a game of snowballing. They carried men past me down to the cockpit to the surgeon, and a solid shot tore through the hammock netting within a few yards of me, killing two men and strewing the brains, even the head of one, all over the deck, yet it seemed all in place."[38]

Now, with the flashes of the guns illuminating the darkening sky, the scene from the shore was spectacular. The *Congress* was ablaze, her men now finally getting to shore as her loaded guns discharged one by one as the fires reached them. The embattled *Minnesota* "seemed a huge monster at bay" to Colonel Colston. "The entire horizon was lighted by the continual flashes of the artillery," he wrote; "clouds of white smoke rose in spiral columns to the skies, illumined by the evening sunlight, while land and water seemed to tremble under the thunders of the cannonade."

Now the *Minnesota*'s misfortune in grounding worked to her advantage. The *Virginia* could not get directly to her because of the shallow water between them. The only way to get within less than a mile of the ship would be to steam through the south channel, below the middle ground, and then come back up to the frigate. But with the ironclad's great draft, getting close to her would have been tricky in broad daylight. With the growing darkness now, the *Virginia*'s pilots advised Jones that it was no longer safe to remain in the Roads, for fear of grounding themselves in the dark. Still he fired on the frigate as he brought the ironclad back toward the mouth of the Elizabeth. "We fought until it was so dark that we could not see to point the guns with accuracy," Jones would write. Then, at six-thirty, having passed through the south channel, the *Virginia* fired her last gun and moved on to anchor under the guns of the Confederate batteries on Sewell's Point. Behind her lay a fleet in shambles. Afloat and ashore, thousands of men in blue stood stunned by what they had seen. Somewhere amid the smoke, and flame, and blood of the last few hours, the centuries-long era of the wooden warship had passed forever. "The IRON and the HEAVY GUNS did the work," wrote an ecstatic Lieutenant Minor. "It was a great victory."[39]

CHAPTER 8

"We Vowed Vengeance on the *Merrimac*"

"A pretty good day's work," Lieutenant Eggleston said to Jones as the latter made his rounds of the *Virginia,* now anchored off Sewell's Point. "Yes," Jones answered, "but it is not over." Indeed it was not. Everyone understood that tomorrow they would have to go out again, this time to finish off the *Minnesota* where she lay aground, and then to destroy the *Roanoke* and the *St. Lawrence.*

But, for now, there was other work to do. As soon as the ironclad came to anchor, Jones sent off her dead and wounded along with Surgeon Phillips. Miraculously, this ship had passed close to hell that day, yet she suffered only two men killed—one, Dunbar, through his own foolishness—and eight wounded. All but Buchanan and Minor were taken ashore. Total casualties aboard the *Beaufort* and the *Raleigh* came to only ten, while the *Teaser* and the *Jamestown* took no injuries at all and the *Patrick Henry* suffered only seven. In all, just twenty-seven men killed or wounded in the entire fleet, and against this the *Beaufort* now disgorged twenty-three Federal prisoners taken from the *Congress* alone. How many Yankee seamen lay bleeding or dead in the wake of the *Virginia* no one could say.

Once the wounded and dead were gone, Jones had Parker turn over the Federal prisoners to Major William Norris of the Signal Corps. He would take them to the naval hospital at Norfolk. It was a long, hard pull, though, and on the way two wounded Federals died, victims of the well-intentioned bullets of the 20th Indiana. Meanwhile, inside the iron monster, Buchanan and Minor suffered in the cabin. The lieutenant was the far more seriously wounded of the two, but he took it lightly. In three days he would tell Brooke that "a 'spell' of a few weeks will put me on my pins again." Buchanan, despite his great victory, was in much lower spirits. As his officers gathered about him this evening, he would say with considerable emotion, "My brother, Paymaster Buchanan, was on board the Congress." Few expected that he had survived.[1]

It was almost 8 P.M. when the *Virginia* dropped anchor at Sewell's Point, and necessary business kept the crew so occupied that the cooks and stewards did not get the supper fires started until after ten. Another hour and a half passed before the crew, "begrimed with powder, dirt and blood," sat down to their meal. Though exhausted, the men could hardly sleep and, despite their exhaustion, many sat up on the deck until well after midnight watching the spectacle of the burning *Congress*.

After all the vessels had come to anchor, the men on the several ships began looking for comrades aboard the others. Aboard the *Virginia,* all the officers met in reunion to exchange recollections of the fight. Lieutenant William Webb, commanding the *Teaser,* displayed his uniform ridden with bullet holes. Civilians such as the Wises crowded around the shore, talking anxiously with Jones and others about the fight, and received "a full and graphic description."[2]

Jones himself had very little time to talk. With Buchanan bedridden, the duty of inspecting the ship's damage and making a report to Captain Forrest fell upon him. This evening, probably even before eating, he checked out every corner of the ironclad, and then sat down to write. He was concise, to the point, brief, probably because he was dead tired. All concerned with the day's battle had served well, he said; "in fact it could not have been otherwise after the noble and daring conduct" of Buchanan.

Surveying the vessel, Jones found a small leak in the bow where the ram had been wrenched off, leaving behind some twisted iron that could not immediately be repaired. But somehow he missed seeing that the ram itself was missing, thinking it only twisted. The anchors, flagstaffs, and howitzers were shot away, while the smokestack and the steam vent pipe were riddled through with holes. Both of the ship's boats were lost, Minor having abandoned his when he and his wounded men boarded the *Teaser*. Of course, there were the two guns with their muzzles shot away. And if Jones had light enough to survey the outside of the casemate, he would have found ninety-eight indentations where enemy balls struck. Yet, for all that, the *Virginia*'s casemate had stood the test.

Not so the rest of her, however, though it was discovered that Brooke's rifles could stand twice the recommended powder charge "without the least complaint." The ship simply did not prove adapted for anything but river defense. According to Norris, she "was not weatherly enough to move in Hampton Roads, at all times, with safety, and she never should have been found more than three hours sail from a machine shop." Her great draft, combined with slow speed and a sluggish helm, made her impossible to maneuver in a close fight. As for seaworthiness, Buchanan now believed that "should she encounter a gale, or a very heavy swell, I think it more than probable she would founder." This alone effectively put an end to any thoughts of the ironclad steaming up the coast to New York. Then, worst of all, there were the ship's engines. Under Ramsay's constant attention they had performed adequately during the fight, but most of her officers agreed with Lieutenant Wood that "We could not depend upon them for six hours at a time. A more ill-contrived or unreliable pair of engines could not have been found."[3]

Jones and his command tried to get what sleep they could, watched the burning *Congress,* and looked forward to even greater glory on the morrow. Few of them knew that one of the *Virginia*'s pilots had spied "a strange looking craft, brought out in bold relief by the brilliant light of the burning ship." What was this curious vessel that had joined the Federal fleet? Perhaps they would find out in the morning.[4]

For those who could not sleep, there was the grandeur of the burning *Congress.* Ramsay was eloquent in describing it:

All the evening we stood on deck watching the brilliant display of the burning ship. Every part of her was on fire at the same time, the red-tongued flames running up shrouds, masts, and stays, and extending out to the yard arms. She stood in bold relief against the black background, lighting up the Roads and reflecting her lurid lights on the bosom of the now placid and hushed waters. Every now and then the flames would reach one of the loaded cannon and a shell would hiss at random through the darkness. About midnight came the grand finale. The magazines exploded, shooting up a huge column of firebrands hundreds of feet in the air, and then the burning hulk burst asunder and melted into the waters, while the calm night spread her sable mantle over Hampton Roads.

Colonel Colston, still watching from the shore, found himself equally captivated. A second-quarter moon shone over the water, yet the burning *Congress* illuminated the entire scene. "As the flames crept up the rigging, every mast, spar, and rope glittered against the dark sky in dazzling lines of fire. The hull, aground upon the shoal, was plainly visible, and upon its black surface each porthole seemed the mouth of a fiery furnace." Then came the explosion, "one of the grandest episodes of this splendid yet somber drama."[5]

Other eyes than the Confederates' watched that flaming frigate. For the men on the other side of Hampton Roads it was a taunting reminder of the defeat they had suffered that day. Colonel Cannon, at Fort Monroe, found that "the whole aspect at headquarters was gloomy." The garrison were all volunteers, the armament out of date and "as useless as musket-balls against the ironclad." Precious stores were sitting on the parade ground where enemy shells could reach them, and the wooden barracks could easily be put aflame by the *Virginia*'s hot shot. "The success of the Merrimack gave her the control of the Roads," Cannon lamented, "and if she could get sufficient elevation to her guns, she had the ability to shell and destroy the vast stores in and about the fort without the least power on our part to resist her."

Already, a frustrated Wool had sent word of the disaster to Washington. A telegraph line connecting Fort Monroe with the capital had been completed, interestingly enough, this very same day. Even before the fight ended, he had wired to Secretary of War Stanton the news of the loss of the *Cumberland* and the *Congress,* and with *Minnesota* and *St. Lawrence* aground, he warned that "probably both will be taken." His only cause for thanks was the light losses his own command had suffered. One man's foot was accidentally crushed when a gun carriage ran over it, and another soldier's leg was amputated by a piece of shell.[6]

The losses aboard the ships, however, were terrible. The *Roa-*

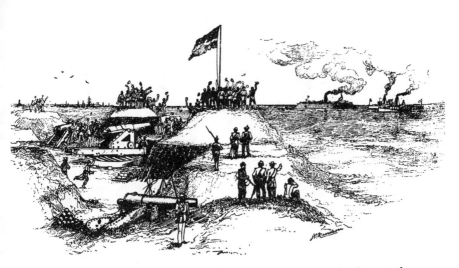

23. Artist's depiction of the *Virginia* passing Craney Island to attack the Federal fleet, March 8, 1862. (*Century Illustrated Monthly Magazine,* XXIX, March 1885.)

24. The *Virginia* ramming the *Cumberland.* (*Century Illustrated Monthly Magazine,* XXIX, March 1885.)

25. Midshipman Hardin B. Littlepage, who ably served one of the *Virginia*'s guns. (Courtesy of Alvan C. Macauley, Grosse Pointe Farms, Michigan.)

26. Midshipman Henry H. Marmaduke, injured when the muzzle was shot away from his gun aboard the *Virginia*. (Courtesy of Jon Nielson, Orono, Maine.)

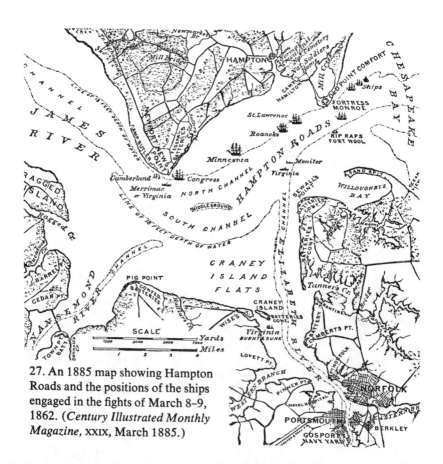

27. An 1885 map showing Hampton Roads and the positions of the ships engaged in the fights of March 8–9, 1862. (*Century Illustrated Monthly Magazine*, XXIX, March 1885.)

28. Union Assistant Secretary of the Navy Gustavus V. Fox came to Fort Monroe in time to witness the *Monitor-Virginia* fight. (Courtesy of the Naval Photographic Center, Washington, D.C.)

29. Lieutenant Thomas O. Selfridge, Jr., fought on the *Cumberland* to the very last, and later witnessed the great battle of March 9. (Courtesy of the MOLLUS-Mass. Collection, U. S. Army Military History Research Collection, Carlisle Barracks, Pennsylvania.)

30. The *Monitor* and the *Virginia* at close quarters. The drawing is reasonably accurate, though it erroneously shows the *Virginia* with boat davits. (*Century Illustrated Monthly Magazine,* XXIX, March 1885.)

31. Captain Josiah Tattnall, who succeeded the wounded Buchanan in command of the *Virginia*, and who eventually ordered her destroyed. (*Harper's New Monthly Magazine*, XCVII, October 1898.)

32. A small pennant from the *Virginia*, saved from the flames of the dying ship by Midshipman Littlepage. (Courtesy of Alvan C. Macauley, Grosse Pointe Farms, Michigan.)

33. A crude depiction of the last minutes of the CSS *Virginia*. (Courtesy of the Naval Photographic Center, Washington, D.C.)

noke and the *St. Lawrence,* fortunately, lost no one. On the tugs serving them and the other ships, the wounded were very few, and none killed. But the poor *Congress* bled pathetically. All afternoon and evening, boats went back and forth trying to carry away all the wounded and stranded men who could be found. There was neither time nor space to take away the dead, but the body of Lieutenant Joseph Smith was secretly placed on a cot and covered by friends so that it was taken off along with the wounded. A friend retrieved from the deck Smith's watch and the shoulder strap that had been blown away by the shell that killed him. They would go to his father.

Some of the ship's officers stayed aboard until the end, being forced to jump into the icy water to swim ashore when the last boat could not hold them. Behind them lay "our poor old ship, deserted by all but the dead." Once ashore, officers and men gathered around their wounded and dying in the hospital at Newport News. From them they heard accounts of the fight. To them they gave what comfort they could as the surgeons went about their bloody work. Limbs were taken off without anesthetic, while men whose bodies were burned in the fires had to lie and suffer, and die, in their pain. Pendergrast went about the work of tallying his losses. As best he could determine, out of a ship's complement of 434 that morning, 110 were either dead, or missing and presumed dead; only twenty-six wounded had been found to bring ashore, and of them ten more would die in days ahead. And in a few hours the burning *Congress* died, her explosion sounding to some like "the eruption of a volcano," shaking the buildings at Newport News and for miles around with its force, and showering Fort Monroe, over seven miles away, with falling fragments.[7]

For the sunken *Cumberland,* matters were just as bad. Commander Radford left to return to his ship as soon as he learned of the *Virginia*'s appearance. He reached Newport News just in time to see her go down and to help with the wounded. Lieutenant Morris, once ashore, began the unhappy task of counting the survivors. Of 376 men known to be aboard when the fight began, he could account for 255, including the wounded. That meant 121 Yankee seamen had gone to the bottom with their ship. Including the wounded, *Cumberland*'s losses approached 150.

Minnesota, too, had suffered, but little in comparison. No more than a dozen men had been hit, two or three of them fatally. Eleven enemy shells had penetrated her sides, one of them striking the mainmast and carrying away a third of it. Once the action ended, Engineer Rae and others had mustered some cheese and crackers and started coffee boiling in the engine room. After a while, the shock of battle subsiding somewhat, the men gathered below to smoke and talk of the fight. "We enjoyed ourselves," said Rae, "for none cared to look forward to the morrow, as there was but one termination possible as far as we knew then." The men got their papers ready to destroy in case of disaster, while others went topside to watch the burning *Congress*. They were almost casual as some of the shells fired by the burning ship's red-hot guns arched high over their heads. Van Brunt, meanwhile, had exhausted every effort to refloat the ship. Failing in this, he reported to Marston and Wool that he proposed to land part of her crew to save them, while with the remainder—surely volunteers—he would stay aboard and fight her to the last should the *Virginia* reappear, as he knew she must. To keep the *Minnesota* from being captured, he would blow her up if necessary.[8]

There was little sleep afloat or ashore that night. "It was a long and dreary night to us," wrote one who escaped from the *Congress*. "We all expected to be taken prisoners the next day." There was word that Magruder would attack Newport News when the *Virginia* came out again and, caught between the two, the Federals might have little choice but surrender. Orphaned sailors wandered about all through the dark night, while refugees from Newport News and elsewhere walked to Fort Monroe for what protection it could offer. The one hotel near the fort was overcrowded with women and children, and private homes opened up all around to take in the fleeing. "The night was not half so heavy as our hearts, nor so dark as our prospects," wrote a reporter at the fort.

Then something happened to lift the spirits of hundreds—something quite unexpected. "All at once a speck of light gleamed on the distant wave," wrote the same reporter. "It moved; it came nearer and nearer." And then, he penned joyfully, *"the Monitor appeared."*[9]

From the moment that Worden first heard the firing at Hampton Roads, he ordered his ship cleared for action and the *Monitor*'s turret "keyed" up off the brass ring, ready to turn. Upon learning of what was happening in the Roads, many at first disbelieved. As they came closer, however, and saw the *Congress* aflame, all doubts vanished. "Our hearts were so very full," wrote Greene a few days later, "and we vowed vengeance on the *Merrimac*."

At 9 P.M. the *Monitor* entered Hampton Roads and anchored near the *Roanoke*. Immediately, Worden and Stimers went aboard the frigate to confer with Marston. The captain gave them an account of what had happened that day, stating his conviction that the *Virginia* would be back again in the morning to finish up on the grounded *Minnesota*. Here, too, Worden learned for the first time that Gideon Welles had ordered him to the defense of the Potomac at Washington. Even before the ironclad left Brooklyn, Welles had ordered Marston not to let the experimental ship go under fire "except for some pressing emergency." Then, on March 6, he sent Paulding orders to send the *Monitor* to Washington instead. Apparently, fears of what the *Virginia* might do if she passed Fort Monroe and came up the Potomac made Welles change his mind. Fortunately, however, Welles's order arrived at Brooklyn just hours after the ironclad steamed south. History records few examples of bad timing that proved more fortuitous. If Worden had obeyed Welles's order, March 9, 1862, surely would have turned Hampton Roads into a Federal graveyard.

Even now, Marston had urgent orders from Welles to send the *Monitor* to Washington immediately. He and Worden conferred on the matter, and the captain proposed that they ignore the order and keep the ironclad here to defend the *Minnesota* and keep the Rebel monster from wreaking even more havoc. Worden happily agreed. At once, Marston ordered Worden to take his ship next to the grounded frigate to be ready for what must come in the morning. First, Worden took a few minutes to report his arrival to Welles by telegraph. Then, at 10 P.M., just before going back aboard the *Monitor,* he wrote a brief note to his wife. For all he knew, it might be his last. "The Merrimac has caused sad work amongst our vessels," he told her. But then he spoke with iron confidence: "She cant hurt us."[10]

Lieutenant Greene went ahead of his ship in a small cutter, hailing the *Minnesota* at 11 P.M. Going aboard, he found that Van Brunt expected to make another attempt to get afloat at 2 A.M., when the tide would be high. Greene assured him that the *Monitor* would do all she could to protect him from the *Virginia* the next morning, should the attempt to float the frigate fail. Then he returned to the ironclad, still anchored near the *Roanoke*.

Now there came a problem. Worden could not find a pilot to guide the *Monitor* through the shoals to the grounded frigate. Nearly two hours were consumed in the attempt to locate one. Complicating the search was the knowledge that anyone going aboard this tiny vessel tonight would surely be with her when she faced the *Virginia* on the morrow. The Rebel ironclad was a proven terror that no one was anxious to face. The *Monitor* was not. But finally, about 11 P.M., Acting Master Samuel Howard of the bark *Amanda* volunteered, and Worden put out for the *Minnesota*.

The *Monitor* came alongside the frigate about 1 A.M., March 9, and dropped anchor. About this same time her crew heard the thunder of the *Congress'* explosion. "It went straight to the marrow of our bones," wrote Greene. Their determination to revenge themselves on the *Virginia* was redoubled by the sight.[11]

Now the ironclad's crew bedded down for what they hoped would be their first real sleep in over forty-eight hours. Greene and Worden remained on the top deck keeping a watch for the *Virginia* should she appear before dawn. Meanwhile, the reaction to her arrival among the men of the *Minnesota* was mixed. "We found the crew of the Minnesota very dejected and dispirited," wrote fireman Ellis, and for some the appearance of the ironclad did little. "How insignificant she looked," lamented one observer; "she was but a speck on the dark blue sea at night, almost a laughable object by day." Others, however, found hope in the little vessel next to them. When the *Minnesota's* chief engineer went below to tell his men that the *Monitor* was coming, "what a jump our hearts gave," wrote Rae. Going on deck, he looked at the ironclad, "the little black 'Pill Box' on a 'shingle,'" he called her. "The *Monitor* is alongside," he yelled down to the engine room, "and they gave a cheer that might have been heard in Richmond."

Worden went aboard the frigate for a brief time, and brought back with him a detailed account of the day's fight. This alone was enough to keep his men wakeful with anticipation. Then, throughout the night, occasional reports came in saying that the *Virginia* was coming. On top of this, just as some men were finally getting to sleep, the *Minnesota* hailed the ironclad and said she was finally getting afloat and that the *Monitor* was in her way. Worden backed his ship out into the north channel and remained there for an hour before it was determined that the frigate was still stuck and could not pull free. For some of the men it was 5:30 A.M. before they could finally lie down in their hammocks. "No one slept," Keeler wrote his wife.[12]

Had the news of the March 8 fight reached Washington that evening, no one there would have slept either. But the new telegraph line was rather haphazard, and the messages from Wool and Worden were delayed in arriving until morning, March 9. That morning, Sunday, Gideon Welles was at the Navy Department looking over the latest dispatches when Assistant Secretary of War P. H. Watson ran into the room with Wool's telegram to Stanton from Fort Monroe. Carefully Welles read the message of disaster, and just as he finished it a summons came from the White House. Lincoln was calling a cabinet meeting to deal with the emergency.

Welles hurried to the Executive Mansion, to find that Stanton, Secretary of State William Seward, and Treasury Secretary Salmon P. Chase were already there. All were excited and alarmed. Stanton, observed the President's secretary John G. Hay, "was fearfully stampeded. He said they would capture our fleet, take Ft. Monroe, be in Washington before night." Even Lincoln was unusually perturbed, and had sent for Dahlgren and Quartermaster General Montgomery C. Meigs to counsel with them.

Welles had never liked Stanton, and now he found him "inexpressibly ludicrous." Stanton paced the room back and forth, his eyes always on Welles, hardly concealing his contempt at the Navy Secretary's cool manner. The *Virginia* would wreck every ship they had, he said, force extorted contributions from every northern coastal city, prevent an anticipated army movement up the James peninsula, and then destroy Washington, New York, and Boston. Frequently Stanton walked over to a window that looked out on the Potomac. "Not unlikely we shall have a shell or cannon-ball from her guns in the White House before we leave this room," he said. Not given to panic, Lincoln, too, occasionally stepped to the window, as if expecting to see the Rebel monster steaming up the river any moment.

All wanted to know what the Navy could do to stop the *Virginia.* All wanted Welles to give them some hope. All he could give them was the *Monitor,* and an assurance that the *Virginia* drew too much water for her to come up the Potomac to the capital. Seward was cheered by this last, but Stanton was not.

"What is the size and strength of this 'Monitor,'" he asked, "how many guns does she carry?" Welles explained as best he could her dimensions and character. When he came to the point of saying that she carried only two guns, however, Stanton abruptly turned away from him with what Welles thought was a look of "amazement, contempt, and distress, that was painfully ludicrous." Others there asked for further details on the craft and her capabilities, but Stanton was plainly disgusted that the Navy expected a two-gun experiment to stop the ship that had ruined a Federal fleet. Throughout it all, Welles remained composed, "and yet," he wrote in his diary, "there was throughout the whole day something inexpressibly ludicrous in the wild, frantic talk, action, and rage of Stanton as he ran from room to room, sat down and jumped up after writing a few words, swung his arms, scolded, and raved."

Soon Lincoln went over to the navy yard to confer further with Dahlgren and other officers, and then all came back again to the White House. Dahlgren took a reasonable attitude toward the emergency. "We were too much interested here to be mortified or dejected about the loss of vessels at Old Point," he wrote his son two days later, "for it well behoved [sic] us to take care of the consequences." Dahlgren, Meigs, and Major General George B. McClellan were ordered to agree upon a plan of defense for Washington. Then the meeting broke up. "When I left," said Dahlgren, "it was with no despair of the Republic, though all of us were thoughtful enough."[13]

Welles was more than thoughtful when he left. He had a duty to perform. It was still a little before noon and, going around to St. John's Church, Welles sent in a message asking Commodore Joseph Smith to come out and see him. Quietly Welles told him of the destruction of the *Congress*.

"The 'Congress' sunk," said Smith calmly. He methodically buttoned his coat against the chill. "Then Joe is dead."

Welles disagreed, reminding Smith that no casualty lists were in yet, and that Lieutenant Smith might have survived.

"You don't know Joe as well as I do," the commodore replied. "He would not survive his ship." Before long, a watch and a lieutenant's shoulder strap would come to confirm Smith's unhappy prediction.[14]

Meanwhile, a panicky Stanton was sending wires to the governors of New York, Massachusetts, and Maine, advising them of the supposed danger from the *Virginia* and proposing that they prepare to defend their ports with heavy batteries and large timber rafts to obstruct the ironclad's passage. He also called for proposals on how to capture or destroy the ship. Meigs began proposing offensive action against the *Virginia*. He feared she would appear at Annapolis and suggested that every steamer there should run up and send men to board her and throw shells down her smokestack. "Sacrifice the steamers in order to retake the Merrimac," he said. "Promotion, ample reward awaits whoever takes or destroys her."

The cabinet met again that day, and Stanton again scoffed at Welles's confidence in the *Monitor*. Instead, he proposed to sink heavily loaded canal barges in the Potomac. Welles disapproved but, with Lincoln's tacit approval, Stanton went ahead and had Dahlgren begin the work. When Welles later pointed out that the sunken boats would not only prevent the *Virginia* from coming up the Potomac but also stop all Federal shipping to or from the capital, Lincoln ordered that they not be sunk unless and until the *Virginia* actually approached. Some weeks later, Lincoln, Stanton, and others were on a boat going downriver when they passed a long line of these barges lying along the shore. "That is Stanton's navy," said the President playfully. "Stanton's navy is as useless as the paps of a man to a sucking child. There may be some show to amuse the child, but they are good for nothing for service."[15]

The people of the North, however, saw little humor in the situation when word of the disaster at Hampton Roads reached the newspapers. "The Merrimac affair," Count Adam Gurowski, constant critic of Lincoln's, called it. "Terrible evidence how active and daring are the rebels, and we sleepy, slow, and self-satisfied." "What next," lamented a New Yorker. "Why should not this invulnerable marine demon breach the walls of Fortress Monroe, raise the blockade, and destroy New York and Boston?" The only reason, it seemed, why the *Virginia* might not accomplish all this and more was the *Monitor*. Even as the people of the North speculated on what would happen, and as Welles, Stanton, and Lincoln searched for a course to follow, the issue was being decided in Hampton Roads.[16]

CHAPTER 9

"One of the Greatest Naval Engagements"

The boatswain's pipe shrilly awakened the sleeping crew of the *Virginia* before dawn, March 9. "It seemed as though we had scarcely been asleep," lamented Surgeon Phillips. While the fife and drum were still sounding to awaken the men, they hurriedly dressed and went to a hearty breakfast. For those who wanted it, the morning meal was rinsed down with two jiggers of whiskey per man.

As soon as he finished eating, Phillips went to see Buchanan and Minor. The captain was loath to leave his ship, wanting to be aboard during the day's fight, but Phillips remonstrated with him at such length that eventually Buchanan consented that he and Minor should be put ashore at Sewell's Point and then conveyed to the hospital at Norfolk. Besides, the space thus vacated might be needed for more wounded before this day was done.

Phillips accompanied them ashore and turned them over to the Confederate surgeon there. On his return, he did not go aboard the *Virginia* immediately but, rather, rowed his boat once around her, surveying the damage from the day before. He saw all that Jones had found the previous night, counting, as well, ninety-eight indentations from the impact of enemy solid shot. The smokestack was so riddled that it "would have permitted a flock of crows to fly through it without inconvenience."

Shortly after sunrise, about six-thirty, Phillips was back on board his ship, and she was ready to leave. Far off in the distance, they could dimly see that the *Minnesota* was still aground. She, and any other Federal ships the Confederates might engage, should be easy victories. Jones got her steam up, weighed anchor, and put out into

Hampton Roads. The Roads was still covered by the early-morning fog, just now dissipating under the warm rays of the rising sun. It was going to be another unusually beautiful day. Off in the distance, they could hear the signal gun at Fort Monroe awakening the garrison. It promised to be a great day for the Confederate States of America.[1]

Accompanied by *Patrick Henry, Jamestown,* and *Teaser,* Jones steamed due north at first, toward the fort. The *Raleigh* had to go back to Norfolk for repairs, but joining them were a number of smaller craft filled with spectators. Captain James Byers of the steam tug *J. B. White* had a number of Confederate officers and civilians board his boat in Norfolk that morning, ordering him to run out to see the ironclad finish off the *Minnesota*. He stood off Craney Island to watch the show, his passengers in high spirits as they anticipated a splendid entertainment. Once again, the banks were lined with people and soldiers who had come early to get a place to view the spectacle.

Aboard the moving squadron, however, something else shortly came into view. As Jones steamed north into the Roads, he and his men suddenly saw that the *Minnesota* was not alone. "There was an iron battery near her," he reported. Despite his later claims that he knew the *Monitor* had arrived thanks to his pilot's spotting her in the light from the *Congress* the night before, it is obvious that the appearance of Ericsson's ironclad took the Confederates quite by surprise. Looking out his gun port, Eggleston thought her "the strangest looking craft we had ever seen before." "We could see nothing but the resemblance of a large cheese box," recalled another. Hunter Davidson at first exclaimed with glee that "the Minnesota's crew are leaving her on a raft." Littlepage frankly admitted that "we were taken wholly by surprise." At first he thought it was a raft on which Van Brunt was sending one of his ship's boilers ashore for repairs.

The surprise extended to the other ships and ashore as well. "We could not tell what the Monitor was," complained Byers. Aboard the *Patrick Henry,* her executive officer, Lieutenant James H. Rochelle, saw next to the Federal frigate "such a craft as the eyes of a seaman never looked upon before—an immense shingle floating in the water, with a gigantic cheese box rising from its center; no sails, no wheels, no smokestack, no guns. What could it be?" Some suspected that it was a water tank supplying the *Minnesota*. Others thought it a floating magazine, reloading her. "A few visionary characters," wrote Rochelle, "feebly intimated that it might be the *Monitor*."

Colonel Colston, determined to have a better view of this day's fighting than yesterday's, sent during the night for a twelve-oar barge that he used when inspecting his river batteries. At dawn he had gotten into it and had his rowers head toward the grounded frigate, "confident of witnessing her destruction or surrender." Then he saw the *Monitor*. "No words can express the surprise with which we beheld this strange craft, whose appearance was tersely and graphically described by one of my oarsmen, 'A tin can on a shingle.'"

Once the surprise at seeing the *Monitor* was done, however, there were those aboard the *Virginia* who wondered what lay ahead. Lieutenant Wood spoke for many: "She could not possibly have made her appearance at a more inopportune time."[2]

Those on the opposite shore might have disagreed. The Federals, still exhausted from the day before, awoke to see the sun, "red and angry," rising over the foggy Roads. The camps were astir as soon as the signal gun from Fort Monroe was fired, regiments forming into line and the survivors of the two warships taking places at the shore batteries. Then the fog finally lifted and melted under the sun, "as if purposely to afford an uninterrupted view of a sight which the world had never seen before," thought one refugee from the *Congress*.

This morning gave the men the first opportunity to view the *Monitor* as she lay at anchor near the *Minnesota*. Many were not encouraged. "No one in our camp seemed to know what it was or how it came there," wrote Surgeon Edward Shippen of the *Congress*, "but at last it was conceded that it must be the strange new ironclad which we heard was being built in New York by Ericsson." Yet, he lamented, "she seemed so small and trifling that we feared she would only constitute additional prey for the leviathan." Another former *Congress*-man confessed that "to tell the truth, we did not have much faith in the 'Monitor.'"

Aboard the ship itself, those who had managed to get to sleep during the hectic night awakened early and had a 7 A.M. breakfast. There was a good deal of bustle about, since already several tugs had come alongside the *Minnesota*. Onto them, the frigate's men were throwing their hammocks and duffel bags and the ship's stores. Much of what was thrown overboard missed, and was seen bobbing up and down in the water.

Already the *Monitor* had her steam up and, while some men ate, others raised her anchor. Slowly she steamed along the *Minnesota* towering above her. Those on top of the turret looked up *Minnesota*'s sheer, lofty side. Men were now leaving the ship, getting into small boats to go ashore. Some of the frigate's guns were being thrown overboard to prevent the enemy from getting them. "Everything seemed in confusion," wrote Keeler. As an ominous reminder of the power of the *Virginia,* he and others on the turret could see the splintered holes made by the ironclad's shells as they penetrated the frigate's wooden side.

As the fog lifted, Keeler and others got their first glimpse of the *Virginia* steaming north from Sewell's Point. It was nearly 8 A.M. Some were still eating their breakfast, but at the word that the ironclad was in sight, "our coffee was forgotten." Worden called up to Van Brunt to ask what he intended to do. There was still half an hour perhaps before the *Virginia* reached them. Van Brunt hoped to throw off enough material to lighten his ship and float her. If not, he would destroy the *Minnesota*. "I will stand by you to the last if I can help you," Worden yelled, but Van Brunt, agreeing with Keeler that "the idea of assistance or protection being offered to the huge thing by the little pigmy at her side seemed absolutely ridiculous," replied that the *Monitor* could do nothing for him.

Immediately, the ironclad's crew came to life, battening down all the deck hatches, removing the smokestacks and vent stacks, and putting the stoppers in the deck lights. Every man went to his post. Worden, with the pilot Howard and Quartermaster Peter Williams to steer, would occupy the pilothouse. Greene would command in the turret, with Stimers and Stodder helping direct the two guns. Isaac Newton would manage the engine and boiler rooms. Keeler, who had no battle station, remained on top of the turret along with a few others. By now they could see the *Virginia* clearly. "There was no mistaking her slanting, rakish outlines," said Truscott. Then they saw a puff of white smoke jet out from her bow port and heard the howl of a shell as it passed over them and hit the *Minnesota*. Peeved at the foolishness of the men staying exposed on the turret,

Worden now came up and said sternly, "Gentlemen, that is the *Merrimac*, you had better go below."

All raced down into the turret, Worden coming down last and pulling shut the iron hatch after him. Once in the turret, they could see that the gunners were loading the guns. A 175-pound, 11-inch projectile was just then being lifted into the mouth of one of the guns. "Send them that with our compliments, my lads," Worden encouraged them.

The scene in the turret just now was eerie, unforgettable. A few rays of sunlight filtered in through the gratings on top of the tower, while dim lanterns provided just enough additional illumination to cast misshapen shadows of men and guns on the turret's interior. The men all stood perfectly still—almost like statues, thought Keeler. "The most profound silence reigned," he wrote, "if there had been a coward heart there its throb would have been audible, so *intense* was the stillness." The paymaster was baffled by the feelings he experienced. It was not exactly fear. It was inexplicable. "We were enclosed in what we supposed to be an impenetrable armour —we knew that a powerful foe was about to meet us—ours was an untried experiment & the enemy's first fire might make it a coffin for us all." Making matters worse was the fact that, with the gun-port shutters closed, no one in the turret could see the *Virginia*. They waited in the silent darkness, expecting every moment to hear a Rebel shell strike their untried iron. "The suspense was awful," Keeler recalled.

Soon they heard the firing of a gun, followed by two or three other shots, and then what sounded like a broadside from the *Minnesota* in reply. The *Monitor*'s speaking tube was not working now, so Greene sent Keeler forward to the pilothouse to ask Worden if he could open fire. "Tell Mr. Green [sic] not to fire till I give the word, to be cool & deliberate, to take sure aim & not waste a shot."

Worden headed his craft straight for the *Virginia*. Now he sent the word to Greene: "Commence firing." The engines stopped, Stodder laboriously turned the wheel that controlled the turret, and the great iron tower turned until its guns pointed at the enemy ship. Greene ordered a gun-port stopper moved, ran out a gun, and pulled the lanyard. Quartermaster Truscott peered out after that first shot. "You can see surprise on a ship just the same as you can see it in a human being," he declared, "and there was surprise all over the Merrimac."[3]

The *Virginia* indeed was surprised by the appearance of the *Monitor,* but Jones did not change his original intention. He told his pilots to take the ship to within a half mile of the *Minnesota,* from which distance he could easily destroy her. But the pilots would never get him any closer than a mile. Even from this distance, however, he could eventually accomplish his object, and he ordered the ironclad's first firing to commence when the enemy frigate was nearly one and a half miles distant. Simms was the first to fire, with his bow gun, once again. Onward the ironclad went on her course, heading for the *Minnesota.* When the Confederates saw the puff of smoke of the *Monitor's* first shot, some still did not believe that it was an enemy ship. Littlepage, still thinking that the strange ship was actually the frigate's boiler being removed for repairs, thought that perhaps it had exploded.

Jones knew what it was, but decided at first to ignore it and keep trying to reach the *Minnesota.* But when it appeared that his pilots could not get him close enough to suit him, the lieutenant decided instead to try a fight with the enemy ironclad, which now peppered the *Virginia* constantly with its shells. It was about 8:45 A.M. now, and for the next two hours the two iron monsters gave each other their undivided attention.

At first they fired at long range, but before long the ships closed to within fifty yards, then began circling each other in spirals, now opening the distance to 100 yards or more and then closing until they almost touched. Thanks to her light draft and better engines, the *Monitor* moved about at will, steaming much faster and steering considerably better than the *Virginia.* Indeed, during the fight Jones complained repeatedly that he could not bring his guns to bear on the antagonist, because she presented such a relatively small target and moved and maneuvered so quickly. As for the enemy's armament, Eggleston declared that "we never got sight of her guns except when they were about to fire into us." As soon as the *Monitor's* guns were fired, the turret revolved them out of view to reload. Jones marveled at how proper aim could be taken by the Yankee gunners when their guns stopped such a short time on target. Yet the sound of the enemy shells ricocheting off the *Virginia's* side gave ample proof that Greene was sending his shots true.

The *Virginia*'s gun deck took on the aspect of a scene from Dante as the Confederates began battling the Yankee iron monster. In the dim light, figures bustled about in the dense smoke, silent, begrimed with sweat, soot, and burned powder. Commands from sometimes unseen officers sternly put the men through their tasks. Below, in the boiler room, the furnaces spewed fire and smoke while the firemen, looking to Ramsay like gladiators, worked their controls to get more heat. "The noise of the crackling, roaring fires, escaping steam, and the loud and labored pulsations of the engines, together with the roar of battle above and the thud and vibration of the huge masses of iron being hurled against us, altogether produced a scene and sound to be compared only with the poet's picture of the lower regions."[4]

The inside of the *Monitor*'s turret presented a scene far more calm, particularly after the first shots from the *Virginia* rebounded harmlessly off its sides. When the first shot struck, a wave of consternation coursed over the men in the turret. They told Greene where the shot had struck and showed him the indentation that it made in the iron. Greene, in turn, reported it to Stimers, since he was better acquainted with the ship's construction.

"Did the shot come through?" asked the engineer.

"No sir, it didn't come through," Greene replied, "but it made a big dent, just look a there sir!"

"A big dent," exclaimed Stimers, "of course it made a big dent— that is just what we expected, but what do you care about that so long as it keeps out the shot?"

"Oh! it's all right then of course sir." Stimers noticed immediately a feeling of relief in the turret, as the men felt safe. Greene admitted that now "a look of confidence passed over the men's faces." Soon there were boasts that the *Virginia* would be whipped in short order.

The men working the guns stripped to the waist as the heat from engines, boilers, and guns rose inside the turret. Powder and smoke soon turned their bodies black. Keeler could see "the perspiration falling from them like rain." They loaded and fired the guns as fast as possible. Greene himself aimed and fired each gun personally. Because of a problem with the port stoppers, only one gun could be fired at a time. Then too, thanks to the closing of the ports as soon as the guns recoiled, no one could see what effect the shots were having, since the only way to see out at all was over the guns as they were aimed. Consequently, after each shot Greene sent Keeler forward to the pilothouse to ask Worden the effect it had, if any. Here, at last, the paymaster found his niche in battle. "The situation was novel," Greene admitted, with a captain and his executive officer being cut off from direct communication while engaged in mortal combat. Yet he found that Keeler, assisted by D. Toffey, Worden's clerk, did the work "with zeal and alacrity," though he noticed that, both of them being unexperienced at sea, some of the technical nautical information being passed came out garbled or miscarried entirely.

Other problems soon reared up. As feared earlier, Greene found that he could not fire at the *Virginia* when she was directly bow on—in front of the *Monitor*'s bow—because the pilothouse was in the way. Then there were the ports. When they closed, the gun muzzles were too close to them to allow the free use of long-poled rammers and sponges. Consequently, with this in mind, Ericsson had provided small holes in the stoppers just large enough for a rammer or swabber to insert the end of his pole, run it out through the hole until the end with the sponge or ram could be inserted in the muzzle, and then proceed with his task. From the outside this gave the appearance of two poles feverishly running in and out of the stoppers. Then, this process concluded, the gun was ready for firing. Here came the problem. The stoppers were so heavy that it took an entire crew to move them, a slow, laborious process that interfered with the turret's fire power, since one crew had to raise while the other ran out the gun and fired it. Finally, Greene decided to leave both ports open.

This decision was in part necessitated by yet another difficulty. When the *Monitor* nearly foundered on the trip to Hampton Roads, the incoming sea water drenched the machinery that turned the turret, which in turn quickly rusted. Poor Stodder tried his best to control the wheel that operated it all, but he simply was not powerful enough. Now Stimers, whom Greene found to be "an active, muscular man," took over, discovering that he could turn the wheel. "He is a trump of the very first water," Fox would say of the engineer, but soon even he could not manage it. Eventually the turret could not be stopped with any precision at all, making it impossible to give a well-directed fire. Consequently, Greene finally decided to leave the stoppers open permanently and then discharge the guns "on the fly," as the turret revolved the guns past his target. It was a method not well calculated to enhance the accuracy of the *Monitor*'s guns, but it did allow the crews to maintain a relatively rapid fire, shooting both guns once every seven or eight minutes. As he fired at the *Virginia,* Greene more than once mused on the fact that his old friend and roommate in the Naval Academy at Annapolis, Walter R. "Butsy" Butt, was now a lieutenant in the Confederate Navy, commanding one of the guns that was firing back at him.

Worden had ordered that everyone aboard remain silent during the fight, so that any orders shouted could be heard clearly. For the most part his instructions were observed, but at least once the silence was broken. Hearing what sounded like the rattle of hailstones falling on the iron top deck, a gunner stuck his head outside one of the ports briefly, then pulled it back in to announce with a grin, "Well, the d——d fools are firing canister at us." What he, Greene, and others, actually saw, however, must have been fragments of exploded shells. No one aboard the *Virginia* was foolish enough to suppose that canister would have any effect on the *Monitor.*

But while the men remained silent, not so Worden and Greene, and poor Keeler racing back and forth between them. The messages he conveyed capture vividly the scene that only Worden could see.

"Tell Mr. Green that I am going to bring him on our Starboard beam close along side [the *Virginia*]."

"That was a good shot, went through her water line [incorrect]."

"Don't let the men expose themselves, they are firing at us with rifles."

"That last shot brought the iron from her sides."

"She's too far off now, reserve your fire till you're sure."

The men were performing magnificently. During the past forty-eight hours none had enjoyed any real rest, and but little food. Many had been hard at work during the night, getting nothing for breakfast but some hard bread and coffee. Greene himself estimated that he had not slept in fifty-one hours. "But after the first gun was fired, we forgot all fatigue, hard work, and everything else—& went to work fighting as hard as men ever fought."[5]

Greene would have been a little pleased to know that the *Virginia* was operating under some severe handicaps too. Thanks to the loss of her ram the day before, and from other causes, she was now leaking badly, her pumps constantly in operation. With the added weight of the water in her hold, she steered miserably. Her helm was sluggish, and the men aboard could feel the lack of responsiveness in the way she jerked and vibrated under their feet when turning. It took nearly fifteen minutes for her to make a simple maneuver to turn a broadside toward the *Monitor.* Some men aboard thought she was actually close to sinking all through the fight. Worse yet, the smokestack was so perforated that it no longer served to provide the draft necessary to draw in the needed fresh air for the fires. Ramsay was having a great deal of trouble in keeping up steam. "Our ship was working worse and worse," lamented Lieutenant Wood.

The Confederates could take comfort, however, in the fact that the *Monitor* so far had done them very little damage aside from a few cracked plates on the casemate. In fact, some aboard could actually see where the enemy ironclad was missing her opportunities to deliver telling blows, perhaps fatal ones. In particular, they felt that Greene's gunnery was bad. Wood thought that the *Monitor* should be concentrating her fire on one particular spot on the *Virginia's* casemate. Since several shots struck and broke or cracked armor plates, successive shots in the same place could have broken through the wooden backing, allowing a shell to get inside to wreak havoc. One of the Rebel ironclad's lieutenants declared that "another shot or two from the *Monitor,* following up two or more that she had placed between my two guns on the starboard side, would have brought down the shield about our ears." At the same time, a few shots placed at the *Virginia's* water line might have gone under the barely submerged eaves to hole her unprotected hull. Of course, the men on the *Virginia* could not know the difficulties Greene was having with the turret and port stoppers. To them it simply seemed that "not a shot appeared to have any 'Motif.'"

After nearly two hours of this, little damage had been done to either vessel, and clearly the fight was far from finished. Then, about ten-thirty, when still a mile distant from the *Minnesota,* the Rebel ironclad met calamity. With all the circling and maneuvering, her pilots became confused and allowed the *Virginia* to run aground in shoal water. She stuck fast.

"Our situation was critical," said Ramsay. The *Virginia* was drawing twenty-two feet of water now, while the *Monitor*'s draft was just half that. Now that the Rebel monster was grounded, the "cheese box" could still steam around her, firing at will from any position without fear of herself running aground. And that is what she did. "In she came," wrote Ramsay, "and began to sound every chink in our armor." The enemy ironclad seemed to Surgeon Phillips to circle the *Virginia* "like a fice dog."

Ramsay, in particular, was apprehensive. The coal consumption of the two days' fighting had used up several tons of the ballast needed to keep the *Virginia*'s eaves submerged. Now the unprotected submerged deck at the bow was almost at the surface, as were the sides of the ship below the casemate. "Lightened as we were," said Ramsay, "these exposed portions rendered us no longer an ironclad."

Soon the *Monitor* took a position close enough to deliver telling blows, yet so situated that none of the *Virginia*'s ports allowed the Confederates an opportunity to fire back. Here, for fifteen minutes, Greene fired gun after gun, at least five or six short-range shots that raked the enemy casemate. Some nearly entered the open ports, while others struck in the same general area, cracked the iron plates, and began forcing in the timber backing. A few more minutes of this would have meant the end of Jones's ship.

Ramsay was all the while expending every effort to get the ship off the mud. "We had to take all chances," he said. He tied down the steam safety valves which prevented the boiler from building too much pressure. Ramsay wanted all the steam he could get now, and safety was no longer a consideration. Fast-burning combustibles were thrown into the furnaces, already raging with flames, to raise the heat to produce even more steam pressure. The pressure gauge went far past the danger point. The propeller churned the water and mud with frenzy, yet still the ship stayed aground. Ramsay began throwing into the fires anything he could find that would burn faster and hotter than coal—oiled cotton waste, splinters of wood, probably even turpentine. "It seemed impossible the boilers could long stand the pressure we were crowding upon them."

Meanwhile, on the gun deck the men were standing quietly, apprehensive. "Every one was watching and waiting," said Phillips, "with an impatience which may well be imagined to be relieved of the horrible night-mare of inactivity, from which we all suffered." Ramsay was finally at the point of despair, when suddenly he felt a slight movement. Then the men on the gun deck "felt the old vessel give one Samsonian effort," and then she pulled free. A loud cheer broke out from hundreds of voices as the *Virginia* backed out into deeper water once more. "We were saved."[6]

As the *Virginia* continued to build up speed again, her gunners opened fire once more, all, that is, except Eggleston. He told his men to rest. Jones, coming past his station, asked, "Why are you not firing, sir?"

"It is quite a waste of ammunition to fire at her," Eggleston replied. "Our powder is precious, sir, and I find I can do the Monitor as much damage by snapping my finger at her every five minutes."

Now Jones revealed for the first time a new resolve. "Never mind," he said, "we are getting ready to ram her." Had his inspection of the *Virginia* the night before been more thorough, he would have known that she no longer had her iron ram. Without it he would have been foolish to attempt now to ram, with a wooden bow, an iron vessel.

Jones called Ramsay to him, and ordered that the engines be reversed the second that Ramsay felt her hit the *Monitor*. Then he began to maneuver for position. The ironclad required at least a mile of water to get up full headway, but she would have only one half mile or less now. "Go ahead!" "Stop." "Astern." Jones gave his short, sharp commands to the helmsman as he tried to turn the vessel into the *Monitor*'s midships. As usual, the *Virginia* proved unresponsive. "The ship was as unwieldy as Noah's ark," complained Wood. But finally, gauging that he had his position, Jones called out, "Go ahead, full speed," and drove the *Virginia*'s bow straight toward the *Monitor*.[7]

Aboard the Federal ironclad, Greene and his men had methodically kept up their fire on the enemy throughout the grounding and freeing of the *Virginia*. Now Worden, looking out from his pilot-house, could see Jones maneuvering to come around and ram. "Look out now," he told Keeler, "they're going to run us down, give them both guns."

As the paymaster ran back to the turret to give Greene the message, he felt real fear for the first time. "This was the critical moment, one that I had feared from the beginning of the fight—if she could so easily pierce the heavy oak beams of the *Cumberland,* she surely could go through the ½ inch iron plates of our lower hull." He gave Greene his message. Worden put the helm hard away from the *Virginia,* hoping her blow would strike obliquely and glance off. "A moment of terrible suspense" settled over the Federals, wrote Keeler, and then "a heavy jar nearly throwing us from our feet."[8]

In fact, according to Ramsay, Jones doomed the attempt to ram even before the blow was struck. Fearing that, as with the *Cumberland* the day before, he would have trouble extricating himself once he rammed the *Monitor,* Jones decided not to hit her full force. Several seconds before the impact, he signaled to Ramsay to back the engines. As a result, the Confederates struck the enemy only a halfhearted blow. Worden's turning of the *Monitor* lessened its effect even more, causing the *Virginia*'s prow to strike obliquely and glance off. Aboard the *Monitor,* everyone felt the impact and immediately cast their eyes about looking for a hole and an inrushing torrent of water. Instead, they found nothing. "We were safe," exulted Keeler.

At first the Confederates thought they had done great damage. Phillips believed that they had made the *Monitor* "reel beneath our terrible blow," leaving her staggering in shock. Confederates ashore agreed, thinking the enemy ironclad seriously wounded. In fact, however, the only sign of the *Monitor*'s iron deck's being struck at all was a few splinters from the *Virginia*'s wooden bow sticking to a nut and screw, and a very slight indentation in the iron. The worst damage done by the ramming was done to the Confederate vessel. Right after impact, the ship's carpenter reported to Jones that there was a leak in the bow. The lieutenant sent for Ramsay, who assured him that, while there was some water in the hold, there was no great danger. A little later Jones asked him again, but the pumps and bilge injectors were working more than well enough to keep them afloat for hours, even should her hull be penetrated. On the gun deck, Wood found a much greater danger narrowly averted. Just as the *Virginia* rammed the *Monitor,* Greene followed Worden's orders and gave the enemy both guns almost simultaneously. The shells struck halfway up the casemate next to Wood's after pivot gun. The side was forced in two or three inches by the impact, while the concussion from it knocked over most of the men in the after gun crews, who arose bleeding from nose and ears. "Another shot at the same place would have penetrated," declared a shaken Wood.[9]

Aboard the *Monitor* the firing never stopped. "The sounds of the conflict at this time were terrible," wrote Keeler. Clouds of smoke filled the turret. The howling of shells fired from the *Minnesota* as they passed overhead mingled with the roar of the ship's own guns and the terrible sound of the *Virginia's* shot striking her. "The din inside the turret was something terrific," said Truscott. "The noise of every solid ball that hit fell upon our ears with a crash that deafened us."

As yet no one inside the turret had been injured, though several were bruised when the nuts on the inside of the tower flew off their bolts on the impact of enemy shells. "Had anybody been hit in the face or eyes they would have been done for," said Truscott, but fortunately all injuries were slight, not even requiring the men to leave their posts.

As the *Virginia* resumed her fire, Stimers, Stodder, and Truscott were conversing, all three of them leaning against the turret wall. At that moment a shot from the enemy ironclad struck the outside of the turret directly opposite them. The impact knocked all three of them to the deck. Stimers, who only had his hand resting against the wall, sprang back up again, uninjured. Stodder, however, had rested his knee against it. "I was flung by the concussion clean over both guns to the floor of the turret," he recalled. Unconscious, he was taken below, where he remained for an hour before awakening. Truscott was the most seriously injured of all. His head, while not against the turret, was only inches from the point which the shell struck. "I dropped over like a dead man," he wrote. He remained semiconscious for quite some time, while Dr. Logue constantly bathed his head. Eventually, he also regained full consciousness and was found to have suffered no permanent injury.

About this time Worden pulled the *Monitor* out of the fight and stood off for half an hour. The supply of shot in the turret had been exhausted, and must be replenished from the lockers below. To do this, the turret must stand stationary to align its hatchway with the one in the main deck so the powder and shot could be hauled up. Probably at this same time Paymaster Keeler, on orders from Worden, opened the spirit room and doled out to every man aboard half a gill—an eighth of a pint—of whiskey. Keeler, himself an abstainer, concluded that "if liquor ever does good to any one & is ever useful it must be on some such occasion."[10]

While the *Monitor* was out of the fight, Jones took advantage of the opportunity to turn his full attention to the *Minnesota*. Though he could never get closer than a mile, he had been throwing occasional shots at her all during the fight. Now, about 11 A.M., Simms fired his bow pivot gun at her, the shell tearing through four rooms aboard the frigate, exploding two charges of powder and starting a fire, which was quickly extinguished. Simms's second shot struck the boiler of the tug *Dragon,* alongside the frigate, exploding it. Meanwhile, Van Brunt kept up a constant but ineffectual fire on the ironclad. Constant reports on the progress of the fight were sent below to the *Minnesota*'s crewmen. Occasionally one of them could get to a port or open deck to see it for himself, as did Rae. Getting an opera glass, he watched the fight. "It was really laughable. The *Merrimac* was making strenuous efforts to get down to us, but always just before her was the diminutive 'Pill Box' waiting every chance and putting in a shot at each." This was before the *Monitor* hauled off. Back below, Rae narrowly missed being injured by Simms's first shot.[11]

As soon as the supply of shot in the turret was replenished, Worden turned the *Monitor* back between the *Minnesota* and the *Virginia*. "At it we went again as hard as we could," wrote Greene. "The shot, shell, grape, canister, musket, and rifle, balls flew about in every direction, but did us no damage." The ships closed to within a few yards of each other once more, and Greene claimed that they actually touched at least five times.

By now Jones was convinced that he could do the enemy ironclad no injury, and some of his officers instead suggested attempting to board the *Monitor*. Wood called for volunteers to go with wedges and hammers, driving the former between the turret and the deck to freeze the tower in place. A man at Littlepage's gun, Seaman John Hunt, actually jumped into the open port and was on his way outside when Littlepage stopped him. Hunt proposed to jump aboard the *Monitor*—the "bloody little iron tub," he called it—and put his sea jacket over the viewing slits in the pilothouse. It might have worked, but Littlepage kept him from trying.

The possibility of being boarded had already been considered by Worden. Since the only way into the *Monitor* during battle was through the top of the turret, and boarders on her main deck would be sitting targets, hand grenades had been prepared which could be tossed out the ports at the Confederates, who would find no shelter except by jumping into the water.

Consequently, when Wood called away his boarders, Worden detected the beginnings of the movement. "They're going to board us," he told Keeler; "put in a round of canister." Greene replied that both guns were already loaded with solid shot. "Give them to her then," came Worden's reply. Meanwhile, Greene announced to the men in the turret, "they are going to board us." They met the news with perfect calm. "Let 'em come," one said, "we will amuse them some." Before the Confederates could step out of their casemate, however, the *Monitor* steamed past the *Virginia* and the opportunity was gone.[12]

Now Worden decided to attempt to ram. It was nearly eleven-thirty. He had been fighting the *Virginia* for almost three hours, yet aside from a few cracked plates on her casemate, there was no indication that he was doing any real damage to the Rebel ironclad. With the *Monitor*'s superior speed and maneuverability, he should be able to seriously injure her. And he knew just where to strike. The weakest point in the *Virginia*'s defenses, her most vulnerable spot, was her stern. A powerful thrust well delivered could wreck her rudder and propeller, thereby leaving the ironclad adrift, unable to move or steer. Since none of the other wooden Confederate vessels was any sort of match for the *Monitor,* the *Virginia* would clearly be beyond help, with no choice but to surrender or float at the whim of the currents.

Worden ordered the helm put around to aim his ship for the *Virginia*'s stern. At full speed they headed directly toward their target. Then, just before reaching the Confederate ironclad, the *Monitor*'s steering apparatus somehow malfunctioned, causing her to sheer off, just missing the *Virginia* by a few feet. Most of the Confederates agreed that if the Federal ship had struck her, the fight would have been over.[13]

Just as quickly now, the advantage turned for a time to the Confederates. Some time before, Jones had ordered his gunners to concentrate their fire on the *Monitor*'s pilothouse. It seemed the only target they might damage. Now, as the enemy ironclad glided past the *Virginia*'s stern, Wood trained his after pivot gun on the pilothouse and, at a distance of about twenty yards, fired.

Keeler was standing near the pilothouse, awaiting orders, when Wood's shell struck and exploded. "A flash of light & a cloud of smoke filled the house," he wrote. Then he saw Worden put his hands to his eyes, and ran up to him to ask if he was injured.

"My eyes," Worden answered; "I am blind."

With help from Logue, Keeler took Worden down from the pilothouse and sat him down at the foot of the ladder, at the same time sending to the turret for Greene, the next in command. "I went forward," wrote Greene, "& there stood as noble a man as lives at the foot of the ladder, of the Pilot House. His face was perfectly black with powder & iron & he was apparently perfectly blind." When Greene asked what had happened, Worden explained that a shell had struck and exploded right outside a viewing slit through which he was looking.

By now, several of the ship's officers had gathered around Worden, from whose blackened face blood mixed with powder was running profusely. Quartermaster Williams, meanwhile, had without orders turned the ship away from the *Virginia* the minute Worden was struck. As the officers consulted, the *Monitor,* her guns silent, quickly steamed farther and farther away from her adversary.

Greene wanted to know what he should do. "Gentlemen," said Worden, "I leave it with you, do what you think best. I cannot see, but do not mind me. Save the *Minnesota* if you can." At once Greene led Worden back to his cabin and laid him on his sofa. Then he went up to examine the damage to the pilothouse. Wood's shell had struck the second nine-by-twelve-inch iron log from the top, cracking it in two, knocking the iron hatch on top up and back several inches. Another shot placed there might well penetrate and kill anyone in the pilothouse. Yet, despite this, the officers who had gathered about Worden agreed in consultation that they should continue the fight. Greene took over in the pilothouse, and Stimers would direct entirely the operations of the turret.[14]

Just how much time passed between Worden's wounding and Greene's assumption of command is unknown, but it was at least half an hour. By noon, when Greene turned the *Monitor* back around to head back into the fight, the ship had gone into shoal

34. Officers of the *Monitor* photographed in front of the turret, July 9, 1862; back row, left to right: George Frederickson, Mark Sunstrom, Paymaster William Keeler, Isaac Newton; middle row: Lieutenant Samuel D. Greene, Master Louis N. Stodder, Edwin V. Gager, William Flye, Surgeon Daniel C. Logue; bottom row: Robinson Hands and Albert Campbell. (Courtesy of the MOLLUS-Mass. Collection, U. S. Army Military History Research Collection, Carlisle Barracks, Pennsylvania.)

35. The same officers rearranged and clowning a little. (Courtesy of the MOLLUS-Mass. Collection, U. S. Army Military History Research Collection, Carlisle Barracks, Pennsylvania.)

36. Officers surveying shot marks in the turret made by the *Virginia's* fire. In the background can be seen part of the new, sloping pilothouse built by Stimers after the square one was damaged. (Courtesy of MOLLUS-Mass. Collection, U. S. Army Military History Research Collection, Carlisle Barracks, Pennsylvania.)

37. Campbell and Flye taking a closer look at the turret. The pilothouse shows well here, as does a plate at the edge of the hull, just below Flye, where it was struck by the *Virginia*. (Courtesy of the MOLLUS-Mass. Collection, U. S. Army Military History Research Collection, Carlisle Barracks, Pennsylvania.)

38. The none-too-popular Lieutenant William N. Jeffers, who commanded the *Monitor* during the summer of 1862. (Courtesy of the MOLLUS-Mass. Collection, U. S. Army Military History Research Collection, Carlisle Barracks, Pennsylvania.)

39. Crewmen of the *Monitor* cooking a midday meal aboard ship. (Courtesy of the MOLLUS-Mass. Collection, U.S. Army Military History Research Collection, Carlisle Barracks, Pennsylvania.)

40. The *Monitor*'s crew relaxing on deck. (Courtesy of the MOLLUS-Mass. Collection, U. S. Army Military History Research Collection, Carlisle Barracks, Pennsylvania.)

41. The hulk of the *Monitor*, lying off Cape Hatteras, as photographed by a Duke University-National Geographic Society team in 1973. The turret is visible at lower left. (Courtesy of National Geographic Society.)

water much too shallow for the *Virginia* to follow. Indeed, the Confederates believed that she had been retreating, declining to continue the fight. "The fact is, the *Monitor* was afraid of the *Virginia,*" one would claim, though others thought it a trick to lure their ship into running aground again.

Regardless, seeing that the *Monitor*'s running into the shoals "prevented our doing her any further injury," as Jones put it, he turned his vessel back toward the *Minnesota*. But now new problems presented themselves. The pilots still could get her no closer than a mile away from the frigate, and at this distance it would take some time to reduce Van Brunt's ship. Yet the pilots also now warned Jones that they could stay out in the Roads no longer. The tide was receding, and was still just barely high enough to allow the *Virginia* to pass back over the sand bar at the mouth of the Elizabeth. If they stayed out much longer, they would be unable to return until the next morning, for to risk a passage on the midnight high tide would be too difficult. While still heading for the *Minnesota,* Jones passed along the gun deck holding informal counsels with his lieutenants. "The Monitor has given up the fight and run into shoal water; the pilots cannot take us any nearer to the Minnesota; this ship is leaking from the loss of her prow; the men are exhausted by being so long at their guns; . . . I propose to return to Norfolk for repairs. What is your opinion?" All but Wood agreed, he suggesting instead that they run down to Fort Monroe to attack the frigates anchored there. Jones's opinion prevailed, and he gave Ramsay orders accordingly. The pressure in the boilers could be reduced now, relieving the strain they had endured for nearly four hours. Shortly past noon, the *Virginia* turned away from Hampton Roads and steamed off toward the Elizabeth River. "Had there been any sign of the Monitor's willingness to renew the contest," Jones declared, however, "we would have remained to fight her."[15]

Once Greene had the *Monitor* turned around again, he saw the *Virginia* steaming off toward Sewell's Point. Where Jones had interpreted Williams' sheering his vessel off after Worden's wounding as a retreat, now Greene believed that the *Virginia*—whose commander actually thought the *Monitor* had quit—was herself abandoning the fight. "We had evidently finished the *Merrimac,*" Greene wrote home. It was one of history's curious cases of mutual misapprehension. Both ironclads felt that they had won the day.

Of course, the shells were still flying. Wood fired his stern gun as his ship moved away, while the *Monitor* kept up her fire at the withdrawing adversary. Now there was a dilemma. Worden's orders —now Greene's orders—had been explicit. They were to defend the *Minnesota,* nothing more. On no account were they to pursue the *Virginia* into her own waters. Then, too, the pilothouse was damaged, presenting a weak spot in the *Monitor*'s defenses. And no one could judge immediately of the seriousness of Worden's wounds. Certainly, however, he needed better facilities than those available aboard his ship.

All these influences decided Greene, now exercising his very first independent command, to break off, cease firing, and return to the side of the *Minnesota.* At last the guns in the turret were silent, its turning stopped. The hatches sprang open, and out onto the deck stepped men gasping for fresh air, longing for the light of day after hours of hellish darkness. The deck beneath their feet lay strewn with fragments of Rebel balls that had exploded or shattered against the turret. Keeler began gathering up a box of them as mementoes, when a last shell fired from the departing *Virginia* passed about twenty feet over his head and burst some one hundred feet away. A shower of shell fragments rained down upon the deck. A gunner standing nearby respectfully touched his hat and said coolly, "Paymaster there's some more pieces."[16]

Aboard the *Virginia* the men now came out for air too. As soon as all hands were "piped down," or relieved from battle stations, many hurried out onto the roof of the casemate. They looked longingly at the *Minnesota,* a prime bloom unplucked. They also looked for the *Monitor,* which was soon "a mere little speck to the naked eye." Back with the *Virginia* came her consort ships, who had been engaged throughout the morning mostly with keeping up an ineffective fire on the *Minnesota.* Back also came the tugs full of sightseers, some of them more sober than when they went out that morning. Some of those aboard grudgingly admitted that the *Monitor* was "a wicked thing."

For those Confederates afloat and ashore who had watched the day's battle, most sensed that they had seen something most unusual, that history was being made. It was a "great success," a

Georgia boy wrote home, a day of "stirring events." Colonel Colston, out in his barge, spent the better part of the morning in danger of being hit by one or the other of the ironclads. Several shots struck close enough to throw spray into his craft, "but the grandeur of the spectacle was so fascinating that they passed by unheeded." Wise and his son were witnesses to this day's fight, and marveled that the *Monitor* survived. "We could not doubt that the Merrimac would, either by shot or by ramming, make short work of the cheese-box; but as time wore on, we began to realize that the newcomer was a tough customer." When Jones was seen steaming back toward Sewell's Point, a cry of dismay escaped them. Not realizing the circumstances acting upon the *Virginia*, Wise thought that "dear old Buchanan would never have done it." Yet no one would argue with the newspaper reporter who declared that "the battle was altogether terrific." The editor of the *Day Book* was there to watch, and he sensed perhaps better than anyone the meaning of what he saw. "This successful and terrible work," he wrote, "will create a revolution in naval warfare, and henceforth iron will be the king of the seas."[17]

To watching Federals, the battle seemed much the same. It was almost forgotten that Magruder actually made a halfhearted move toward Newport News that day. "The Mermick and Ericsson Battery . . . fought like tigers for four hours," wrote a soldier at Fort Monroe, in "one of the greatest Naval Engagements that has ever ocured [sic] since the Beginning of the world." It seemed to some like David and Goliath afloat. Many men watched the fight from treetops, or the rigging and spars of their frigates. "To tell the truth, we did not have much faith in the 'Monitor,' " wrote one, "we all expected to see the 'Merrimac' destroy her." What he saw, however, was "one of the grandest fights between two war vessels that the world had ever seen." Of course, some did not see it that way. O'Neil of the *Cumberland* viewed it from Marston's *Roanoke*. While the battle was "a notable affair," he said, "it seemed tame enough to me as seen at a distance of three or four miles." Perhaps so, but few were disappointed with the results. The *Minnesota* was saved, the *Virginia* had gone back to her lair, and for the time being at least the *Monitor* seemed to command Hampton Roads. If she could not herself destroy the Rebel ironclad, she could prevent the *Virginia* from seriously damaging other Federal vessels. "Never was

a greater hope placed upon apparently more insignificant means,"
wrote a war correspondent, "but never was a great hope more tri-
umphantly fulfilled."[18]

The battle was a curious one, bringing different results on
different planes. In terms of the immediate missions of the two
ships, it was an unqualified victory for the *Monitor.* She had been
ordered to protect the *Minnesota,* and protect her Worden did. The
Virginia's object was the destruction of that frigate and any other
Federal warships she could engage. In this she failed. Of course,
the Confederates would claim that the *Monitor* had nothing to do
with their failure to destroy the *Minnesota.* They were only prevented from doing so by the fact that the water was too shallow for
their ironclad to approach nearer than one mile from the frigate.
But this argument disintegrates in the face of the damage the
Virginia did do with the few shots fired at Van Brunt from that
distance while engaged with the *Monitor.* Had Worden's ship not
been there, nothing else in Hampton Roads could have prevented
the *Virginia* from taking her time in slowly reducing the *Minnesota*
to rubble.

From a tactical vantage point, assessing the fighting itself, the
verdict appears different. The *Virginia* left the fight in almost exactly the same condition as when she entered it. Aside from some
cracked plates and the leak in her bow, she was relatively uninjured, and reported no casualties other than a very few walking
wounded. Jones could have continued the fight had he wished, and
according to Chief Engineer Ramsay, Jones actually intended at
first to withdraw only to Sewell's Point, there to wait for the tide to
come in again so he could safely renew the attack. As for the *Monitor,* however, she took serious, though hardly incapacitating,
damage in a vital spot, the pilothouse, and ended the fight with her
captain badly wounded. Greene could have continued fighting had
the *Virginia* not withdrawn, but only at the risk of losing his own
and several other lives should another Rebel shell strike the injured portion of the pilothouse. Clearly, in terms of damage done,
the *Virginia* emerged slightly the victor.

As for how the battle of the two iron monsters influenced the
broad strategic picture in Virginia, for the moment it seemed a
draw. The Federals still controlled Hampton Roads; the Confederates still held securely to the James, Nansemond, and Elizabeth,

and with the last, Norfolk. So long as the two ironclads remained afloat, the *Monitor* and her sister vessels stood no better chance of taking Norfolk by water and regaining the navy yard than did the *Virginia* and her consorts of escaping Hampton Roads to the Chesapeake to break the blockade.

But it was a draw whose real effects would be far-reaching, particularly for Federal strategy in the months to come, and even more so for a world in which naval warfare would never again be the same.

CHAPTER 10

"The *Virginia*
No Longer Exists"

What a hero's welcome awaited Jones and his men as they steamed back up the Elizabeth toward Norfolk! Crowds lined the shores on both sides, waving flags and handkerchiefs, shouting cheers until they were hoarse. Scores of small boats, bedecked with colorful banners, joined the *Virginia* on her return, turning it into a procession. When one boat with the editor of the Norfolk *Day Book* came close alongside, its occupants gave the ironclad three cheers. Jones mustered most of his command on the top deck of the casemate and returned the shout. Forrest came alongside in another boat, offering his compliments to Jones, who stood "looking as calm and modest as any gentleman within the jurisdiction of Virginia." Then on they all steamed. "As the ships, grouped against the soft, hazy sky, followed the Virginia," wrote a witness, "the picture was one never to be forgotten, the emotions excited such as can never be described."

Once the *Virginia* reached Norfolk, the scene was much the same. "No conqueror of ancient Rome ever enjoyed a prouder triumph than that which greeted us," wrote one of the ironclad's men. "The whole city was alive with joy and excitement," Lieutenant Parker discovered. People swarmed in the streets and on the wharves, while the shore batteries fired repeated salutes. Once stopped, Jones mustered the entire crew and spoke to them briefly to compliment their actions. The men responded with three cheers for their lieutenant commanding. Then, with the ship secured, he dismissed them, allowing most to go ashore to their friends and families. Young John Wise was amazed to find them "walking about the streets of Norfolk, or sitting at their firesides, as if unaware that fame was trumpeting their names to the ends of the earth." Indeed, they were the heroes of the hour, but some among them felt grave disappointment. They had not taken or destroyed either the *Monitor* or the *Minnesota.* "I remember feeling as though a wet blanket had been thrown over me," Ramsay recalled. Wood believed that "the battle was a drawn one," but that the advantage actually was with the Federal ironclad. Jones privately told Major Norris of the Signal Bureau that he felt "the destruction of those wooden vessels was a matter of course especially so, being at anchor, but in not capturing that ironclad, I feel as if we had done nothing." "And yet," Jones concluded, "give me that vessel and I will sink this one in twenty minutes."[1]

The next day, at noon, the Reverend J. H. Wingfield, assistant rector of Portsmouth's Trinity Episcopal Church, came aboard at the request of the *Virginia*'s officers and crew. The whole ship's complement gathered on the gun deck to hear him give a prayer of thanksgiving. "The sunshine of a favoring Providence beams upon every countenance," he declared; "the fierce weapons of our insolent invaders are broken." As he spoke, the officers and men all fell to their knees. The ceremony was, said Wood, "beautiful & impressive."[2]

Buchanan was extremely pleased. Though some reports had him dead, he was actually enjoying a slow but steady recovery at the Norfolk hospital. When he learned that the *Virginia* was back, he sent for Wood and dictated to him a brief report of the two days' action to take to Mallory. On his way to Richmond, Wood found himself repeatedly called on to tell the story of the fight. Once in the capital, he told the story yet again, this time before Mallory, Davis, Secretary of War Judah P. Benjamin, and others. "In the *Monitor*," he told them, "we had met our equal." The results of another engagement with her would be doubtful. After telling his story, Wood brought out and unrolled the flag captured from the *Congress.* For the first time, it was discovered that the banner was saturated with blood. Quickly he rolled it again and sent it to the Navy Department for safekeeping. Before Wood left, Mallory gave him the welcome news that Buchanan would shortly be promoted to the rank of admiral.[3]

Mallory could not have been more pleased. His faith in the *Virginia,* "a novelty in naval architecture, wholly unlike any ship that ever floated," was reinforced. She had won, he would claim, "the most remarkable victory which naval annals record." The Richmond *Enquirer* agreed, declaring that the *Virginia*'s success vindicated Mallory from the charges of sloth that had been laid to him. But then the *Examiner* of that same city only saw in it a clear example of how slow the Navy Department had been. By this time it could and should have had several more such ironclads built from other frigate hulks. It seemed that Mallory could hardly please everyone.

Benjamin, who on March 18 became Confederate Secretary of State, was more than satisfied. Here in the demonstrated ability of the *Virginia,* and particularly in her destruction of the *Congress* and the *Cumberland,* he had proof of the strength of the Confederacy and of its ability to break the Union blockade. Such a demonstration could have great diplomatic importance in his attempt to persuade England and France to grant the South formal recognition and the military aid without which the Confederacy could not hope to survive. "The *Virginia's* performances were more extraordinary than the printed reports exhibit," he claimed. Her success "evinces our ability to break the much-vaunted blockade, and ere the lapse of ninety days we hope to drive from our waters the whole blockading fleet." To his diplomats in London and Paris, Benjamin sent detailed accounts of the battles to be used for propaganda. One of his agents in England soon reported that "the success of the *Virginia* has caused great excitement here." Two days after the news arrived, the British Admiralty declared that no more wooden ships would be built, that England must have an ironclad navy. A lively debate began in British service journals over the battle at Hampton Roads, but in most quarters the verdict was the same as that expressed by the London *Times:* "Whereas we had available for immediate purposes one hundred and forty-nine first-class war-ships, we have now two, these two being the *Warrior* and her sister *Ironside.*" To Benjamin's dismay, however, the British showed more interest in the design and performance of the *Monitor* than that of the *Virginia.*[4]

In the aftermath of the fight, others were disappointed as well, chief among them being John Porter. Most of the Confederate press, as well as Mallory and others in the Navy Department, accorded the lion's share of the credit for the *Virginia* to Brooke.

Porter was incensed. Brooke had done nothing, he declared, but oversee the production of the guns and armor, and continually got in the way of the actual construction. The real design for the iron-clad was all Porter's. The constructor began a newspaper campaign to claim that portion of the limelight which he felt rightfully belonged to him. Brooke far more temperately defended himself against the accusations, and as is so often the case, the dispute was never settled to the satisfaction of either.[5]

While the *Virginia* went into dry dock for repairs, Buchanan sent Surgeon Phillips to Richmond with a confidential letter to Mallory. In it he recommended that the opening of the James River be obstructed as soon as possible, since the heavy draft of the *Virginia* would not allow her to go up the river to prevent Federal ships from entering it to move toward Richmond. Phillips found Mallory singularly uninterested for some reason. "That rotten official," he said, cast aside Buchanan's appeal and thereafter ignored it. Two months later the men of the *Virginia* actually did much of the work themselves.[6]

Buchanan also replied to Mallory's earlier inquiry about the *Virginia* steaming to New York. It was impossible. "The 'Virginia' is yet an experiment," he wrote, "and by no means invulnerable as has already been proven." The *Monitor,* he believed, was fully her equal. The *Virginia* had survived the guns of the Federal ships, but she might not withstand the much heavier cannon at Fort Monroe. In a gale, once at sea, she would probably founder, and if not she would be followed and harassed by the *Monitor* and other ships without mercy. Then too, her draft was too great to enter New York Harbor without experienced pilots, and no New Yorker would likely volunteer. Certainly, if she did actually get inside the harbor, the Federals would block it up and never let her out. "I consider the 'Virginia' the most important protection to the safety of Norfolk," he concluded, "and there she should remain. Most of Buchanan's officers, even Parker, whom he did not esteem, agreed with him. The *Virginia* would stay where she was.[7]

Amid a continuing hail of acclaim, including the official thanks of the Confederate Congress, repairs on the *Virginia* proceeded. Captain Sidney Smith Lee, brother of General Robert E. Lee, had been appointed to command at Norfolk, and he would oversee the work. She was not materially injured, he believed, and was still fit for service. Wood, however, found Lee "wanting in force, energy & vim, he allows every one to brow beat him." Still, Lee ordered that the work on the *Virginia* go on night and day; "spare no expense." Constructor Porter found one hundred indentations in her armor, twenty of them made by the *Monitor*. Six of the outer iron plates were cracked, and some of the timber backing was damaged enough to require reinforcing. Porter replaced the damaged armor, substituted new guns for the two with broken muzzles, went to work on a new and better-designed iron prow, provided a new anchor, and added a four-inch width of two-inch iron around the ship's knuckle, the vulnerable part just below the casemate eaves. Flagstaffs, ship's boats, steampipes, and a host of other accouterments had to be added as well. It was April 4 when the *Virginia* was ready to leave the dry dock, still unfinished.

One aspect of the ship that no one could fault was her battery. Jones had done his job well, but there were complaints about the projectiles fired. The *Virginia* had used only exploding shells, fine for wooden ships but lacking in the penetrating power needed for iron. If she was to meet the *Monitor* again, bolts of solid wrought iron or steel were necessary. A rush order went to Tredegar, who supplied the bolts as well as the repair plate and the iron shutters that were finally to be installed. When finished, the *Virginia* would be a much more formidable antagonist than on March 9.[8]

While the repairs went ahead, life in Norfolk went on. Wood's wife had borne him a baby girl on March 6. He had not seen her yet and anxiously awaited the time when he could get away. Poor Eggleston was down abed with the mumps. Jones went to Richmond. Buchanan, still too unwell to perform active duty, would have to be relieved. Rumors of who his replacement would be circulated through the command. Wood, of course, preferred Jones to anyone else, but the lieutenant was not old enough and there was no getting around the seniority system. Finally the command went to Commodore Josiah Tattnall, though some thought him Jones's inferior in ability. A sixty-seven-year-old Georgian, Tattnall had joined the United States Navy in 1812, served in the Mexican War, and in 1857 commanded the East India Squadron. When the war broke out, he resigned his U.S. commission and took command of Georgia's little navy. Named captain in March 1861, he was one of the most senior officers in the Confederate Navy, and so naturally stood well in line for Buchanan's post. So far in the war he had not done great things, and many suspected the mental and physical ability of a man of his age in such a responsible position, but Mallory had implicit faith in him. "Do not hesitate or wait for orders," the Secretary told Tattnall, "but strike when, how, and where your judgment may dictate."⁹

Until it was time to strike, however, until the Virginia came out of dry dock, the Confederates could only wait. Meanwhile, Brooke mused that perhaps it was best that the *Monitor* was not sunk or captured in their first fight. Now the enemy would regard their ironclad as a model—which Brooke felt she was not—and pattern all future ironclads after her. "She is not strong enough," he believed. The *Virginia* could yet finish her. Until they met again, though, no one could say for sure. "In these times," Wood wrote his wife, "we cannot tell what may occur from one day to another."¹⁰

The ovations and compliments proved equally plentiful on the northern side of Hampton Roads. When it became apparent that the fight was over, Greene turned the *Monitor* toward the *Minnesota,* coming alongside shortly after 1 P.M. She was literally surrounded by small craft of every description, filled with men anxious to see the effects the titanic fight had had upon her armored sides. Already, one tug had come alongside carrying the Navy Department's assistant inspector of ordnance, Lieutenant Henry A. Wise, a lifelong friend of Worden's. Jumping down the deck hatch, he ran to Worden's cabin to find him reclining "with the surgeon sponging away the blood and powder from his closed eyes and blackened and swollen face." Throwing his arms about his old friend, Wise declared that the *Monitor* had fought the most remarkable battle in naval history. "Have I saved that fine ship, the Minnesota?" asked Worden.

"Yes, and whipped the Merrimack to-boot."

"Then I don't care what happens to me," Worden replied.

But Wise did care, and immediately had a couch prepared aboard his tug to take Worden ashore. When the wounded man was brought up on deck for transfer to the tug, still blind, the *Monitor's* crew came out as well to give him cheer after cheer. Then, once he was gone, the ship's stewards went to the galley to prepare dinner, which was served at the usual hour, as if nothing had happened that day. Men who emerged from battle blackened even to their underclothes by the powder, now sat down to steak and peas.

On hailing the *Minnesota,* Greene found that Assistant Secretary Fox was aboard her. He had arrived at Hampton Roads with Wise at 6 A.M. As soon as he saw the *Virginia* coming out, he took over direction of affairs and started sending all the transports and other Federal ships that could move out of the Roads, in case the *Monitor* should fail. That done, at 11 A.M. he took two tugs to the *Minnesota* and started trying to get her afloat, experiencing at first hand the fire of the *Virginia.* In this he failed, but he was there to greet the *Monitor* now when she came alongside.

"Well, gentlemen," he said, "you don't look as though you were just through one of the greatest naval conflicts on record."

"No Sir," Greene replied, "we haven't done much fighting, merely drilling the men at the guns a little."

That little bit of drill left a crew of exhausted men, some so worn out that they could not eat or sleep. Greene ached in every bone and joint of his body. He had trouble standing steady. "My nerves and muscles twitched as though electric shocks were continually passing through them and my head ached as though it would burst. Sometimes I thought my brain would come right out over my brows." He tried to sleep. "I might as well have tried to fly."

Fox, meanwhile, reported to Welles over the newly completed telegraph, which managed to break down once during the day. From what he had seen of the fight, the assistant secretary felt that the Federal ironclad was hardly impregnable, but "the Monitor is more than a match for the Merrimac."[11]

Worden was taken by steamer to Washington that evening, while his shipmates tried to get some rest. It was a troubled night. The steamer *Whitehall,* hit earlier in the day, exploded, in the process accidentally firing one of her guns into the hospital at Fort Monroe. "Few of us slept that night," wrote a reporter. Perhaps the only bright spot in those dark hours came at 2 A.M., when the high tide and Van Brunt's continuing efforts finally floated the *Minnesota* free of the shoal. She left for Fort Monroe at once, then dropped anchor, injured but safe and ready for service.

The *Monitor,* too, was ready for service. In examining the effects of the *Virginia*'s shells upon her, all present marveled at how little damaged she was. Two shots had struck at the edge of the deck, tearing the iron a bit and denting it two or three inches. The rest of the deck showed scars where shells had struck and glanced off. The pilothouse sustained the most damage, while the turret withstood several shots with nothing more to show than a few indentations. In all, the ironclad had taken twenty-two hits, most of them on the turret. On her part, like the *Virginia,* the Federal ironclad had not been firing the most effective projectiles. Where Jones had only shells, Worden had both solid cast-iron and wrought-iron shot. He was allowed to use only the former, firing forty-one in all, because Dahlgren and others feared that the wrought-iron missiles—though they would surely have penetrated the *Virginia*—weighed so much that there was danger of bursting the guns in firing. Had that happened, everyone in the turret must have been killed.[12]

When the news reached Washington and the North, a great sigh of relief replaced the anxiety of the previous day. People all over were found "collecting in knots at corners, from which one is sure to hear in passing the words *Merrimac* or *Monitor.*" Welles was overjoyed, though at the same time greatly disappointed in Goldsborough. At the time of crisis he had been absent in North Carolina, "purposely and unnecessarily absent, in my apprehension, through fear of the Merrimac." Goldsborough himself, upon hearing of the two days' fight at Hampton Roads, immediately left North Carolina and hurried back to the Roads. Within four months Welles would relieve him of his command.

Worden, of course, became the hero of the hour. Wise took him to his own home in Washington to be tended by Mrs. Wise. Then on March 10, in company with Welles, Wise went to see Lincoln to give him a full account of the fight. When the lieutenant had finished, the President said, "Gentlemen, I am going to shake hands with that man." Lincoln and Wise walked the short distance to Wise's house, where they went up to Worden's second-floor room. Seeing the wounded man lying in bed, his face covered with bandages, Wise said, "Jack, here's the President, who has come to see you." Worden raised up on one elbow as Lincoln took his hand.

"You do me great honor, Mr. President, and I am only sorry that I can't see you," said Worden.

Lincoln's tall form bent over Worden, still holding his hand. The President's voice quivered slightly from emotion. "You have done *me* more honor, sir," he said, "than I can ever do to you." Then

Lincoln sat on the edge of the bed to hear the whole story again from Worden. Before leaving, the President told him that, if he could do so, he would see that Worden would be promoted to captain. Later that year, in December, he would recommend that the seaman be voted the thanks of Congress for his actions, and on February 3, 1863, Congress gladly complied. And on March 14, his ship having met and passed the final test, John Ericsson was paid the last installment due him in his contract with the Navy Department.[13]

The news of the fight had a profound effect in the Navy and War departments. Dahlgren immediately ceased his barge-sinking project, deciding he had better check with Welles now that the danger from the *Virginia* was diminished. Welles withheld his approval, leaving Stanton's "navy" stranded along the Potomac's banks as a constant reminder of his panic. Welles did, however, remain cautious enough to suggest that nets and heavy hawsers be stretched across the narrowest part of the river's channel, just in case. Stanton, meanwhile, still uncontent to rely on the Navy to do its own business, called millionaire shipowner Cornelius Vanderbilt, who volunteered his own 1700-ton side-wheel steamer *Vanderbilt* for use in stopping or destroying the *Virginia*. Just how this wooden steamer would do the job at which the *Cumberland* and the *Congress* had failed is conjecturable, though Vanderbilt thought he might ram the ironclad and sink her. Under authority from Stanton, the *Vanderbilt* steamed south to Hampton Roads, where, in the coming months, she did precisely nothing.

"It was a serious business," Dahlgren wrote, "and if the Merrimac were successful no one could anticipate the consequences to our side." Taking no chances, Welles now ordered his naval commanders on the Mississippi River to be on their guard against other Confederate ironclads known to be under construction. At the same time, he formulated strategy for the immediate future in Hampton Roads. Worden, in speaking to Lincoln, had warned that the *Monitor* was quite susceptible to boarding, since her turret could easily be wedged immobile, while water poured in the vents could drown and stop the machinery. On this account, Worden recommended that the ironclad not be sent "sky-larking up to Norfolk." Consequently, on March 10 Welles directed that the policy in Hampton Roads be a defensive one and that the *Monitor* not be risked in any attempt on Norfolk or against the *Virginia* that was not unavoid-able. This attitude was confirmed by an inspection of the ironclad by Goldsborough. "It will not do, in my judgment, to count too largely on her prowess. She is scarcely enough for the 'Merrimac.'" He feared that a good ramming would be the end of the *Monitor.* "Would to God we had another iron clad vessel on hand," he told Fox. Meanwhile, to prevent the *Virginia*'s escaping from Hampton Roads, Welles ordered hulks loaded with stone to be sunk in the channel between Fort Monroe and Rip Raps. "How frightened they must be, with all of their Forts & 3 or 400 vessels in their Navy to be afraid of our vessel," mused Lieutenant John Taylor Wood.[14]

There were changes to take place aboard the *Monitor.* Thinking Greene's youth precluded his holding permanent command of the ironclad, Fox ordered Selfridge of the *Cumberland* to relieve him on March 10. Then, two days later, Selfridge was in turn relieved by Lieutenant William N. Jeffers, a thirty-eight-year-old veteran of twenty-two years' service. He had been a graduate in the first class at Annapolis, in 1846, and since then an ordnance expert of distinc-tion. The men of his new command found him capable enough, but he "lacked that noble kindness of heart & quiet unassuming manner to both officers & men which endeared Capt. Worden to all on board," thought Keeler.

Stimers stayed with the ship until April 17, working to repair and remodel the pilothouse. He altered it so that its sides, instead of being perpendicular, were now sloping at roughly thirty degrees, so that, greased with tallow, it would glance off all shot and shell. Beyond this, a variety of small arms were brought aboard, including hand grenades, rifles, and bayonets. The men of the *Monitor* would be prepared for anything. Obviously, their greatest fear, as Wor-den's, was of being boarded. With these weapons, they might fight off their attackers.[15]

Even while the two ironclads repaired and refitted, they exercised a considerable influence upon military affairs, particularly the strat-egy of General McClellan's forthcoming spring campaign. It was his intention to take his Army of the Potomac, land it at Fort Monroe, and move up the Peninsula, between the James and York rivers, to take Richmond. The success of the *Virginia* on March 8 endan-gered this plan, since it threatened his base at the fort, but the *Monitor*'s performance the next day changed the picture. "I have such a lively faith in the gallant little Monitor," McClellan told Fox, that he would go ahead as planned. "The Monitor justifies this course." However, he would have to rely upon the York for his water communications, since the *Virginia* could still deny the James to Federal shipping. This was all right, just so long as the Rebel ironclad could not get out of Hampton Roads to the York. On this account, Goldsborough agreed to "neutralize" the *Virginia* if possible. Meanwhile, the Confederates were allowed to think that McClellan would try to move up the James. There followed three weeks of inconclusive waiting, and repeated rumors that the *Virginia* was coming out to fight, while the Confederates regarded themselves and their ship as the "cock of the walk" at Norfolk. No one would dare challenge the *Virginia*.[16]

Then came intelligence of McClellan's intention to change his principal invasion route to the York. This meant that, somehow, Tattnall needed to get his ship out of Hampton Roads and up to the York to be of any use in this campaign. To do so, however, he would have to destroy or capture the *Monitor*. He settled on the latter course. On April 6 he spoke to a council of war with the captains of *Raleigh, Beaufort, Patrick Henry,* and *Jamestown.* He outlined to them the weak spots in the *Monitor*'s defenses and proposed that blankets or sailcloths could stop the smokestack and blind the pilothouse, while wedges driven in at the deck could stop the turret. Bottles of turpentine ignited with matches could then be thrown into the turret through its top and through the stacks. He proposed that the *Virginia* should engage the ironclad's attention, and then at the proper signal the other four ships would surround her and board with gangs of men each assigned a specific task. Some, in addition, were to run hawsers around the tower to secure the ironclad to the other ships so she could not get away. The *Virginia*'s midshipmen dreamed of the glory of capturing the enemy ironclad and returning to Norfolk in triumph. Then they would turn the *Monitor* against New York and Boston. Others were not so sure. One man in the detail to take the *Monitor* recalled that "I . . . would have made out my will but that I had no property." Tattnall, though, was certain, almost obsessed. Stamping up and down the deck of the *Virginia,* he muttered through gritted teeth, "I will take her! I will take her if hell's on the other side of her!"[17]

At 6 A.M., April 11, the *Virginia* and her consorts steamed down the Elizabeth toward Hampton Roads. Tattnall made a brief speech to his men and then said, "Now you go to your stations, and I'll go to mine." His was an armchair he had placed rather foolishly on the top deck. When the ironclad came to Sewell's Point and into view of the Federal ships, Tattnall was disappointed to find that most of the enemy transport ships, which he had hoped to take while fighting the *Monitor,* were snugly anchored outside the Roads and under the guns of Fort Monroe. Still, there were three ships inside the entrance, and these were soon taken by Commander Joseph N. Barney in the *Jamestown.*

The Federals had anticipated the *Virginia*'s advance, and the *Monitor* was ready. She fired a signal gun and steamed slowly toward the Roads. Keeler, on the turret, watched the *Virginia* as she approached the Roads "like some huge gladiator." The Federal ships seemed "like a flock of wild fowl in the act of flight," to some aboard the Rebel ironclad.

In fact, each ironclad hoped to entice the other into making an attack on its own ground. "They stood on the edge of the arena, each hesitating to advance, neither caring to retreat." Tattnall wanted to lure the *Monitor* into his own waters, where not only the *Virginia* and the other ships could attack, but also the batteries at Sewell's Point and Craney Island could come into play. Jeffers, on the other hand, wanted Tattnall to attack him where Fort Monroe's guns could aid in reducing the *Virginia.* Each commander accurately surmised the intentions of his opponent, and just as correctly refused to take the bait. Tattnall actually steamed in a large circle out into the Roads and nearly to Newport News, but Jeffers would not budge. As a result, well into the afternoon the two vessels ranged back and forth at their boundaries. Finally, in disgust, Tattnall hoisted the flags of the captured transports under his own banners as a gesture of contempt, fired a single gun at the *Monitor* as a parting shot of defiance, and steamed to Craney Island for the night. Tattnall, of course, was greatly disappointed. No opportunity even to try his plan for capturing the *Monitor* presented itself, but then, perhaps, that worked in his favor. "It is just as likely that the *Monitor* would have towed us to Fortress Monroe if she had not sunk the whole concern before we reached her," wrote one of the prospective boarders. The Federals, too, were unhappy. Jeffers wanted to take his chances with the *Virginia,* but was restrained by his orders from Goldsborough not to risk his ship, but to protect the entrance to the Roads. "It is a great mistake that superannuated old men are given the control of such important measures," lamented Keeler. If Jeffers were given his head, he would take the *Virginia*. What made matters worse was that the people back in the North, unaware of Goldsborough's orders, could not understand why the *Monitor* declined to fight. "The public are justly indignant at the conduct of our navy in Hampton Roads," declared the press.[18]

Now Mallory asked Tattnall to keep his ship at all times ready to make a dash past the fort and up to the York if possible. The *Virginia*'s captain hardly wanted to do so, for it would leave Norfolk virtually at the mercy of Goldsborough and the *Monitor*. However, despite Sidney Smith Lee's belief that the ironclad was essential to protect Norfolk, his brother Robert E. Lee became more and more convinced that the *Virginia* was needed to help stop McClellan's advance up the Peninsula via the York. According to Ramsay, Tattnall himself finally went to Richmond to decide, with Mallory and Davis, what to do. No record of their meeting exists, but when Tattnall came back, shortly after the April 11 fiasco, he ordered the *Virginia* to get up steam and head for Hampton Roads. After nightfall, the ironclad entered Hampton Roads and was on its way out the channel between Fort Monroe and Rip Raps. Just then, Jones received a lantern signal from one of the batteries on Sewell's Point. "We have been ordered to return, sir," said Jones.

The order came from Major General Benjamin Huger, army commander in Norfolk, and apparently with the authority of the Navy Department. But Tattnall, looking through his glass at the nearing fort, pretended not to hear.

"The order is peremptory," Jones added.

Tattnall seemed to Ramsay to weigh the possibilities of disobeying, but finally he muttered, "Old Huger has outwitted me. Do what you please, I leave you in command. I'm going to bed." Back went the ironclad, never to attempt this passage again. Yet, even stuck in the Elizabeth River where she was, she continued to exercise a powerful influence over Federal strategic thinking as McClellan moved up the Peninsula. The men of the *Virginia* paid for it, though, in boredom and endless routine, interspersed with constant repairs. There was no light and little ventilation inside the ironclad. They had nowhere to walk except on the top of the casemate. "A modern prison is far more comfortable," complained Ramsay. Sometimes the seamen waded in the water that covered the fore and aft decks by a few inches, giving rise to the claim among some of the superstitious slaves ashore that these men of the "debble ship" could walk on water.[19]

Faced by an advancing McClellan, General Joseph E. Johnston, exercising over-all command of Confederate forces on the Peninsula, was forced to withdraw toward Richmond. For a variety of reasons, this made necessary as well the evacuation of Norfolk, and on May 3 Johnston gave the order. In fact, the work of removing stores and machinery from the navy yard had begun several days before. That which could not be taken away would be burned or destroyed, including the buildings and the dry dock. "What a terrible necessity this is," lamented Wood. "This is war, stern, terrible War, which our sires have brought upon us."

To help cover the evacuation, the *Virginia* almost daily went down to the Roads to attract the attention of the enemy. Her only purpose was to show herself, which she did. What the Confederates could not know was that they were showing themselves to someone new, President Abraham Lincoln. At about 8:30 P.M., May 5, Lincoln, Stanton, Chase, and others arrived and immediately went aboard the *Minnesota* to speak with Goldsborough about the *Virginia* and other matters. Lincoln said he wanted the *Monitor* and the ironclad *Galena,* now here, to go up the James to open it to Federal traffic. Goldsborough wanted to wait until he had more ships, but Stanton demanded immediate action. Then the commodore raised the specter of the *Virginia.* There were some reports that her officers and crew had deserted and that she could easily be beaten. "If I can only get a fair crack at the Merrimac, I feel certain of crushing her," he had told Fox. But then, after Lincoln's arrival seemed about to force him into action, Goldsborough suddenly came up with a prediction that the ironclad would be able to get out to do mischief among the Federal ships and perhaps escape to the York.

Lincoln and Stanton gave him no choice. They visited the *Vanderbilt,* now strengthened with an iron ram, and laid plans for the *Virginia*'s destruction. Then a deserter brought word of the evacuation of Norfolk. To put the news to the test, Lincoln ordered Goldsborough to have his ships bombard Sewell's Point to see if the batteries there were still manned and to attempt to lure the *Virginia* out.

On the morning of May 8, Goldsborough's ships, including the *Monitor,* got up steam and headed across the Roads. Lincoln, Stanton, and Chase went by tug to Rip Raps to watch the bombardment. Jeffers took his ship right up to the point, while the other five ships stood behind him and threw their shells into the still-manned earthworks. Soon the ironclad's shells started fires in the enemy's buildings and almost completely silenced their guns. Then, from Rip Raps, Chase saw smoke curling up over the woods some miles down the Elizabeth. "There comes the Merrimac," said someone.

Tattnall had been at the navy yard when he heard the firing, and immediately he got up steam and brought his vessel down the river. It was about 2:45 P.M. when he reached Sewell's Point, to find that the *Monitor* was almost within range. For a brief few minutes, it looked as though there would finally be another battle between the two, but then Goldsborough sent out the signal to "resume moorings," and the entire fleet slowly retired toward Fort Monroe, much to the chagrin of Jeffers and Tattnall both. The *Virginia* stayed out in the Roads until sometime after 4 P.M., and then went to her moorings at a much damaged Sewell's Point. Some, like Littlepage, were relieved that there had been no fight. Tattnall, disgusted that the enemy would not fight, ordered Jones to fire a shot to leeward in defiance. Wood, disappointed that another opportunity to battle the *Monitor* had passed, declared that "it was the most cowardly exhibition I have ever seen . . . Goldsborough & Jeffers are two cowards."[20]

At Norfolk, matters were now frantic. Another ironclad had been under construction for some time there, christened the CSS *Richmond.* It was yet incomplete, and on the night of May 6 the *Jamestown* and *Patrick Henry* managed to tow it out into the Roads and up the James to Richmond without being discovered. To many, it seemed that this was the only course the *Virginia* herself could pursue. On May 9 Tattnall met with six army and two navy officers to agree on what should be done with the ironclad when Norfolk was abandoned. It was their unanimous decision that she should remain off Sewell's Point for the present, preventing the enemy from ascending the Elizabeth. Once Norfolk was thoroughly evacuated, then her best course was to follow the *Richmond* up the

James to the Confederate capital. Pilots assured Tattnall that if he could reduce the ship's draft to eighteen feet, they could get him up the river. Wood agreed with the plan, and even the Federals actually believed the *Virginia* could do it, though Fox, on May 8, doubted that Tattnall would make the attempt.

The Federals were doing a lot of speculating on just what would happen to the *Virginia* now that they knew Norfolk was being abandoned. The attack of May 8 had shown that a movement against Norfolk from that point seemed impractical. Now Chase, and even Lincoln, personally conducted reconnaissances to find a suitable spot for landing troops to move on Norfolk without fear of interference from the *Virginia.* Lincoln himself found it, with the aid of a local pilot, and on the morning of May 10 Wool and four regiments of infantry were landed. Chase accompanied them, and by late that afternoon Norfolk was again a Union-held city. Huger, ready to evacuate anyhow, had withdrawn before Wool with almost no resistance. Alas for Tattnall, he had also withdrawn without giving the agreed-upon signal that would tell the *Virginia* that Norfolk was lost.[21]

On the morning of May 10, at 10 o'clock, Tattnall noticed that there was no flag flying at Sewell's Point and that his signals to the garrison were not answered. He immediately sent Lieutenant J. Pembroke Jones to Craney Island, where the flag was still flying, to find out what had happened, and here Jones learned of the Federals' advance on Norfolk. Sewell's Point had been abandoned. Tattnall sent Jones back up the river to Norfolk to ask Huger and Lee what should be done, but Jones arrived just after Huger had left. Norfolk was in flames, and Wool's force was just half a mile away, advancing unopposed. By the time Jones got back to the *Virginia,* Craney Island, too, had been abandoned.

It was now 7 P.M., and there was little time. Whatever Tattnall did, he must do it this night, or the morning would find him stranded between Federal forces at his back in Norfolk and in his front in Hampton Roads. Going up the James was the only hope. On the assurances of his pilots that the ship could make it to within forty miles of Richmond if properly lightened, he set his crew to work while he, ill, went to bed. Between 1 and 2 A.M., May 11, Catesby Jones awoke Tattnall with ill tidings. By throwing all her ballast overboard, the *Virginia* had been lightened to twenty feet, and the men were still at work disgorging everything but powder and shot from her. But now the pilots had changed their minds. Eighteen feet of draft would get her over the sand bar at the mouth of the James when the wind was blowing from the east, forcing water from the Roads back over the bar. But now the wind was from the west and actually pushed the water away from the bar and into the Roads, making it far more shallow at the bar. They could never get the *Virginia* across.

Now, with nowhere to go, Tattnall also had a ship whose lightened draft made her sit high enough in the water that two feet of unprotected hull was exposed all around, as well as her rudder and propeller. She was just as susceptible as any other wooden ship now. She was, said Ramsay, "now no longer an ironclad." Poor Tattnall had commanded this ship for only forty-five days, during only thirteen of which she was not in dock under repair for one reason or another. Never did he get his opportunity to meet the enemy and make the reputation he so longed for. Now, instead, he faced the undeniable fact that he must destroy her to prevent the ship falling into enemy hands. All his officers concurred in the decision, but it provided small comfort.

Tattnall headed the ship for Craney Island, the best place to land the men for their retreat toward Huger's army at Suffolk. As close to the island as possible, he ran the *Virginia* ashore, and then began debarking the men. Since she was too far from shore for them to wade, the two ship's boats had to go back and forth for hours before her three-hundred-odd men were safely off. Jones and Wood were the last to leave her, as they packed the inflammable cotton and other combustibles and set the powder trains. Midshipman Littlepage, before leaving, happened to see the ship's flags lying out on the gun deck. Taking off his knapsack, he threw out his own clothes in order to pack and save her banners. Then Jones set the match, jumped into the last boat with Wood, and "by the light of our burning ship we pulled for the shore." The ship's company, tired, hungry, dejected, set out on the twenty-two-mile march to Suffolk. As they walked, they could hear behind them the guns of the ironclad discharging as the fires reached them. Then, shortly before 5 A.M., there came a roar that shook the forests and houses for miles around as the fire reached the ship's magazine. Sadly Tattnall reported to Mallory, "The *Virginia* no longer exists."[22]

She "was utterly unseaworthy," Eggleston would write. "She had never been the effective fighting machine that the hopes of her friends and the fears of her enemies had made her." This is true, but still she had been for the Confederacy the first of her kind, a prototype, albeit not the best. Almost all future Rebel ironclads would follow her basic pattern; all would try to live up to the reputation she made in just two days of fighting. Her loss was felt like a hammer blow, particularly following hard on the abandonment of Norfolk and the loss to the South of the vital navy yard and its equipments. Mallory, stricken, could only compensate for the feeling of loss by blaming Tattnall. He had destroyed the ship prematurely, without trying to save her. "May God protect us and cure us of weakness and folly," the Navy Secretary lamented to his diary the night of May 11, 1862. Eventually Tattnall would go before a court-martial to answer for his actions this day. Once all the evidence was in, however, it could do naught but exonerate him. Indeed, it offered him its compliments for his fidelity to duty.[23]

Now, though, all this was in the future. Tattnall marched his men to Suffolk, took the train from there to Petersburg, where they got their first meal in many hours, and then proceeded on to Richmond, arriving on May 12. They had barely arrived in the capital when word came that Goldsborough's fleet was ascending the now unprotected James. Quickly the men of the *Virginia* moved down the river to Drewry's Bluff, the first high ground on the river below Richmond. Here they spent the next two days in the rain and mud mounting the guns that Buchanan had suggested be emplaced back in March. The *Jamestown* and other vessels were sunk in the channel as obstructions. Here, by May 15, when the Federal ships appeared, Catesby Jones and his men had five heavy guns mounted ready to meet them. And only here did the men of the *Virginia* and the *Monitor* meet again in battle, for as the *Monitor* and other ships steamed up to fight at Drewry's Bluff, Littlepage unfurled the *Virginia*'s scarred flags to the breeze once more.[24]

CHAPTER 11

"The *Monitor* Is No More"

The news of Norfolk's fall was received with wild cheers in Golds-borough's fleet off Fort Monroe, and throughout the Union. Of more immediate concern to the men of the *Monitor,* however, was the fate of the *Virginia.* Shortly after 2 A.M., May 11, Keeler saw a bright light over by Craney Island. It increased in brilliance until after 4 A.M., "when a sudden flash & a dull heavy report brought us all on deck to conjecture & Surmise till the morning light should reveal the mysteries of the night." Yet when morning brought the definite news of the *Virginia*'s demise, many, like Keeler, felt a sort of dismay. They had regarded the Rebel ironclad as their special game. They had hoped one day to capture and then examine her in detail. At the worst, they felt that "she would die game rather than fall by her own hand."

Shortly after sunrise, the *Monitor* received orders to proceed up the Elizabeth to Norfolk, which she did, coming to rest at the *Virginia*'s old moorings. Several other ships followed her, the last of them, the *Baltimore,* carrying Chase, Stanton, and Lincoln. As he passed the *Monitor,* the President took off his hat and bowed. Before leaving Norfolk later that day, both Lincoln and the *Monitor* passed by the blackened hulk that was all that remained of the *Virginia.* Keeler and some of the others stopped to take a few souvenirs.[1]

With the fall of the *Virginia,* whole new avenues were opened to the Federals, and little time was wasted. The *Virginia* could no longer protect the James, and Goldsborough immediately ordered the *Monitor,* the *Galena,* and three wooden ships to steam up the river toward Richmond. On May 15 they came to the obstructions in the river at Drewry's Bluff, just eight miles from the Confederate capital. The *Galena* took the lead, the *Monitor* following close behind, and as soon as they came in range of the Rebel batteries the fight started.

Because of the narrowness of the river, the ironclads could not maneuver freely, and finally had to run in close to the batteries and drop anchor. For four hours, from 7:30 A.M. on, they suffered "a perfect tempest of iron raining upon & around us," as Keeler described it. Aboard the *Monitor* everyone remained below deck, and the ship itself took only three, harmless hits. Their only casualties were from heatstroke in the close, foul air. The *Galena,* however, took a terrible beating. The Confederate balls began to penetrate her iron sides as the men of the *Virginia* concentrated the fire of their guns upon her.

The *Virginia*'s men, led by Jones, were so exhausted that many of them carelessly exposed themselves. Jones actually dozed while sitting on a shell box next to his gun. Then, about 11 A.M., Littlepage saw a flash come out of the *Galena*'s gun ports, and immediately after, a signal was raised from her halyards. He awakened Jones, and they agreed that one of their shells must have penetrated to her powder room and that she was now signaling to pull out of the action.

In fact, what Littlepage saw was just the explosion of one of the Confederate shells inside the *Galena*, but she was pulling out just the same, her ammunition nearly exhausted. Seeing the ironclad's plight, Jeffers had steamed the *Monitor* ahead of her briefly to draw the enemy fire but discovered that his own guns could not be elevated sufficiently to train them on the Rebel batteries. After a few minutes more, both ships pulled out of the fight and steamed back down to City Point, on the James. The *Galena* was proved a failure as an ironclad, with eleven men wounded and thirteen killed in the fight. Keeler went aboard her after the action. "She looked like a slaughter house . . . of human beings," he wrote, spattered everywhere with brains and blood and pieces of limbs.

This had been Jeffers' first action in the *Monitor* and, true to his personality, he found a great deal of fault with his ship. He complained of having little control over the guns from the pilothouse, while in the smoke of battle he could not see the effect his firing was having so as to correct the turret's aim. He was only able to aim accurately by himself going out exposed on top of the turret and, placing himself above the gun ports, sighting along the joint lines of the iron plates. His only protection was a barrier of hammocks to absorb the enemy rifle fire. Then too, both guns could not be fired at the same time, and the ports so confined the guns that their muzzles could not be elevated toward high targets. Perhaps worse, because of inadequate ventilation in battle and under steam, the heat in the turret stood at 140° during the fight. In all, he did not entertain a high opinion of his ship, even fearing that she was not fit to engage another ironclad and that, despite her "exaggerated" success at Hampton Roads, "for general purposes wooden ships . . . have not yet been superseded."[2]

The *Monitor* did, indeed, need repairs and refitting, but it would be a long time before she got them. Goldsborough—"old Guts" he was called, in derision of his girth—would not let her go. Instead, the summer months passed, for the most part, in utter boredom for her crew. A few minor repairs were made on the spot, though Jeffers rejected a number of suggestions from Ericsson. Flies and mosquitoes settled in the ship's bowels in the summer heat, making the men miserable, while the humidity forced some of them, like Keeler, to prefer sleeping outside on the iron deck. There was a small fire aboard in June, with little damage, a visit from Lincoln again in July, and a visit from a photographer that same month that turned most of the officers and men out for photos in front of the turret. Meanwhile, just as in the days before the *Virginia* first sortied from Norfolk, rumors constantly came down the river that the Confederate ironclad *Richmond*—called by many the *Merrimack II* —would be coming to attack. "Some of us will die off one of these days with *Merrimac*-on-the-brain," wrote Keeler. "The disease is raging furiously."[3]

Finally, in August, the *Monitor* was rid of the much disliked Jeffers. "The *Monitor* under her present commander will never be what she was under Capt. Worden," lamented Keeler in June. "We have all been greatly disappointed in our present Captain. He will sit at the table & entertain us with plans of the most magnificent conception, but he is most sadly deficient either in ability or power to carry them out." In April the ship's crew had actually sent Worden a letter expressing their sorrow that he was not still with them.

"Since you left us we have had no pleasure on Board of the *Monitor*," they said. "We once was happy on Board of our little *Monitor*." Finally, on August 9, the Navy Department relieved Jeffers, replacing him temporarily with Commander Thomas Stevens, a capable and experienced officer much more to the liking of everyone aboard.[4]

Finally, on September 30, 1862, orders came directing the ironclad to proceed to the navy yard at Washington for repairs. Her bottom was so fouled with marine growth that she had to be towed there by a tug, but she arrived in good order on October 3, and under her fourth, and final, captain. On September 11 Stevens had turned the ship over to Commander John P. Bankhead, a forty-one-year-old South Carolinian who had remained loyal to the Union. He was a cousin to General John Bankhead Magruder. For nearly six weeks the ship would remain at the capital, most of the men taking well-earned furloughs while the *Monitor* saw some changes made. Davits and cranes were added to hold new ship's boats, the old smokestacks were replaced with new, telescoping ones, and the shot marks from enemy balls were covered with iron patches. Markings were placed on each patch, "Merrimac," "Merrimac's Prow," "Minnesota," to show the source of the dent. And on the guns, words were engraved.

"MONITOR & MERRIMAC   WORDEN" on one, and
"MONITOR & MERRIMAC   ERICSSON" on the other.

As would be expected, the *Monitor* proved quite a tourist attraction while at Washington. Carriages lined the wharves to look at her, and on the one day that the ship was thrown open to visitors, her decks were jammed for hours. "Our decks were covered & our ward room filled with ladies," wrote Keeler, "& on going into my state room I found a party of the 'dear delightful creatures' making their toilet before my glass, using my combs & brushes. We couldn't go to any part of the vessel without coming in contact with petticoats. There appeared to be a general turn out of the sex in the city, there were women with children & women without children, & women—hem—expecting, an extensive display of lower extremities was made going up & down our steep ladders." When the day was over, the men discovered that the visitors had taken souvenirs. "When we came up to clean that night," wrote Stodder, "there was not a key, doorknob, escutcheon—there wasn't a thing that hadn't been carried away."[5]

By early November, the *Monitor* was back at anchor off Newport News, looking to the prospect of a dull winter. A few more improvements were made aboard ship. At Keeler's suggestion, work was begun on an iron "breastwork," or shield, to go around the top of the turret to protect those standing on it from enemy rifle fire. Meanwhile, rumors came in that the ship would soon be sent off to the south, perhaps to South Carolina, to assist the blockading fleet there. They were expecting the first of the new "Monitor" class of ironclads, patterned after their ship, to arrive shortly, one of them now commanded by a recovered Worden. And then Christmas came. The officers sat at their holiday dinner for three hours in the wardroom, talking long and loud, making plans, and winning the war in a variety of ways. It was jovially decided that when the South was conquered, the ironclads would divide it up and reign over the various states. "In fact," said Keeler, "we arrived at the conclusion that the Star Spangled Banner next to us 'iron clads' is about the 'biggest thing' to be found just now outside of Barnum's Museum."[6]

On December 25, Christmas Day, orders were received to take the *Monitor* in tow under the USS *Rhode Island* and proceed south to Beaufort, North Carolina, to assist with the blockade there. Bad weather held up the departure until December 29, when the two ships steamed off at 2 P.M. on a smooth sea. Just hours after they left, Worden arrived with the *Montauk,* barely missing the last opportunity he would ever have to see his old ship.

The first evening out proved a beautiful one, and the men felt high spirits at the prospect of seeing a new field of operations and an opportunity for more action. But, the next morning, clouds were seen off to the south and west, and the wind increased throughout the day. Still, the ship remained watertight and weathered the rising swells. The officers sat down to their supper at 5 P.M. as usual, laughing and joking, and altogether presenting a perfect picture of conviviality and confidence. Then, between seven-thirty and eight the wind rose ferociously, causing the waves to dash across the deck and break against the turret and pilothouse with terrible force. It was too dangerous for anyone to remain outside the ship. As the vessel rose in the swell, her wooden hull at times coming out of the water, she fell back with a mighty thump, jarring the whole ship and loosening the joint between the hull and the iron deck. Now water began coming in through several openings. The pumps were started, but they could not keep up with the leaks, even when a pump that could handle three thousand gallons a minute was put in operation. The cracks opened, widened constantly under the unrelenting beating of the storm. A few anxious men stood behind the breastwork atop the turret, awaiting the report from the pumps below. "The water is gaining on us, Sir," it came, again and again. Finally, at ten-thirty, Bankhead had no choice but to signal to the *Rhode Island* that he was in distress and needed assistance.

By now, bucket brigades were at work bailing even as the pumps worked. The water was a foot deep in the engine room and was rising rapidly in other parts of the ship. Soon it would extinguish the boiler fires, leaving her helpless. At the signal flare, the *Rhode Island* tried to come back alongside, but the hawser by which she had been towing the ironclad made it difficult. Stodder volunteered to go forward with a hatchet and cut the line. Two men followed him, and both were swept overboard by a giant wave as Stodder began hacking at the thirteen-inch line. "It was not an easy job, and while I was hacking at it a big sea came over the bow," wrote Stodder. He managed to hold on and finish the job.

Bankhead continued to signal to the now freed *Rhode Island,* but now she did not seem to hear his hailing. "Send your boats immediately, we are sinking," he cried. Again and again this and the flare signals were repeated, with no sign of recognition. "Words cannot depict the agony of those moments as our little company gathered on the top of the turret, stood with a mass of sinking iron beneath them, gazing through the dim light, over the raging waters with an anxiety amounting almost to agony for some evidence of succor from the only source to which we could look for relief," wrote Keeler. "Seconds lengthened into hours & minutes into years."

Now the water had come up to the furnaces, extinguishing the fires. To attempt to curtail the ship's pitching in the seas, Bankhead ordered the anchor dropped. This helped steady her somewhat, but it also jarred some watertight packing out of the hawse hole, and now more water poured in through it and into the wardroom. Keeler now led a bailing party in the futile attempt to keep up with the rising water level. Meanwhile, some of the men, seeing that the

Rhode Island was not responding to their signals, felt abandoned, and actually wanted to fire on her in their desperation.

Finally, through the gloom they sighted boats approaching. They would be saved. Hoping to bring away his pay records and the money entrusted to his keeping as paymaster, Keeler went below a last time. It was pitch-dark in the turret and, feeling for the hatchway down to the berth deck, he actually fell through it. Lanterns dimly lit the berth deck, and by their hazy light he groped his way to his cabin, now waist-deep in water. "It was a darkness that could be felt," he wrote. "The hot, stifling, murky atmosphere pervaded every corner." He managed to gather his books and papers, but then found that they were so bulky and unmanageable that the attempt to save them might endanger his own chances. Reluctantly, he left them behind. He did save his watch, and took the key to the safe containing the Federal "greenbacks" entrusted to him, only to find that in the darkness he could not work the lock. Now it was time to get out. Overhead, he could hear the crashing of the waves over the deck. Before him lay a dark, narrow passage through the wardroom in which the deep, rolling water and the mass of floating and bobbing furniture threatened to injure him if caught in their violent surging. Groping his way through the hazardous dark, he finally regained the top of the turret.

Nearly everyone was out of the ship's interior now, but Bankhead sent a man below to look for anyone left. One man, seasick, was lying in his bunk, watching the water rise, almost resigned to dying. "Is there any hope?" the sailor asked. Bankhead's man answered that, of course, there was, but unaccountably he went on without trying to get the sick man up and out. He would die where he lay. Master's Mate George Frederickson gave back a watch he had borrowed from Quartermaster Williams. "Here, this is yours; I may be lost," he said. Before the night was over, he was.

Francis Butts stationed himself in the turret to bail all alone, to the accompaniment of the wailing of the ship's cat. Annoyed by it, he put the cat in the barrel of a gun and stuffed a wad in after it, but still he heard the mournful sound. Then, in the act of handing up another bucket of water, he found that there was no one on top of the turret to take it.

Just before Keeler went below, the first boat from the *Rhode Island* came alongside, followed by the steamer herself. She actually

got too close in the rough seas and nearly crushed the lifeboat between herself and the *Monitor*. Then she pulled away, and Bankhead ordered his men to start filling the boat. Keeler was to lead the
first party, which meant leaving the safety of the turret, descending
the companion ladder down its side, and braving a walk across the
open deck with no protection from the waves. Immediately, a wave
passed over, carrying Keeler clear away from the ship and ten or
twelve yards beyond, and then another dashed him back against the
ironclad's side. He managed to grab one of the deck stanchions and
hold on, and then slowly and carefully made his way to the lifeboat
and jumped in. Others had already gotten in, and soon they were on
their way to the *Rhode Island*.

Coming up out of the turret, Butts saw another of the lifeboats
alongside, loading with men. Some of them had to gauge the waves,
as they lifted and dropped the lifeboat, and then jump. A few misjudged, and instead of landing in the boat, dived into the sea, from
which it was nearly impossible to rescue anyone. Butts also found a
few men still on the turret after all, men terrified at the sight of their
shipmates who had been washed over the side and drowned while
trying to reach the lifeboat. They preferred to take their chances
aboard the sinking ship rather than brave the passage across the
deck.

Now the last men headed for the lifeboat. Truscott went down
the companion ladder, a friend ahead of him, and they ran for the
lifeboat. Then the friend jumped, missed the boat, barely managed
to yell out, "Oh, God," and disappeared beneath the surface. Truscott made it safely, leaving only Butts, Bankhead, and one or two
others aboard the ship, except for those, clinging to the turret, who
would not leave. Bankhead and Butts were both carried overboard
by a wave, yet each managed to stay afloat long enough to be pulled
into the lifeboat by Greene, who had himself only been saved simi-
larly sometime before by being thrown a line by the new ship's surgeon, Dr. Grenville M. Weeks. Then they were off.

Bankhead had begged the men still clinging to the turret to take
their chance on getting to the lifeboat, but they refused. As he set
off now, the men of the *Rhode Island* who were managing it promised to come back one more time to take them to safety. "As we
pulled away," recalled Truscott, "I saw in the darkness some black

forms I knew to be men clinging to the top of the turret." He was perhaps the last to see them alive.

Once in the lifeboats, the passage to the *Rhode Island* was perilous in itself, particularly when the boats came alongside the towering hull of the steamer. The waves threatened to dash them against its sides, throwing all into the sea. Most of the men who could had to haul themselves up by ropes let over the sides, while others, such as Keeler, who had hurt his hand, were pulled up by looping ropes around themselves. Dr. Weeks had let his right arm dangle over the side of the lifeboat, and a sudden wave brought the boat crashing against the side of the *Rhode Island* to crush three of his fingers and dislocate the arm at the shoulder. "An arm was a small price to pay for life," he would write.

Once aboard the steamer, the orphaned seamen received the kindest treatment, warm blankets, dry clothing, hot coffee and food. Weeks's ruined fingers were carefully amputated and his shoulder set by the ship's surgeon. Most of the men, even the wounded Weeks, then lined the steamer's rail to look for their ship. In the darkness they could see the red and white lights hanging above the turret. A score of times they disappeared, blocked by the high seas, only to reappear. Huddled under those lights, invisible in the gloom and distance, a few men still clung to life. The *Rhode Island*'s boat had gone back for them, but lost its course in the storm. Twice it got close to the *Monitor,* but was pulled away abruptly by the raging water. A third time it headed for the ironclad, to find nothing but an eddy "apparently produced by a sinking vessel." The lifeboat and its crew would be found and themselves rescued the next day.

Finally, about 1 A.M., December 31, 1862, the men on the *Rhode Island* saw the ironclad's lights disappear for the last time. For long minutes, they looked in vain for them to reappear. They did not. Almost within sight of land, she sank in 220 feet of water, fifteen miles south of Cape Hatteras, North Carolina. As she slowly settled toward the bottom, she turned over and the turret came loose, touching bottom first, while the hull settled at an angle on top of it. All this, of course, was unknown to the men on the *Rhode Island,* but one thing Keeler and the others did know: "The *Monitor* is no more."[7]

CHAPTER 12

"Ram Fever"

Interestingly enough, neither the *Monitor* nor the *Virginia* lived to see a first anniversary. Neither went down in glorious battle. Neither was able fully to test her potential. Yet both proved something of vital importance in this war, and for all of naval history to come. The Confederate ship displayed conclusively that wooden ships, no matter how powerful their armament, were no match for ironclads. Ericsson's vessel went further yet, to show that only an iron ship could stop another iron ship, and that speed, mobility, a low target profile, and a 360° radius of fire for even a few guns, were more than a match for sheer size and weight and numbers of guns. The *Virginia* proved a case study in the potential—and limitations—of ersatz shipbuilding for a Confederacy that would always have to make do with the materials at hand. The *Monitor* brought together the most innovative yet unproven ideas of a number of inventive people to provide for the world a model for the warship of the future.

Both of the warring sections in this conflict followed substantially the patterns set by these two ships. The ironclads of the Confederacy varied little from the *Virginia,* largely because constructor Porter himself designed most of them. The number of guns varied, but, beyond that, all were built upon the casemated design of the *Virginia,* incorporating a few improvements, among them the abandonment of the submerged fore and after decks. Two ships were begun, late in the war, that featured two casemates, one fore and one aft, mounting pivot guns to fire out of eight different ports, but they were never completed. In February 1865 Mallory even authorized the construction of a Confederate model based on the *Monitor,* but the war ended before any work started. In all, during the war, the Confederate Navy began or planned some fifty ironclads, of which twenty-two actually were commissioned. None of them ever really escaped the problems that plagued the *Virginia*—lack of materials, bad engines, low speed, poor maneuverability. As for their contribution to the southern war effort, it lay more in the fear they generated in Federal officers than in actual damage done. As Keeler noted, *"Merrimac*-on-the-brain," or "ram fever," as some called it, raged through Union naval circles throughout the war. The fears of what the Rebel ironclads might do far exceeded anything that they might have done, and so, in its peculiar way, did much to preserve ports and rivers protected by these dread rams from attack. But of course the Confederacy failed, and as it died, so did the Confederate ironclad. Conceived and built for a specific purpose at a specific time, its usefulness died with its cause. It had little or nothing to offer to the future.[1]

Not so the *Monitor*. She, too, served as a prototype, and yet she was only a beginning. After her, sixty more "monitors" were built, her name becoming the sobriquet for all turreted ironclads built after her. Their variety was great, going to two and even three turrets per vessel. As was the practice when building wooden ships, the Navy Department frequently built several ships of the same model, or "class," all of them being designated after a single ship. Thus the *Passaic* class followed immediately after the *Monitor* itself. Worden's *Montauk* was one of them, and they were almost identical to his first ship. Then came the *Miantonomoh* class, four ships with double turrets, and following it the *Canonicus* class, substantially an improvement on the original *Monitor* design, incorporating improvements based on her battle experience. A failure followed in the *Casco* class, twenty ironclads largely based on designs by Stimers that proved barely serviceable. Five actually had their turrets left off to make them at all useful. After *Casco* came the *Kalamazoo*, a class of 345-foot giants, and the *Neosho, Marietta,* and finally the *Milwaukee* class. The last, the Milwaukees, were by far the greatest refinement of the monitor design in the Civil War. Double-turreted, one of them was an Ericsson turret much like that on the original *Monitor*. The other was designed by a more agreeable engineering genius, James B. Eads, whom Ericsson regarded as a fraud who paid others to think for him. It featured a gun platform inside of, and free of, the revolving turret itself. This platform mechanically lowered into the ship for loading, and then steam engines raised it to the gun ports, providing maximum efficiency with a minimum of human labor and risk. Beyond these classes, several single monitors of other design were produced, including the three-turreted *Roanoke,* and a few ships actually designed for ocean travel. The service that these ships performed aided the Union war effort materially. From 1863 until the end, almost every port taken by the Federals in their ever-tightening grasp on the Confederate seacoast, was taken in part by monitors. They fought, served, and sometimes sank in virtually every river and harbor of the South as the Union waged its war to victory. In the process, they battled again with the Confederacy's casemated monsters but, as in the fight at Hampton Roads on March 9, the results were generally inconclusive. The time when one iron ship could sink or destroy another must wait for the future and the development of more powerful guns and shells.

That time came, of course, thanks to what the *Monitor* and the *Virginia* began. After March 8–9, 1862, no major naval power in the world was safe, even against a second- or third-rate nation, if that lesser power's fleet could boast an ironclad. Consequently, all the world's great navies not already engaged in testing ironclads rushed to the making of ships of iron and steel. For a time they still built on the conventional, old frigate design, but as the years passed, more and more they came around to lower, sleeker, turreted warships. From mere coast-defense ships, the ironclad passed quickly to a seagoing warship. By the end of the century, wood was used only for interior construction, as the hulls themselves were made from steel. Yet they still displayed most of the basic elements that Ericsson combined in the *Monitor:* revolving gun turrets, low profiles, speed and maneuverability instead of mammoth weight for its own sake, and a few guns of immense power rather than whole broadsides of weaker caliber. And so it would continue, on into the modern battleship of the twentieth century, and even beyond to the time when technology developed weapons of war more devastating than the shell gun. From now until the end of time, no matter what their armament, warships will be of steel. This, and so much more, they owe in large part to those now seemingly primitive ironclads that battled like gladiators in Hampton Roads, Virginia, in 1862.

Of course, the war went on for the crews that manned those

ships. Most of their officers stayed in the ironclad service, though some did not. Lieutenant John Taylor Wood, in command of the privateer *Tallahassee,* eventually became one of the most dreaded of Confederate commerce raiders as he preyed upon Federal shipping. Minor went on to a desk job in the Navy Department in Richmond for a time. Littlepage, after serving aboard the ironclad *Chattahoochee* in Florida, went on a diplomatic mission to France hoping to induce the French to build ironclads for the Confederacy. His greatest contribution to the cause came in the 1890s, when, working for the United States Navy Department, he undertook the collection and copying of the personal Civil War papers of almost every major Confederate naval officer of the war. To his efforts, as much as anyone's, is due the amount of material available to historians for the study of the Confederate Navy.

Jones, made a captain, went to command other ships, and finally directed the Confederate cannon foundry at Selma, Alabama. After the war, he was one of the first of the *Virginia*'s officers to attempt to set down a true history of her career. Tattnall, though exonerated in his court-martial, never personally commanded another ship, instead finishing the war in charge of the naval defenses of Georgia. Buchanan, on the other hand, following his slow recovery and appointment as admiral, went on to command the CSS *Tennessee,* an ironclad almost as feared as the *Virginia*. With it and a small fleet, he defended Mobile Bay, Alabama, against the Federal fleet of David G. Farragut until August 1864. Then, in combat with, among others, the monitor *Tecumseh* and a much repaired *Galena,* his ship was rammed and forced to surrender. Buchanan had, at least, the small satisfaction of seeing the fight end with his ship still afloat, while the *Tecumseh* sank thanks to yet another innovation with great potential for the future, an underwater mine.

The men who fought the *Virginia*'s valiant crew, the men of the *Monitor,* also spread in divergent directions following their rescue and reassignment. Stimers finally fell out not only with the Navy Department over his *Casco* class of monitors, but with Ericsson as well. Keeler, Greene, and Bankhead would all subsequently serve on the USS *Florida,* a conventional side-wheel steamer that Bankhead would command while Greene served as his executive officer. Greene eventually died by his own hand in 1884, and Bankhead died four years after the war, still in the service. The ever-quotable

Keeler eventually moved to Florida after the war, said little about his naval service, and instead styled himself "major" until his death in 1886. Stodder lived well into the twentieth century, the last surviving officer of his ship. Jeffers went to a desk job in the Navy's Bureau of Ordnance after he left the *Monitor,* while Captain Stevens eventually rose to rear admiral following a distinguished career. As for John L. Worden, he too rose to rear admiral before his death in 1897. After commanding the *Montauk* until June 1863, he served out the war with sight in only one eye, and afterward commanded the Naval Academy at Annapolis for five years. He was one of the chief movers in 1882 in an attempt to have Congress grant the surviving crew of the *Monitor* some two hundred thousand dollars in prize money for the destruction of the *Virginia.* Quite a battle was waged in the press over how much real influence the ironclad had on Tattnall's destruction of his own ship, and the bill eventually failed.

And the great iron ships themselves? The *Virginia* did not remain for long where her crew left her. She sat where she was until the end of the war, and then in 1868 the work of salvaging portions of her began. The iron prow was recovered, along with some of her plate, the drive shaft, and some of her machinery. In 1874 and 1875 the work resumed, this time conducted by the Baker brothers of Norfolk, who originally raised the *Merrimack* for conversion into the *Virginia.* They brought up cannon and several tons of other metal, and then raised the remainder of her hull and towed it into the same dry dock from which the ironclad had emerged in 1862. There she was cut up for scrap, but fortunately some of her parts, including the anchor, the drive shaft, and a few dented armor plates, survived to end up eventually in museums. The *Virginia* ended exactly where she began.[2]

Not so the *Monitor.* Safe where she sank from salvors and souvenir hunters, she would remain the object of considerable curiosity, and occasional searches, for well over a century. Many times, hunters believed they had found her, only to lose the scent. Then, in 1973, a group of marine scientists studying the ocean floor off Cape Hatteras in the ship *Eastward* located a wreck on the bottom. The harsh currents made underwater photographing of the hulk difficult, but, in September, it was tentatively announced that this might be the *Monitor.* After another five months of scrutiny, further photographic probings, and careful analysis, the team of National Geographic Society and Duke University scientists declared their belief that this was definitely the *Monitor*.

It is a historical find of the century. Its discoverers hope eventually to be able to raise all or part of the hulk, though it lies in a difficult and dangerous place for underwater work. Also, present technology may not be capable of adequately protecting the ship from disintegrating during salvage, or of preserving the remains from deterioration once raised. But if not, she will be safe enough in the watery home that has held her for over a century, until man shall develop the necessary tools and experience to bring her up. And then, perhaps, like the Phoenix, the *Monitor* will rise again.

DOCUMENTATION BY CHAPTER

CHAPTER 1

1. John Taylor Wood, "The First Fight of Ironclads," in Robert U. Johnson and C. C. Buel, eds., *Battles and Leaders of the Civil War* (New York, 1887–88), I, p. 696.
2. William N. Still, *Iron Afloat: The Story of the Confederate Armorclads* (Nashville, 1971), p. 24.
3. Robert W. Daly, ed., *Aboard the USS Monitor, 1862: The Letters of Acting Paymaster William Frederick Keeler* (Annapolis, 1964), p. 28.

CHAPTER 2

1. Wood, "First Fight," p. 692; *American Annual Cyclopaedia and Register of Important Events, 1861* (New York, 1862), pp. 502–3.
2. G. A. Ballard, "British Battleships of the 1870's: the *Warrior* and *Black Prince*," *Mariner's Mirror*, XVI (April 1930), pp. 168–86; John Ericsson, "The Building of the 'Monitor,'" in *Battles and Leaders*. I, p. 730; Edward A. S., Duke of Somerset, "The Merrimac and Monitor," *Southern Historical Society Papers*, XVI (1888), pp. 218–20. This last periodical is hereafter cited as *SHSP*.
3. *American Annual Cyclopaedia, 1861*, pp. 504, 508.
4. John S. Long, "The Gosport Affair," *Journal of Southern History*, XXIII (May 1957), pp. 155–72; Howard K. Beale, ed., *Diary of Gideon Welles* (New York, 1960), I, pp. 41–46; John Niven, *Gideon Welles, Lincoln's Secretary of the Navy* (New York, 1973), pp. 340–45.
5. Richmond *Daily Enquirer*, April 22, 1861.
6. Joseph T. Durkin, *Stephen R. Mallory, Confederate Navy Chief* (Chapel Hill, N.C., 1954), pp. 63–64, 150; James D. Bulloch, *The Secret Service of the Confederate States in Europe* (New York, 1884), I, pp. 41, 46–48; U. S. Navy Department, *Official Records of the Un-*

ion and Confederate Navies in the War of the Rebellion (Washington, 1894–1922), Series II, Volume 2, p. 69. This last source will hereafter be cited as *O.R.N.*, with series and volume references listed as in *O.R.N.*, II, 2, p. 69.

7. Still, *Iron Afloat*, pp. 10–11; George M. Brooke, Jr., "John Mercer Brooke, Naval Scientist," unpublished doctoral dissertation, University of North Carolina library, Chapel Hill, II, p. 760.

8. *O.R.N.*, II, 1, p. 783; Brooke, "Brooke," II, p. 763.

9. John M. Brooke, "The Plan and Construction of the 'Merrimac,'" *Battles and Leaders*, I, pp. 715–16; John M. Brooke, "The Virginia or Merrimac: Her Real Projector," *SHSP*, XIX (1891), pp. 3–5.

10. Brooke, "Plan and Construction," p. 716; *O.R.N.*, II, 2, p. 174.

11. John W. H. Porter, *A Record of Events in Norfolk County, Virginia, from April 19th, 1861, to May 10th, 1862* (Portsmouth, Va., 1892), pp. 327–31; James P. Baxter, *The Introduction of the Ironclad Warship* (Cambridge, Mass., 1933), pp. 226–27.

12. *O.R.N.*, II, 1, p. 783; *O.R.N.*, II, 2, p. 174; Brooke, "Brooke," II, pp. 771–73; Richmond *Enquirer*, March 29, 1862.

13. Brooke, "Plan and Construction," p. 716; Porter, *Norfolk County*, pp. 331–32; *O.R.N.*, II, 1, p. 784; *O.R.N.*, II, 2, pp. 147–75.

14. Porter, *Norfolk County*, pp. 333–34; Brooke, "Plan and Construction," p. 716; *O.R.N.*, II, 2, p. 175.

15. Boston *Evening Transcript*, June 14, 1855; *O.R.N.*, II, 1, pp. 141–42; Edward E. Barthell, Jr., *The Mystery of the Merrimack* (Muskegon, Mich., 1959), pp. 29–30.

CHAPTER 3

1. Niven, *Welles*, pp. 364–65; *Congressional Globe*, 37th Congress, 1st Session (Washington, 1861), p. 347.

2. Gideon Welles, "The First Iron-Clad Monitor," in *Annals of the War* (Philadelphia, 1879), p. 18; *American Annual Cyclopaedia, 1861*, pp. 503–5.

3. C. S. Bushnell to Gideon Welles, March 9, 1877, Gideon Welles Papers, Henry E. Huntington Library, San Marino, Calif. This is also published in *Battles and Leaders*, I, pp. 748–49.

4. See William C. Church, *The Life of John Ericsson* (New York, 1890), I, and Michael Lamm, "The Hot Air Era," *American History Illustrated*, IX (October 1974), pp. 18–23.

5. John Ericsson, "The Monitors," *Century Illustrated Monthly*

Magazine, XXXI (December 1885), p. 298; Ericsson, "Building of the 'Monitor,'" pp. 731–44; David R. Ellis, *The Monitor of the Civil War* (n.p., n.d.), pp. 5–6; "Who Planned the Monitor," *Blackwood's Magazine*, CLXXVII (June 1862), pp. 787–89; Church, *Ericsson*, I, pp. 246–47, 274–75.

6. Bushnell to Welles, March 9, 1877, Welles Papers; Welles, "First Iron-Clad," pp. 18–19; Beale, *Diary of Gideon Welles*, I, p. 214; Ericsson, "Building of the 'Monitor,'" pp. 731–32; "Negotiations for the Building of the 'Monitor,'" *Battles and Leaders*, I, p. 750; Niven, *Welles*, pp. 366–69.

7. Robert MacBride, *Civil War Ironclads* (New York, 1962), pp. 13–14; Beale, *Diary of Gideon Welles*, III, pp. 412–14; Welles, "First Iron-Clad," p. 20; William Tindall, "The True Story of the Virginia and the Monitor," *Virginia Magazine of History and Biography*, XXXI (January 1923), p. 16n.

8. Welles, "First Iron-Clad," pp. 19, 21–22; Beale, *Diary of Gideon Welles*, I, pp. 213–15; Bushnell to Welles, March 9, 1877, Welles Papers; Ellis, *Monitor*, pp. 14–15.

CHAPTER 4

1. *O.R.N.*, I, 5, p. 801; Frances L. Williams, *Matthew Fontaine Maury, Scientist of the Sea* (New Brunswick, N.J., 1963), p. 370; J. F. Shipp, "The Famous Battle of Hampton Roads," *Confederate Veteran*, XXIV (July 1916), p. 305.

2. H. Ashton Ramsay, "Most Famous of Sea Duels: The *Merrimac* and *Monitor*," *Harper's Weekly*, February 10, 1912, p. 11.

3. *O.R.N.*, I, 5, p. 806; *O.R.N.*, II, 2, pp. 77–78, 90, 92.

4. Brooke, "Real Projector," pp. 14–15; Still, *Iron Afloat*, pp. 18–19; Asheville (N.C.) *Times*, Ausust 22, 1926; John S. Wise, *The End of an Era* (Boston, 1902), pp. 191–93; *O.R.N.*, II, 1, p. 757.

5. Baxter, *The Introduction of the Ironclad Warship*, p. 226; *O.R.N.*, II, 2, p. 272.

6. J. Thomas Scharf, *History of the Confederate States Navy* (New York, 1887), p. 152; Porter, *Norfolk County*, pp. 334–35.

7. *O.R.N.*, II, 2, p. 152; *O.R.N.*, II, 1, p. 802; *O.R.N.*, I, 6, p. 772; John B. Jones, *A Rebel War Clerk's Diary* (New York, 1961—reprint), p. 52.

8. Ramsay, "Most Famous of Sea Duels," p. 11; H. Ashton Ramsay, "Interesting Data About the Merrimac," *Confederate Veteran*, XVI (April 1908), p. xvii; *O.R.N.*, I, 7, pp. 758–59.

9. *O.R.N.*, I, 6, p. 728; *O.R.N.*, II, 2, p. 175.

10. Charles B. Dew, *Ironmaker to the Confederacy: Joseph R. Anderson and the Tredegar Iron Works* (New Haven, Conn., 1966), pp. 115–16; Scharf, *Confederate States Navy*, p. 153.

11. Dew, *Ironmaker*, pp. 116–17.

12. *O.R.N.*, II, 1, pp. 785–86; T. Catesby Jones, "The Iron-Clad Virginia," *Virginia Magazine of History and Biography*, XLIX (October 1941), pp. 298–301; Catesby ap R. Jones to Robert D. Minor, September 1861, Minor Family Papers, Virginia Historical Society, Richmond.

13. Charleston (S.C.) *Mercury*, October 30, 1861; Virgil Carrington Jones, *The Civil War at Sea* (New York, 1960), I, p. 390.

14. Dew, *Ironmaker*, pp. 117–18; *O.R.N.*, I, 6, p. 744; *O.R.N.*, II, 2, p. 152.

15. *O.R.N.*, I, 6, pp. 731–32, 743; Dew, *Ironmaker*, pp. 118–19, 130; Wood, "First Fight," p. 694.

16. Wood, "First Fight," pp. 694–95; *O.R.N.*, I, 6, pp. 728, 766.

17. Wood, "First Fight," p. 696; Ramsay, "Most Famous of Sea Duels," p. 11; Sumner B. Besse, *The C.S. Ironclad Virginia: With Data and References for a Scale Model* (Newport News, Va., 1937), pp. 17–20; Richmond *Examiner*, April 3, 1862; Scharf, *Confederate States Navy*, pp. 152–53n; Catesby ap R. Jones, "Services of the 'Virginia' (Merrimac)," *SHSP*, XI (February–March 1883), p. 66; Brooke, "Brooke," II, p. 811.

18. Charleston (S.C.) *Mercury*, March 19, 1862; Ramsay, "Most Famous of Sea Duels," p. 11.

19. John R. Eggleston, "Captain Eggleston's Narrative of the Battle of the Merrimac," *SHSP*, XLI, p. 168; Wise, *End of an Era*, pp. 194–95.

20. Porter, *Norfolk County*, p. 338.

21. Ibid.; William R. Cline, "The Ironclad Ram Virginia—Confederate States Navy," *SHSP*, XXXII (1904), pp. 243–44.

22. Porter, *Norfolk County*, pp. 334–37.

23. Brooke, "Brooke," II, p. 814; William Norris, "The Story of the Confederate States Ship 'Virginia' (Once Merrimac)," *SHSP*, XLII (October 1917), p. 205.

24. Porter, *Norfolk County*, p. 336; Hardin B. Littlepage, Memoirs, in possession of Jon Nielson, Orono, Maine, pp. 6–7; Wise, *End of an Era*, pp. 193–94.

25. Brooke, "Real Projector," p. 31; *O.R.N.*, II, 1, p. 784; Richmond *Examiner*, April 3, 1862; Wise, *End of an Era*, p. 194; Porter, *Norfolk County*, p. 356; Scharf, *Confederate States Navy*, p. 151.

26. *O.R.N.*, II, 2, pp. 175, 271.

27. John Taylor Wood to Mrs. Wood, March 26, 1862, John Taylor Wood Papers, Southern Historical Collection, University of North Carolina library, Chapel Hill; Still, *Iron Afloat,* pp. 23–24; *O.R.N.,* I, 21, p. 898.

28. Beale, *Diary of Gideon Welles,* I, p. 19; Oretha Swartz, "Franklin Buchanan; A Study in Divided Loyalties," *United States Naval Institute Proceedings,* LXXXVIII (December 1962), pp. 62–66.

29. *O.R.N.,* I, 6, pp. 776–77.

30. Still, *Iron Afloat,* p. 24; Eggleston, "Narrative," p. 168; Ramsay, "Interesting Data," p. xvii; Ramsay, "Most Famous of Sea Duels," p. 11; Wise, *End of an Era,* p. 195; *O.R.N.,* I, 21, p. 898.

CHAPTER 5

1. George H. Preble, "Notes for a History of Steam Navigation," *United Service,* VI (May 1882), p. 556; contract of Ericsson et al., October 28, 1861, Smithsonian Institution, Washington, D.C.; Francis B. Wheeler, "The Building of the *Monitor,*" *Magazine of American History,* XIII (January 1885), pp. 59–61.

2. George H. Robinson, "Recollections of Ericsson," *United Service,* New Series, XIII (January 1895), pp. 17, 21; Bushnell to Welles, March 9, 1877, Welles Papers; Church, *Ericsson,* I, p. 136; James W. Gibson, "Cornelius Henry Delamater," *New York Genealogical and Biographical Record,* XX (1889), pp. 131–32.

3. Dana Wegner, "Ericsson's High Priest: Alban C. Stimers," *Civil War Times Illustrated,* XIII (February 1975), pp. 26–34.

4. Preble, "Notes," p. 557; Church, *Ericsson,* I, p. 258; Robert S. McCordock, *The Yankee Cheesebox* (Philadelphia, 1938), p. 34; William H. Cracknell, *United States Navy Monitors of the Civil War* (Windsor, England, 1973), p. 277.

5. Cracknell, *Monitors,* p. 281.

6. Ibid., pp. 278–79; Preble, "Notes," p. 557.

7. U. S. War Department, *War of the Rebellion: Official Records of the Union and Confederate Armies* (Washington, D.C., 1880–1901), Series II, Volume 3, pp. 739–40 (hereafter cited as *O.R.*); *O.R.N.,* I, 6, pp. 515, 516–17, 522.

8. Ericsson, "Building of the 'Monitor,'" p. 731n; Welles, "First Iron-Clad," pp. 22–23; Preble, "Notes," p. 558; *O.R.N.,* I, 6, pp. 517, 538; *O.R.N.,* II, 1, p. 148; Charles Martin, "The Sinking of the *Congress* and *Cumberland* by the *Merrimac,*" *Personal Recollections of the War of Rebellion: Papers Read Before the New York Com-*

mandery, Military Order of the Loyal Legion of the United States (New York, 1891–1912), II, p. 2.

9. Welles, "First Iron-Clad," pp. 19–20; Preble, "Notes," p. 557.

10. Cracknell, *Monitors*, p. 277; *O.R.N.*, I, 6, pp. 525, 534; Samuel Dana Greene, "In the 'Monitor' Turret," *Battles and Leaders*, I, p. 719; Samuel Lewis (Peter Truscott), "Life on the *Monitor*," in William C. King and William P. Derby, comps., *Camp-Fire Sketches and Battle-field Echoes of 61–5* (Springfield, Mass., 1888), pp. 257–58; Daly, *Aboard the USS Monitor*, pp. xiv–xv, 4, 8, 9; Louis N. Stodder, "Aboard the USS *Monitor*," *Civil War Times Illustrated*, I (January 1963), p. 31; Ellis, *Monitor*, pp. 37–38.

11. Stodder, "Aboard the USS *Monitor*," p. 31; Lewis, "Life on the *Monitor*," p. 258; Ellis, *Monitor*, p. 19; Daly, *Aboard the USS Monitor*, p. 8.

12. Cracknell, *Monitors*, p. 282.

13. Ericsson, "Building of the 'Monitor,'" p. 735; Daly, *Aboard the USS Monitor*, pp. 25–26.

14. Cracknell, *Monitors*, p. 283.

15. Ibid., pp. 279–80; *O.R.N.*, I, 6, pp. 525, 529, 604; Welles, "First Iron-Clad," pp. 20–21.

16. Church, *Ericsson*, I, pp. 254–55; *O.R.N.*, I, 6, p. 658.

17. *O.R.N.*, I, 25, p. 757; Naval History Division, *Civil War Naval Chronology, 1861–1865* (Washington, D.C., 1971), II, p. 26.

18. *O.R.N.*, I, 6, pp. 669, 676; *O.R.N.*, I, 1, p. 338; Preble, "Notes," p. 556; Daly, *Aboard the USS Monitor*, pp. 18, 21–22; Ellis, *Monitor*, p. 19; Cracknell, *Monitors*, p. 281.

19. Daly, *Aboard the USS Monitor*, p. 27.

20. Le Grand B. Cannon, *Personal Reminiscences of the Rebellion, 1861–1865* (New York, 1895), p. 75; Beale, *Diary of Gideon Welles*, I, p. 65; *O.R.N.*, I, 5, pp. 747, 748; *O.R.N.*, I, 6, pp. 446, 482–83, 517–18, 535, 543, 640; Albert B. Paine, *A Sailor of Fortune: Personal Memoirs of Captain B. S. Osbon* (New York, 1906), p. 159; *Harper's Weekly*, November 9, 1861; Welles, "First Iron-Clad," p. 20.

21. *O.R.*, I, 5, p. 48; George B. McClellan, *McClellan's Own Story* (New York, 1887), p. 197; Jones, *Civil War at Sea*, I, pp. 395–96; *O.R.N.*, I, 6, pp. 540–41; Gustavus V. Fox, *The Confidential Correspondence of Gustavus V. Fox* (New York, 1919), I, p. 244.

22. *O.R.N.*, I, 6, pp. 659, 679, 684; Ellis, *Monitor*, p. 22.

CHAPTER 6

1. Greene, "In the 'Monitor' Turret," p. 720; Daly, *Aboard the USS Monitor,* pp. 12, 19–20, 22–23, 43, 48–49.
2. Daly, *Aboard the USS Monitor,* pp. 27–31; Alban C. Stimers, "An Engineer Aboard the *Monitor," Civil War Times Illustrated,* IX (April 1970), pp. 29–30; Ericsson, "Building of the 'Monitor,' " p. 741; Ellis, *Monitor,* pp. 23–24; Samuel Dana Greene, "I Fired the First Gun and Thus Commenced the Great Battle," *American Heritage,* VIII (June 1957), pp. 11–13; Greene, "In the 'Monitor' Turret," pp. 720–21.
3. Daly, *Aboard the USS Monitor,* p. 31; Greene, "I Fired the First Gun," pp. 13, 102.
4. *O.R.N.,* I, 6, pp. 233, 248; Beale, *Diary of Gideon Welles,* I, p. 142.
5. *O.R.N.,* I, 6, pp. 282, 313, 603.
6. Ibid., II, 1, p. 65; *O.R.N.,* I, 6, pp. 442, 494, 496, 524, 525, 530, 687; Edward Shippen, "Two Battle Pictures," *United Service,* IV (January 1881), pp. 53–56; *O.R.,* I, 51, Part 1, p. 58.
7. *O.R.N.,* II, 1, p. 145; *Frank Leslie's Illustrated Newspaper,* March 29, 1862.
8. *O.R.N.,* II, 1, p. 193; *O.R.N.,* I, 6, pp. 394, 661; Joseph McDonald, "How I Saw the Monitor-Merrimac Fight," *New England Magazine,* New Series, XXXVI (July 1907), p. 548.
9. *O.R.N.,* II, 1, p. 69; Thomas O. Selfridge, Jr., "The Merrimac and the Cumberland," *Cosmopolitan,* XV (June 1893), pp. 176–80.
10. Louis M. Goldsborough, "Narrative of Rear Admiral Goldsborough, U. S. Navy," *United States Naval Institute Proceedings,* LIX (July 1933), pp. 1022–24; *O.R.N.,* I, 6, pp. 287, 333–34, 363, 375, 437–40, 543; Fox, *Correspondence,* I, pp. 218, 285; *O.R.,* I, 4, p. 620; Cannon, *Reminiscences,* pp. 75–79.
11. *O.R.N.,* I, 6, pp. 536, 624, 663, 672; Cannon, *Reminiscences,* p. 81.
12. Selfridge, "The Merrimac and the Cumberland," p. 180; Moses S. Stuyvesant, "How the *Cumberland* Went Down," *War Papers and Reminiscences, 1861–1865, Read Before the Missouri Commandery, Military Order of the Loyal Legion of the United States* (St. Louis, 1892), I, pp. 205–6; McDonald, "How I Saw the Monitor-Merrimac Fight," pp. 548–49; New Orleans, *Delta,* April 4, 1862; Cannon, *Reminiscences,* p. 81.

CHAPTER 7

1. *O.R.N.*, I, 6, pp. 747–49, 750, 757, 759, 769–70, 771, 772–73, 777–78, 788.
2. *O.R.*, I, 51, Part 2, pp. 479–80; Franklin Buchanan to John B. Magruder (March 2, 1862), Buchanan to John R. Tucker (March 3, 1862), Buchanan to Mallory (March 4, 1862), Franklin Buchanan Letterbook 1861–1863, Southern Historical Collection, University of North Carolina, Chapel Hill; Jones, "Services of the 'Virginia,'" pp. 67–68.
3. *O.R.*, I, 5, Part 2, p. 391; *O.R.N.*, I, 6, pp. 780–81.
4. Littlepage, Memoirs; Eggleston, "Narrative," p. 169; Norris, "'Virginia,'" p. 207; Wood, "First Fight," p. 696; Dinwiddie B. Phillips, "The Career of the Iron-Clad Virginia," *Collections of the Virginia Historical Society*, New Series, VI (1887), p. 201.
5. Eggleston, "Narrative," p. 170; Norris, "'Virginia,'" pp. 206–7; Wood, "First Fight," p. 696.
6. Cline, "Ironclad Ram," p. 244; Porter, *Norfolk County*, p. 359; Wood, "First Fight," p. 696; Ramsay, "Interesting Data," p. xvii; Ramsay, "Most Famous of Sea Duels," p. 11.
7. William H. Parker, *Recollections of a Naval Officer, 1841–1865* (New York, 1883), pp. 252–53.
8. James Keenan to Dear —, March 10, 1862, Georgia Department of Archives and History, Atlanta; Raleigh E. Colston, "Watching the 'Merrimac,'" *Battles and Leaders*, I, p. 712.
9. Parker, *Recollections*, p. 253; Eggleston, "Narrative," pp. 169–70; Wood, "First Fight," p. 696; Phillips, "The Iron-Clad Virginia," p. 201.
10. Phillips, "The Iron-Clad Virginia," p. 201; Ramsay, "Most Famous of Sea Duels," p. 11; Ramsay, "Interesting Data," p. xvii; Eggleston, "Narrative," p. 170.
11. Ramsay, "Interesting Data," pp. xvii–xviii; Cline, "Ironclad Ram," p. 244; Eggleston, "Narrative," p. 170; Littlepage, Memoirs; Parker, *Recollections*, p. 254; Phillips, "The Iron-Clad Virginia," p. 202; Tindall, "True Story," pp. 36–37; *O.R.N.*, I, 7, p. 44.
12. Great Rebellion Scrapbooks, Volume 9, February–April 1862, Collection of the Military Order of the Loyal Legion of the United States, Massachusetts Commandery, U. S. Army Military History Research Collection, Carlisle Barracks, Pennsylvania (hereafter cited as MOLLUS-Mass.).

13. Cannon, *Reminiscences*, pp. 81–82; McDonald, "How I Saw the Monitor-Merrimac Fight," p. 549; Thomas W. Rae, "The Little Monitor Saved Our Lives," *American History Illustrated*, I (July 1966), p. 33; *O.R.N.*, I, 7, pp. 8, 9, 10, 14.

14. Israel N. Stiles, "The Merrimac and the Monitor," *Military Essays and Recollections, Papers Read Before the Commandery of the State of Illinois, Military Order of the Loyal Legion of the United States* (Chicago, 1891), I, p. 125; F. S. Alger, "The 'Congress' and the 'Merrimac,'" *New England Magazine*, XIX (February 1899), p. 688; Charles L. Lewis, *Admiral Franklin Buchanan: Fearless Man of Action* (Baltimore, 1929), p. 184; Great Rebellion Scrapbooks, Volume 9, MOLLUS-Mass.; *O.R.N.*, I, 7, pp. 3, 23.

15. Charles O'Neil, "Engagement Between the 'Cumberland' and the 'Merrimack,'" *United States Naval Institute Proceedings*, XLVIII (June 1922), pp. 863–64; Selfridge, "The Merrimac and the Cumberland," p. 181; Stuyvesant, "How the *Cumberland* Went Down," p. 207; *O.R.N.*, I, 7, p. 21.

16. Henry Reaney, "How the Gun-Boat 'Zouave' Aided the 'Congress,'" *Battles and Leaders*, I, pp. 714–15.

17. Wood, "First Fight," p. 696; Scharf, *Confederate States Navy*, p. 173; Parker, *Recollections*, pp. 254–55; Norfolk *Day Book*, March 10, 1862.

18. Wood, "First Fight," p. 698; Jones, "Services of the 'Virginia,'" p. 68n; Cline, "Ironclad Ram," pp. 24–25; *O.R.N.*, I, 7, p. 44; Stuyvesant, "How the *Cumberland* Went Down," p. 207; Selfridge, "The Merrimac and the Cumberland," pp. 181–82.

19. *O.R.N.*, I, 7, p. 23; Eggleston, "Narrative," pp. 170–71; Shippen, "Notes," p. 642; Alger, "The 'Congress' and the 'Merrimac,'" pp. 688–89.

20. New York *Times*, March 14, 1862; Salem (Mass.) *Register*, March 13, 1862; Frank Moore, ed., *The Rebellion Record* (New York, 1861–68), IV, Documents, p. 272.

21. Ramsay, "Most Famous of Sea Duels," p. 11; Tindall, "True Story," p. 26n; Ramsay, "Interesting Data," p. xviii; Eggleston, "Narrative," p. 171.

22. Jones, "Services of the 'Virginia,'" p. 68; John McI. Kell, *Recollections of a Naval Life* (Washington, 1900), p. 282; Wood, "First Fight," p. 698; Salem *Register*, March 13, 1862.

23. Stuyvesant, "How the *Cumberland* Went Down," pp. 207–8; Selfridge, "The Merrimac and the Cumberland," p. 182.

24. Ramsay, "Most Famous of Sea Duels," p. 11; Ramsay, "Interesting Data," p. xviii.

25. Wise, *End of an Era*, pp. 196, 198–99; Colston, "Watching the 'Merrimac,'" pp. 712–13; Keenan to Dear ——, March 10, 1862, Georgia Department of Archives and History, Atlanta; New York *Times*, March 14, 1862.

26. New Orleans *Delta*, April 4, 1862; Great Rebellion Scrapbooks, Volume 9, MOLLUS-Mass.; Jones, "Services of the 'Virginia,'" p. 68; O'Neil, "Engagement," pp. 866–68; Lansing (N.Y.) *Republican*, April 2, 1862; Stuyvesant, "How the *Cumberland* Went Down," pp. 208–10; *O.R.N.*, I, 7, pp. 22–23; Keenan to Dear ——, March 10, 1862, Georgia Department of Archives and History, Atlanta; *Rebellion Record*, IV, p. 272; Tindall, "True Story," p. 26n; Selfridge, "The Merrimac and the Cumberland," pp. 182–83; Wood, "First Fight," p. 698; Jones, "Services of the 'Virginia,'" p. 68.

27. Littlepage, Memoirs; Wood, "First Fight," p. 698n; Porter, *Norfolk County*, p. 360; Tindall, "True Story," pp. 36–37n; Eggleston, "Narrative," p. 171; Jones, "Services of the 'Virginia,'" p. 68.

28. Ramsay, "Most Famous of Sea Duels," pp. 11–12.

29. *O.R.N.*, I, 7, p. 44; Norris, "'Virginia,'" p. 208; Scharf, *Confederate States Navy*, pp. 160–61, 194–95.

30. Parker, *Recollections*, pp. 254–56; Alger, "The 'Congress' and the 'Merrimac,'" p. 689; *O.R.N.*, I, 7, pp. 8–9, 10, 18–19; Porter, *Norfolk County*, p. 359.

31. Henry Reaney, "The *Monitor* and *Merrimac*," *War Papers; Read Before the Commandery of the State of Michigan, Military Order of the Loyal Legion of the United States* (Detroit, 1893–98), II, pp. 168–70; Wood, "First Fight," p. 698; Shippen, "Notes," p. 642; *O.R.N.*, I, 7, p. 23; Alger, "The 'Congress' and the 'Merrimac,'" p. 689; Norfolk *Day Book*, March 10, 1862; Shippen, "Two Battle Pictures," p. 60.

32. *O.R.N.*, I, 7, pp. 23–24; Wood, "First Fight," p. 698; Great Rebellion Scrapbooks, Volume 9, MOLLUS-Mass.; Reaney, "The *Monitor* and *Merrimac*," pp. 169–70.

33. Eggleston, "Narrative," pp. 172–73; Alger, "The 'Congress' and the 'Merrimac,'" p. 690; *O.R.N.*, I, 7, pp. 24, 45; Parker, *Recollections*, pp. 257–58.

34. Great Rebellion Scrapbooks, Volume 9, MOLLUS-Mass.; Stiles, "The Merrimac and the Monitor," p. 128; *O.R.N.*, I, 7, p. 35.

35. Parker, *Recollections*, pp. 258–59; Shippen, "Two Battle Pictures," p. 61; Alger, "The 'Congress' and the 'Merrimac,'" p. 690.

36. Buchanan to Mallory, March 27, 1862, Buchanan Letterbook; Kell, *Recollections*, pp. 282–83; Brooke, "Real Projector," pp. 6–7.

37. Eggleston, "Narrative," p. 173; Porter, *Norfolk County*, p. 360;

Norfolk *Day Book,* March 10, 1862; Thomas Ransom, "The Monitor & the Merrimac at Hampton Roads," ed. by Doris H. Hamilton, *Hobbies,* LXIV (September 1959), p. 111; Brooke, "Real Projector," p. 7.
38. *O.R.N.,* I, 7, p. 45; Brooke, "Real Projector," p. 7; Rae, "The Little Monitor Saved Our Lives," pp. 33–34.
39. *O.R.N.,* I, 7, p. 45; Scharf, *Confederate States Navy,* p. 182; Brooke, "Real Projector," p. 5.

CHAPTER 8

1. Eggleston, "Narrative," pp. 173–74; *O.R.N.,* I, 7, pp. 42–43; Norfolk *Day Book,* March 10, 1862; Norris, " 'Virginia,' " p. 209; Brooke, "Real Projector," p. 8; Kell, *Recollections,* p. 283.
2. Phillips, "The Iron-Clad Virginia," p. 205; Eggleston, "Narrative," p. 174; Wise, *End of an Era,* pp. 201–2.
3. *O.R.N.,* I, 7, p. 42; *O.R.N.,* II, 2, p. 186; Wood, "First Fight," pp. 694, 700; Porter, *Norfolk County,* p. 339; Dinwiddie B. Phillips, "The Career of the Merrimac," *Southern Bivouac,* New Series, II (March 1887), p. 600; Norris, " 'Virginia,' " p. 206; Buchanan to Mallory, March 19, 1862, Buchanan Letterbook.
4. Still, *Iron Afloat,* p. 33; Parker, *Recollections,* p. 264; Jones, "Services of the 'Virginia,' " pp. 70–71.
5. Ramsay, "Most Famous of Sea Duels," p. 12; Colston, "Watching the 'Merrimac,' " p. 714.
6. Cannon, *Reminiscences,* pp. 85–86; Welles, "First Iron-Clad," p. 24; *O.R.N.,* I, 7, pp. 4–5, 35.
7. Edward Shippen, "Notes on the *Congress-Merrimac* Fight," *Century Illustrated Magazine,* XXX (August 1885), p. 642; Shippen, "Two Battle Pictures," pp. 61–62; Stiles, "The Merrimac and the Monitor," pp. 128–29; *O.R.N.,* I, 7, p. 24; New York *Herald,* March 11, 1862.
8. *O.R.N.,* I, 7, pp. 14, 22, 87; Rae, "The Little Monitor Saved Our Lives," p. 34; Cannon, *Reminiscences,* p. 86.
9. Alger, "The 'Congress' and the 'Merrimac,' " p. 692; Great Rebellion Scrapbooks, Volume 9, MOLLUS-Mass.
10. Greene, "I Fired the First Gun," pp. 13, 102; *O.R.N.,* I, 6, pp. 678–79, 681, 682, 686; *O.R.N.,* I, 7, p. 5; Stimers, "Engineer Aboard the *Monitor,*" pp. 31–32; John Worden to "My darling wife," March 8, 1862, John L. Worden Papers, Lincoln Memorial University, Harrogate, Tenn.
11. Greene, "I Fired the First Gun," p. 102; Greene, "In the 'Monitor' Turret," p. 722; Ellis, *Monitor,* p. 27.

12. Greene, "I Fired the First Gun," p. 102; Ellis, *Monitor*, p. 27; Great Rebellion Scrapbooks, Volume 9, MOLLUS-Mass.; Rae, "The Little Monitor Saved Our Lives," p. 34; Stimers, "Engineer Aboard the *Monitor*," p. 32; Daly, *Aboard the USS Monitor*, pp. 31–32.

13. Welles, "First Iron-Clad," pp. 23–25; Beale, *Diary of Gideon Welles*, I, pp. 61–64; Tyler Dennett, ed., *Lincoln and the Civil War in the Diaries and Letters of John Hay* (New York, 1939), p. 36; John A. Dahlgren to Ulrich Dahlgren, March 11, 1862, John A. Dahlgren Papers, Library of Congress.

14. Welles, "First Iron-Clad," pp. 25–26.

15. *O.R.*, III, 1, p. 923; *O.R.*, I, 51, Part 1, pp. 548–49; Scharf, *Confederate States Navy*, pp. 175–76; Welles, "First Iron-Clad," p. 26; Beale, *Diary of Gideon Welles*, I, pp. 66–67.

16. Adam Gurowski, *Diary from March 4, 1861 to November 12, 1862* (Boston, 1862), p. 168; George Templeman Strong, *Diary of the Civil War 1860–1865* (New York, 1962), p. 210.

CHAPTER 9

1. Phillips, "Career of the Merrimac," p. 600; Phillips, "The Iron-Clad Virginia," pp. 206–7; Cline, "Ironclad Ram," p. 246; Still, *Iron Afloat*, p. 33.

2. *O.R.N.*, I, 7, pp. 46, 49, 53; "The Merrimac and the Monitor," *SHSP*, XIII (1885), p. 101; Eggleston, "Narrative," p. 174; Cline, "Ironclad Ram," p. 246; Porter, *Norfolk County*, p. 361; H. B. Littlepage, "Merrimac vs. Monitor: A Midshipman's Account of the Battle with the 'Cheese Box,'" in King and Derby, *Camp-Fire Sketches*, p. 335; Scharf, *Confederate States Navy*, p. 197; Colston, "Watching the 'Merrimac,'" p. 714; Wood, "First Fight," p. 701.

3. Shippen, "Two Battle Pictures," pp. 62–63; Alger, "The 'Congress' and the 'Merrimac,'" p. 692; Stimers, "Engineer Aboard the *Monitor*," p. 32; Daly, *Aboard the USS Monitor*, pp. 32–35; Greene, "In the 'Monitor' Turret," pp. 722–23; Lewis, "Life on the Monitor," pp. 258–59; Greene, "I Fired the First Gun," p. 102; Ellis, *Monitor*, pp. 29–30.

4. Jones, "Services of the 'Virginia,'" p. 71; Littlepage, "Merrimac vs. Monitor," p. 335; Wood, "First Fight," p. 701; Eggleston, "Narrative," pp. 174–75; *O.R.N.*, I, 21, p. 874; Ramsay, "Most Famous of Sea Duels," p. 12.

5. Stimers, "Engineer Aboard the *Monitor*," p. 33; Greene, "In the 'Monitor' Turret," pp. 723–24; Fox, *Correspondence*, I, p. 254; Wood,

"First Fight," p. 701; Greene, "I Fired the First Gun," pp. 102, 105; Daly, *Aboard the USS Monitor*, pp. 34–36.

6. Littlepage, "Merrimac vs. Monitor," p. 336; Norris, " 'Virginia,' " pp. 210, 219–20; Wood, "First Fight," pp. 701–3; Ramsay, "Most Famous of Sea Duels," p. 12; Phillips, "The Iron-Clad Virginia," pp. 208–9.

7. Norris, " 'Virginia,' " p. 211; Wood, "First Fight," p. 702.

8. Daly, *Aboard the USS Monitor*, pp. 36–37.

9. Ramsay, "Interesting Data," p. xix; Littlepage, Memoirs; Daly, *Aboard the USS Monitor*, p. 37; Phillips, "The Iron-Clad Virginia," p. 209; Phillips, "Career of the Merrimac," p. 601; Norfolk *Day Book*, March 11, 1862; Great Rebellion Scrapbooks, Volume 9, MOLLUS-Mass.; Ramsay, "Most Famous of Sea Duels," p. 12; Wood, "First Fight," p. 702.

10. Daly, *Aboard the USS Monitor*, pp. 39, 50, 64; Lewis, "Life on the Monitor," pp. 259–60; Stimers, "Engineer Aboard the *Monitor*," p. 35; Stodder, "Aboard the USS *Monitor*," p. 34.

11. *O.R.N.*, I, 7, pp. 12, 15; Rae, "The Little Monitor Saved Our Lives," pp. 34–35.

12. Greene, "I Fired the First Gun," p. 103; Eggleston, "Narrative," p. 176; Wood, "First Fight," p. 702; Littlepage, Memoirs; Daly, *Aboard the USS Monitor*, p. 36; Lewis, "Life on the Monitor," p. 259.

13. Cline, "Ironclad Ram," p. 246; Littlepage, Memoirs; Great Rebellion Scrapbooks, Volume 9, MOLLUS-Mass.

14. Wood, "First Fight," p. 701; Ramsay, "Most Famous of Sea Duels," p. 12.

15. Cline, "Ironclad Ram," pp. 247–48; Norris, " 'Virginia,' " pp. 215–16; Eggleston, "Narrative," pp. 175–76; *O.R.N.*, I, 7, pp. 12, 46; Jones, "Services of the 'Virginia,' " p. 72; Ramsay, "Most Famous of Sea Duels," p. 12.

16. Daly, *Aboard the USS Monitor*, pp. 38–39, 47.

17. Littlepage, Memoirs; "The Merrimac and the Monitor," p. 101; Keenan to Dear ——, March 10, 1862, Georgia Department of Archives and History, Atlanta; Colston, "Watching the 'Merrimac,' " p. 714; Wise, *End of an Era*, pp. 202, 204; Raleigh (N.C.) *Standard*, March 12, 1862; Norfolk *Day Book*, March 11, 1862.

18. Ransom, "The Monitor & the Merrimac," pp. 111, 119; Alger, "The 'Congress' and the 'Merrimac,' " p. 692; O'Neil, "Engagement," p. 882; Baltimore *American*, March 12, 1862.

CHAPTER 10

1. Ramsay, "Most Famous of Sea Duels," p. 12; Norris, "'Virginia,'" pp. 218, 221; Norfolk *Day Book,* March 11, 1862; Robert C. Foute, "Echoes from Hampton Roads," *SHSP,* XIX (1891), p. 246; Parker, *Recollections,* p. 267; Wise, *End of an Era,* p. 205; Wood, "First Fight," p. 703.

2. J. H. D. Wingfield, "A Thanksgiving Service on the 'Virginia,' March 10, 1862," *SHSP,* XIX (1891), pp. 249–50; Norris, "'Virginia,'" p. 22; Wood to his wife, March 20, 1862, Wood Papers.

3. Fox, *Correspondence,* I, p. 254; Wood, "First Fight," pp. 703–5.

4. Richmond *Enquirer,* March 11, 1862; Richmond *Examiner,* March 20, 1862; *O.R.,* I, 6, p. 863; *O.R.,* IV, 1, p. 986; *O.R.N.,* II, 2, pp. 129, 181, 184; *O.R.N.,* II, 3, pp. 363–64, 400; "The Late Naval Duel and Its Consequences," *United Service Magazine* (May 1862), pp. 34–48; Wood, "First Fight," p. 692.

5. Porter, *Norfolk County,* pp. 341–57; Brooke, "Real Projector," pp. 3–34.

6. *O.R.N.,* II, 1, p. 625; Phillips, "The Iron-Clad Virginia," pp. 221–22.

7. Buchanan to Mallory, March 19, 1862, Buchanan Letterbook; William H. Parker, "Letter from Captain Parker," *SHSP,* XI (1883), pp. 37–38.

8. Buchanan to Jones, March 21, 1862, Buchanan Letterbook; *O.R.N.,* II, 1, p. 634; *O.R.N.,* II, 2, pp. 170, 186; Wood to his wife, March 21, 1862, Wood Papers; Porter, *Norfolk County,* pp. 339, 364–65; Norris, "'Virginia,'" pp. 206, 222; Wood, "First Fight," p. 706; Dew, *Ironmaker,* p. 120.

9. Wood to his wife, March 18 and 26, 1862; Wood, "First Fight," p. 705; Robert M. Langdon, "Josiah Tattnall—Blood Is Thicker than Water," *United States Naval Institute Proceedings,* LXXXV (June 1959), pp. 156–58; *O.R.N.,* I, 7, p. 757.

10. Brooke to Minor, March 17, 1862, Minor Papers; Wood to his wife, March 18, 1862, Wood Papers.

11. Greene, "I Fired the First Gun," pp. 103–4; Log of the USS *Monitor,* March 9, 1862, Record Group 24, National Archives, Washington, D.C.; John L. Worden Scrapbook, Worden Papers; Daly, *Aboard the USS Monitor,* pp. 39–40; Fox, *Correspondence,* I, pp. 432–33, 439.

12. Daly, *Aboard the USS Monitor,* p. 40; Great Rebellion Scrap-

books, Volume 9, MOLLUS-Mass.; *O.R.N.*, i, 7, p. 12; Worden Scrapbook.

13. Strong, *Diary*, p. 216; Beale, *Diary of Gideon Welles*, i, p. 142; Goldsborough, "Narrative," pp. 1024–25; *O.R.N.*, i, 7, p. 574; Worden Scrapbook; Welles to Worden, March 15, 1862, Worden Papers; Roy P. Basler, comp., *Collected Works of Abraham Lincoln* (New Brunswick, N.J., 1953–55), v, pp. 154, 547; Preble, "Notes," p. 557.

14. *O.R.N.*, i, 5, pp. 24, 29; *O.R.N.*, i, 18, p. 59; *O.R.N.*, i, 7, p. 83; Beale, *Diary of Gideon Welles*, iii, pp. 473–74; Dahlgren to Ulrich Dahlgren, March 11, 1862, Dahlgren Papers; Fox, *Correspondence*, i, pp. 248–49; Wood to his wife, March 18, 1862, Wood Papers.

15. Greene, "I Fired the First Gun," p. 104; *O.R.N.*, i, 7, p. 98; Daly, *Aboard the USS Monitor*, pp. 46, 52, 53; Stimers, "Engineer Aboard the *Monitor*," p. 35.

16. Fox, *Correspondence*, i, pp. 254, 438–39; *O.R.*, i, 5, pp. 24, 51, 64, 742, 751; McClellan, *McClellan's Own Story*, p. 268; Still, *Iron Afloat*, pp. 36–37; Eggleston, "Narrative," p. 177.

17. *O.R.N.*, i, 7, pp. 759–60; Norris, "'Virginia,'" pp. 211–12; Foute, "Echoes," pp. 247–48; Virginius Newton, "The *Merrimac* or *Virginia*," *SHSP*, xx (1892), pp. 19–20; Ashley Halsey, "Seal the Turtle in Its Shell," *Civil War Times Illustrated*, v (June 1966), p. 29.

18. *O.R.N.*, i, 7, p. 223; *O.R.*, i, 11, Part 1, p. 423; Parker, *Recollections*, p. 275; Daly, *Aboard the USS Monitor*, pp. 73–74, 77; Newton, "The *Merrimac*," p. 20; Halsey, "Seal the Turtle in Its Shell," p. 31; Parker, "Letter," p. 35; New York *Herald*, April 15, 1862.

19. *O.R.N.*, i, 7, p. 224; *O.R.N.*, ii, 1, p. 635; *O.R.*, i, 51, Part 2, p. 539; Ramsay, "Most Famous of Sea Duels," p. 12; McClellan, *McClellan's Own Story*, p. 282.

20. Wood to his wife, May 4, 5, 6, 8, 1862, Wood Papers; David Donald, ed., *Inside Lincoln's Cabinet: The Civil War Diaries of Salmon P. Chase* (New York, 1954), pp. 75–79; Goldsborough, "Narrative," pp. 1027–28; Fox, *Correspondence*, i, pp. 265–66; Daly, *Aboard the USS Monitor*, pp. 111–13; *O.R.N.*, i, 7, pp. 335–36; *O.R.*, i, 18, p. 755; H. B. Littlepage, "Statement of Midshipman Littlepage," *SHSP*, xi (January 1883), p. 34; *Rebellion Record*, v, Documents, pp. 121–22; Wood, "First Fight," p. 709.

21. Wood to his wife, May 5 and 7, 1862, Wood Papers; *O.R.N.*, i, 7, pp. 336–37; Fox, *Correspondence*, i, pp. 267–68; Donald, *Inside Lincoln's Cabinet*, pp. 79–83.

22. Phillips, "The Iron-Clad Virginia," pp. 228–30; Wood, "First Fight," p. 710; Ramsay, "Most Famous of Sea Duels," p. 12; Jones, "Services of the 'Virginia,'" p. 73; Littlepage, Memoirs; Robert L.

Preston, "Did the *Monitor* or *Merrimac* Revolutionize Naval Warfare?" *William & Mary Quarterly,* XXIV (July 1915), p. 66; *O.R.N.,* I, 7, pp. 336–37.

23. Eggleston, "Narrative," p. 178; Stephen Mallory Diary (typescript), I, May 11, 1862, Library of Congress.

24. Phillips, "The Iron-Clad Virginia," p. 230; Wood, "First Fight," p. 711; Littlepage, Memoirs.

CHAPTER 11

1. *O.R.N.,* I, 18, p. 736; Daly, *Aboard the USS Monitor,* pp. 119–20, 121–22; Donald, *Inside Lincoln's Cabinet,* p. 85.

2. *O.R.,* I, 11, Part 1, p. 636; Daly, *Aboard the USS Monitor,* pp. 122–30, 136; Wood, "First Fight," p. 711; *O.R.N.,* I, 7, pp. 357–58, 362, 410–13; Littlepage, Memoirs.

3. Daly, *Aboard the USS Monitor,* pp. 155, 160, 161, 189, 192–93, 198, 203, 206, 207; Fox, *Correspondence,* I, p. 287.

4. *O.R.N.,* I, 7, pp. 39–40, 654.

5. Daly, *Aboard the USS Monitor,* pp. 218–19, 224–25, 228, 232; Stodder, "Aboard the USS *Monitor,*" p. 35.

6. Daly, *Aboard the USS Monitor,* pp. 229, 243–44, 247, 249–50.

7. *O.R.N.,* I, 8, pp. 338–39; Daly, *Aboard the USS Monitor,* pp. 253–60; Stodder, "Aboard the USS *Monitor,*" p. 36; Grenville M. Weeks, "The Last Cruise of the *Monitor,*" *Atlantic Monthly,* XI (March 1863), pp. 367–72; Ellis, *Monitor,* pp. 33–36; Francis B. Butts, "The Loss of the 'Monitor,'" *Battles and Leaders,* I, pp. 745–48; Lewis, "Life on the Monitor," p. 261; Durham (N.C.) *Sun,* March 28, 1974.

CHAPTER 12

1. Still, *Iron Afloat,* pp. 99, 227–28. This book is by far the best single source for the story of the Confederate ironclads.

2. Robert A. Jones, "Aftermath of an Ironclad," *Civil War Times Illustrated,* XI (October 1972), pp. 21–23.

A NOTE ON SOURCES

The available literature on the *Monitor*, the *Virginia*, and the career of each, is more extensive than that for any other ships or naval engagement of the Civil War. Nearly five hundred published sources alone have been located, and the number of newspapers and manuscript collections that bear on the subject runs to well over one hundred. A great deal has been written, and yet a great deal of it is worthless or of very questionable value. This is due in large part to fading memories, and as well to old hatreds that did not fade. Then too, there is much duplication, much borrowing between one author and another, and much of what survives in manuscripts, that has been published. As a result, the bibliography that follows is by no means to be taken as comprehensive. It is, rather, a critical selection of those sources found to be most useful for this book.

The field of manuscripts available is surprisingly full, though much of what exists has already appeared in published form in works cited elsewhere in this bibliography. Among those not published, however, some of the best are Confederate. The Franklin Buchanan Letterbook, 1861–1863, Southern Historical Collection, University of North Carolina, Chapel Hill, is excellent, containing his thoughts on his ship and officers, and his plans for meeting the Federals in Hampton Roads. The Hardin B. Littlepage Memoirs, in possession of Jon Nielson, Orono, Maine, are full, valuable recollections by a midshipman aboard the *Virginia*. The Minor Family Papers, Virginia Historical Society, Richmond, contain a few letters of Lieutenant Robert D. Minor, Buchanan's flag lieutenant. Far more useful are the John Taylor Wood Papers, Southern Historical Collection, containing as they do a series of his letters to his wife from March to May 1862. John Brooke's papers are also there, while many useful letters are to be found in an excellent 1956 dissertation, "John Mercer Brooke, Naval Scientist," by George R. Brooke, Jr., in the University of North Carolina library. The March 10, 1862, letter of James Keenan in the Georgia Department of Archives and History, Atlanta, is a fine account of the fighting of March 8–9, while the Stephen R. Mallory Diary (typescript) in the

Library of Congress, Washington, D.C., provides a few sparse but useful overview comments.

For the Federals, sources are more numerous, but qualitatively less useful. The best are the John L. Worden Papers, Lincoln Memorial University, Harrogate, Tennessee, containing his letters and a useful scrapbook, and the Gideon Welles Papers, Henry E. Huntington Library and Art Gallery, San Marino, California. The Logbook of the USS *Monitor*, Record Group 24, National Archives, Washington, D.C., is sparse as would be expected, but does provide good time references for events during the fight with the *Virginia*. The original contract between John Ericsson and his subcontractors is in the collection of the Smithsonian Institution. Also useful are the John Dahlgren Papers, Library of Congress, and the Collection of the Military Order of the Loyal Legion of the United States, U. S. Army Military History Research Collection, Carlisle Barracks, Pennsylvania.

Virtually every newspaper in the nation covered some aspect of the construction of the two great ironclads and their fight, but only those who had eyewitness correspondents present or who published firsthand information have been used. These are Ashville (N.C.) *Times*, Baltimore *American*, Boston *Evening Transcript*, Charleston (S.C.) *Mercury*, Lansing (N.Y.) *Republican*, New Orleans *Delta*, New York *Frank Leslie's Illustrated Newspaper*, New York *Harper's Weekly*, New York *Herald*, New York *Times*, Norfolk (Va.) *Day Book*, Raleigh (N.C.) *Standard*, Richmond *Daily Enquirer*, Richmond *Examiner*, and the Salem (Mass.) *Register*.

Among the basic reference sources used, two of the most helpful are bibliographies—David R. Smith, *The Monitor and the Merrimac: A Bibliography* (Los Angeles, 1968), and Myron J. Smith, Jr., *American Civil War Navies: A Bibliography* (Metuchen, N.J., 1972). Both are excellent finding aids, though the latter must be used carefully due to frequent errors in its listings.

Indispensable, of course, is the U. S. Navy Department, *Official Records of the Union and Confederate Navies in the Civil War* (Washington, 1894–1922), 31 vols. Supplementing it are Frank Moore, comp., *The Rebellion Record* (New York, 1861–68), 11 vols.; Virgil C. Jones, *The Civil War at Sea* (New York, 1960–62), 3 vols.; U. S. Naval History Division, *Civil War Naval Chronology* (Washington, 1961–66), 6 vols.; and J. Thomas Scharf, *History of the Confederate States Navy from Its Organization to the Surrender of Its Last Vessel* (New York, 1887). Of these, Scharf is by far the most useful.

General background to the subject of Civil War ironclads is found in James P. Baxter, *The Introduction of the Ironclad Warship* (Cambridge, Mass., 1933); William H. Cracknell, *United States Navy Monitors of the Civil War* (Windsor, England, 1973); Robert MacBride, *Civil War Ironclads: The Dawn of Naval Armor* (Philadelphia, 1962); William N. Still, Jr., *Iron Afloat: The Story of the Confederate Ironclads* (Nashville, 1971); and G. A. Ballard, "British Battleships of the 1870's: the *Warrior* and *Black Prince*," *Mariner's Mirror*, XVI (April 1930), pp. 168–86. Of these, Baxter and Still are the most informative and useful.

John S. Long, "The Gosport Affair," *Journal of Southern History*, XXIII (May 1957), pp. 155–72, provides good background on the loss of the *Merrimack*, and is supplemented by Edward E. Barthell, Jr., *The Mystery of the Merrimack* (Muskegon, Mich., 1959), which deals mainly with proving that the ship's name is properly spelled with the final "k." For the controversy over who designed the CSS *Virginia*, John M. Brooke, "The Plan and Construction of the 'Merrimac,'" in Robert U. Johnson and Clarence C. Buel, eds., *Battles and Leaders of the Civil War* (New York, 1887–88), I, pp. 715–16; John M. Brooke, "The Virginia or Merrimac: Her Real Projector," *Southern Historical Society Papers*, XIX (1891), pp. 3–34; and John W. H. Porter, *A Record of Events in Norfolk County, Virginia, from April 19th, 1861, to May 10th, 1862* (Portsmouth, Va., 1892), present among them both sides of the matter. Further details on the actual construction itself are found in William R. Cline, "The Ironclad Ram *Virginia*," *Southern Historical Society Papers*, XXXII (1904), pp. 243–49; Charles B. Dew, *Ironmaker to the Confederacy: Joseph R. Anderson and the Tredegar Iron Works* (New Haven, Conn., 1966); Catesby ap R. Jones, "Services of the '*Virginia*' (*Merrimac*)," *Southern Historical Society Papers*, I (February 1876), pp. 90–91, XI (February–March 1883), pp. 65–75; T. Catesby Jones, "The Iron-Clad Virginia," *Virginia Magazine of History and Biography*, XLIX (October 1941), pp. 297–303; Albert B. Paine, *A Sailor of Fortune, Personal Memoirs of Capt. B. S. Osbon* (New York, 1906); Sumner B. Besse, *The C.S. Ironclad Virginia: With Data and References for a Scale Model* (Newport News, Va., 1937); and Robert L. Preston, "Did the *Monitor* or *Merrimac* Revolutionize Naval Warfare?" *William & Mary Quarterly*, XXIV (July 1915), pp. 58–66.

Much material is available on the background and building of the *Monitor*. Among the better sources on its planning are Robert S. McCordock, *The Yankee Cheesebox* (Philadelphia, 1938); *American Annual Cyclopaedia and Register of Important Events, 1861* (New York, 1862); Gideon Welles, "The First Iron-Clad Monitor," in *Annals of the War* (Philadelphia, 1879), pp. 17–31; "Negotiations for the Building of the 'Monitor,'" in *Battles and Leaders*, I, pp. 748–50; Francis B. Wheeler, "The Building of the Monitor," *Magazine of American History*, XIII (January 1885), pp. 59–65; and "Who Planned the Monitor?" *Blackwood's Magazine*, CLXXVII (June 1862), pp. 787–89. Actual construction of the ironclad is well described in John Ericsson, "The Monitors," *Century Illustrated Monthly Magazine*, XXXI (December 1885), pp. 280–99; and John Ericsson, "The Building of the 'Monitor,'" *Battles and Leaders*, I, pp. 730–44, which largely reprints the *Century* article. See also James W. Gibson, "Cornelius Henry Delamater," *New York Genealogical and Biographical Record*, XX (July 1889), pp. 131–32; and George H. Preble, "Notes for a History of Steam Navigation," *United Service*, VI (May 1882), pp. 555–60.

Two general references that provide good background for the military setting of the operations around Hampton Roads, Virginia, are George B. McClellan, *McClellan's Own Story* (New York, 1887); and far more useful, the U. S. War Department, *War of the Rebellion: Official Records of the Union and Confederate Armies* (Washington, 1880–1901), 128 vols.

For what happened in Hampton Roads on March 8, 1862, there are a number of accounts by Federals aboard the *Congress*, the *Cumberland*, and the *Minnesota*. The best are F. S. Alger, "The 'Congress' and the 'Merrimac,'" *New England Magazine*, XIX (February 1899), pp. 687–93; Charles Martin, "The Sinking of the *Congress* and *Cumberland* by the *Merrimac*," in *Personal Recollections of the War of the Rebellion: Papers Read Before the New York Commandery, Military Order of the Loyal Legion of the United States* (New York, 1891–1912), II, pp. 1–16; Charles O'Neil, "Engagement Between the 'Cumberland' and the 'Merrimack,'" *United States Naval Institute Proceedings*, XLVIII (June 1922), pp. 863–93; Thomas W. Rae, "The Little *Monitor* Saved Our Lives," *American History Illustrated*, I (July 1966), pp. 32–39; Henry Reaney, "How the Gun-Boat 'Zouave' Aided the 'Congress,'" *Battles and Leaders*, I, pp. 714–15; Thomas O. Selfridge, Jr., "The Merrimac and the Cumberland," *Cosmopolitan*, XV (June 1893), pp. 176–84; Edward Shippen, "Notes on the *Congress-Merrimac* Fight," *Century Illustrated Monthly Magazine*, XXX (August 1885), p. 642; Edward Shippen, "Two Battle Pictures (A Reminiscence of the First Ironclad Fight)," *United Service*, IV (January 1881), pp. 53–78; and Moses S. Stuyvesant, "How the *Cumberland* Went Down," *War Papers and Reminiscences, 1861–1865; Read Before the Missouri Commandery, Military Order of the Loyal Legion of the United States* (St. Louis, 1892), pp. 204–10.

Accounts by those serving on other ships on March 8–9, 1862, include Virginius Newton, "The *Merrimac* or *Virginia*," *Southern Historical Society Papers*, XX (1892), pp. 1–26; William H. Parker, "Letter from Captain Parker," *Southern Historical Society Papers*, XI (1883), pp. 34–39; and William H. Parker, *Recollections of a Naval Officer* (New York, 1883). Both Parker and Newton were aboard the CSS *Beaufort*. In addition to Henry Reaney's *Battles and Leaders* article already cited, also useful for his view from the *Zouave* is "The Monitor and Merrimac," *War Papers; Read Before the Commandery of the State of Michigan, Military Order of the Loyal Legion of the United States* (Detroit, 1893–98), II, pp. 167–72.

Almost all of the accounts by men of the CSS *Virginia* combine the story of the two days' battles. There are many excellent sources here. In addition to Catesby Jones's article cited above, they include: J. R. Eggleston, "Captain Eggleston's Narrative of the Battle of the Merrimac," *Southern Historical Society Papers*, XLI (1916), pp. 166–78; Robert C. Foute, "Echoes from Hampton Roads," *Southern Historical Society Papers*, XIX (1891), pp. 246–48; Hardin B. Littlepage, "*Merrimac* vs. *Monitor*: A Midshipman's Account of the Battle with the 'Cheeze Box,'" in William C. King and William P. Derby, comps., *Camp-Fire Sketches and Battlefield Echoes of '61–5* (Springfield, Mass., 1880), pp. 335–37; Hardin B. Littlepage, "Statement of Midshipman Littlepage," *Southern Historical Society Papers*, XI (1883), pp. 32–34; Dinwiddie B. Phillips, "The Career of the Iron-Clad Virginia," *Collections of the Virginia Historical Society*, New Series, VI (1887), pp. 193–231; Dinwiddie B. Phillips, "The Career of the Merrimac," *Southern Bivouac*, New Series, II (March 1887), pp. 598–608; H. Ashton Ramsay, "Interesting Data About the Merrimac," *Confederate Veteran*, XVI (April 1908), pp. xvii–xix; H. Ashton Ramsay, "Most Famous of Sea Duels: The *Merrimac* and *Monitor*," *Harper's Weekly*, LVI (February 10, 1912), pp. 11–12; and John T. Wood, "The First Fight of Iron-Clads," *Battles and Leaders*, I, pp. 692–711. While not written by a participant, John McI. Kell's *Recollections of a Naval Life* (Washington, 1900) does contain an excellent letter by Lieutenant Robert Minor written just after the fight. Brooke's article "Real Projector," cited above, also contains an excellent post-battle letter by Minor.

Not quite as numerous are the accounts by participants aboard the *Monitor*, but they are just as good. Of course, standing far above all others is Robert W. Daly, ed., *Aboard the USS Monitor, 1862: The Letters of Acting Paymaster William Frederick Keeler* (Annapolis, Md., 1964). Other excellent sources are D. R. Ellis, "Monitor of the

Civil War," *Papers and Addresses of the Lebanon County Historical Society,* VIII (n.d.), pp. 5–39; Samuel Dana Greene, "I Fired the First Gun and Thus Commenced the Great Battle," *American Heritage,* VIII (June 1957), pp. 10–13, 102–5; Samuel Dana Greene, "In the 'Monitor' Turret," *Battles and Leaders,* I, pp. 719–29; Samuel Lewis, "Life on the Monitor: A Seaman's Story of the Fight with the *Merrimac;* Lively Experiences Inside the Famous 'Cheezebox on A Raft,'" in King and Derby, *Camp-Fire Sketches,* pp. 257–61; "The Merrimac and the Monitor," *Southern Historical Society Papers,* XIII (1885), pp. 90–119; Alban C. Stimers, "An Engineer Aboard the *Monitor,*" ed. by John D. Milligan, *Civil War Times Illustrated,* IX (April 1970), pp. 28–35; Louis N. Stodder, "Aboard the USS *Monitor,*" ed. by Albert S. Crockett, *Civil War Times Illustrated,* I (January 1963), pp. 31–36.

Accounts are numerous by those who witnessed the fight from the shore. Among the best Confederate recollections are Raleigh E. Colston, "Watching the *Merrimac,*" *Battles and Leaders,* I, pp. 712–14; Algernon S. Morrissett, "A Confederate Soldier's Eye-Witness Account of the 'Merrimack' Battle," ed. by Leondra D. Parish and Camillus J. Dismukes, *Georgia Historical Quarterly,* LIV (Fall 1970), pp. 430–32; William Norris, "The Story of the Confederate States Ship *Virginia* (once Merrimac)," *Southern Historical Society Papers,* XLII (1917), pp. 204–33; J. F. Shipp, "The Famous Battle of Hampton Roads," *Confederate Veteran,* XXIV (July 1916), pp. 305–7; and John S. Wise, *End of an Era* (Boston, 1902).

Accounts by Federals are equally good. They include: Le Grand B. Cannon, *Personal Reminiscences of the Rebellion, 1861–1865* (New York, 1895); Joseph McDonald, "How I Saw the Monitor-Merrimac Fight," *New England Magazine,* New Series, XXXVI (July 1907), pp. 548–53; Thomas Ransom, "The Monitor and Merrimac at Hampton Roads," ed. by Doris Hamilton, *Hobbies,* LXIV (September 1959), pp. 110–11, 119; Israel N. Stiles, "The Merrimac and the Monitor," *Military Essays and Recollections: Papers Read Before the Illinois Commandery, Military Order of the Loyal Legion of the United States* (Chicago, 1891–1912), I, pp. 125–33; William Tindall, "The True Story of the Virginia and the Monitor; the Account of an Eyewitness," *Virginia Magazine of History and Biography,* XXXI (January–April 1923), pp. 1–38, 89–145.

The reaction in the northern government and home front to the *Virginia*'s success of March 8 and her fight with the *Monitor* the next day are well covered in Howard K. Beale, ed., *Diary of Gideon Welles* (New York, 1960), 3 vols.; Gustavus V. Fox, *The Confidential Cor-*

respondence of Gustavus V. Fox, ed. by Robert M. Thompson and Richard Wainwright (New York, 1919), 2 vols.; John Hay, *Lincoln and the Civil War in the Diaries and Letters of John Hay,* ed. by Tyler Dennett (New York, 1939); Abraham Lincoln, *Collected Works of Abraham Lincoln,* ed. by Roy P. Basler (New Brunswick, N.J., 1953–55), 9 vols.; Adam Gurowski, *Diary from March 4, 1861 to November 12, 1862* (Boston, 1862); and George Templeman Strong, *Diary of the Civil War 1860–1865,* ed. by Allan Nevins (New York, 1962).

Less extensive is material on the Confederate reactions, though good sources do exist along with some that cover the response abroad. Good are John B. Jones, *A Rebel War Clerk's Diary at the Confederate States Capital* (Philadelphia, 1866), 2 vols.; James D. Bulloch, *The Secret Service of the Confederate States in Europe* (New York, 1884), 2 vols.; "The Late Naval Duel and Its Consequences," *United Service Magazine* [Great Britain] (May 1862), pp. 34–48; and Edward, Duke of Somerset, "The Merrimac and Monitor," *Southern Historical Society Papers,* XVI (1888), pp. 218–22.

The subsequent careers of the *Virginia* and the *Monitor* are covered in many of the sources cited above. Also useful are Salmon P. Chase, *Inside Lincoln's Cabinet: The Civil War Diaries of Salmon P. Chase,* ed. by David Donald (New York, 1954); Louis M. Goldsborough, "Narrative of Rear Admiral Goldsborough, U. S. Navy," *United States Naval Institute Proceedings,* LIX (July 1933), pp. 1023–31; Ashley Halsey, Jr., "The Plan to Capture the 'Monitor'; 'Seal the Turtle in its Shell,'" *Civil War Times Illustrated,* V (June 1966), pp. 28–31; J. H. D. Wingfield, "Thanksgiving Service on the 'Virginia,' March 10, 1862," *Southern Historical Society Papers,* XIX (1891), pp. 248–51.

For the last days and ultimate fate of the ironclads themselves, see Robert A. Jones, "Aftermath of an Ironclad," *Civil War Times Illustrated,* XI (October 1972), pp. 21–23; Francis B. Butts, "The Loss of the 'Monitor,'" *Battles and Leaders,* I, pp. 745–48; and Grenville M. Weeks, "The Last Cruise of the *Monitor,*" *Atlantic Monthly,* XI (March 1863), pp. 366–72.

While a host of biographies are extant covering individuals figuring in this book, only those which contribute information to the subject at hand, rather than provide simple biographical information, have been cited. These include: John Niven, *Gideon Welles* (New York, 1973); William Church, *The Life of John Ericsson* (New York, 1890), 2 vols.; Michael Lamm, "The Hot Air Era," *American History Illustrated,* IX (October 1974), pp. 18–23; George Robinson, "Recollections of Ericsson," *United Service,* New Series, XIII (January 1895), pp. 10–26; Dana Wegner, "Ericsson's High Priest: Alban C. Stimers," *Civil War Times Illustrated,* XIII (February 1975), pp. 26–34. Confederate biographies used are: Joseph T. Durkin, *Stephen R. Mallory: Confederate Navy Chief* (Chapel Hill, N.C., 1954); Charles L. Lewis, *Admiral Franklin Buchanan: Fearless Man of Action* (Baltimore, 1929); Oretha Swartz, "Franklin Buchanan; A Study in Divided Loyalties," *United States Naval Institute Proceedings,* LXXXVIII (December 1962), pp. 61–71; Charles C. Jones, *The Life and Services of Commodore Josiah Tattnall* (Savannah, Ga., 1878); Robert M. Langdon, "Josiah Tattnall—Blood Is Thicker than Water," *United States Naval Institute Proceedings,* LXXXV (June 1959), pp. 156–58; and Frances L. Williams, *Matthew Fontaine Maury, Scientist of the Sea* (New Brunswick, N.J., 1963).

Index